The Definitive Guide To

(Strong) One No Trump Openings, Stayman and Transfers

A Complete Treatment.

♣

♦

♥

♠

Stayman
Jacoby Transfers
Super-accepts
4-way Transfers
Minor Suit Stayman?
Stayman In Doubt?
Extended Stayman?
Puppet Stayman?
Smolen or Quest Transfers?
Gerber or RKCB?
4NT Quantitative
Texas Transfers or South African Transfers?
Extended Texas
Splinters

and much, much more ...

When to open 1NT?
When to use Stayman?
When to transfer?
What do the continuations mean?
5 card major in our NT opening?
Everything is covered.

A comprehensive study by ...   Terrence Quested, B.Sc.

Errors, corrections and additions

If you have any queries regarding NT bidding then e-mail me at terry@pattayabridge.com and I will answer them ASAP. If you find any errors in this book then please do e-mail details to me.

Any such errors or corrections will be posted in www.pattayabridge.com/NTbookcorrections.htm You can access this page by logging into **www.pattayabridge.com** and then navigating via the NoTrump bidding book link and clicking on NT book corrections.

For new material and examples that have occurred after the publication of this book again go to the NoTrump bidding book link and click on NT book additions.

Alternatively, you can simply click the appropriate link in the site-map at the bottom of the links column.

Order this book online at www.trafford.com
or email orders@trafford.com

Most Trafford titles are also available at major online book retailers.

Print information available on the last page.

ISBN: 978-1-4120-9665-2 (sc)

Trafford rev. 10/28/2021

www.trafford.com
North America & international
toll-free: 844-688-6899 (USA & Canada)
fax: 812 355 4082

1NT Openings, Stayman and Transfers …

… when playing a Strong NT

Forward

The intention of this book is to define a complete set of responses to 1NT. The basic responses of Stayman and Jacoby Transfers are well established, but the meaning of bids thereafter is not uniformly defined.

It is perhaps possible to devise a better scheme if you make fundamental changes, but I prefer to keep the well established conventions such as Stayman and transfers.

Many of the concepts are simple and well known, such as the Jacoby Transfers and Stayman mentioned. Others may be rather new and perhaps complex, but they are well worth mastering.

Examples of the latter are the Shape Asking Relays after Stayman (SARS), Quest Transfers, Advanced SID and many more indispensable conventions for the more advanced player.

This book defines a complete bidding system after an opening 1NT, where virtually every possible bidding sequence in an uncontested auction is defined. It is also intended as a reference manual, and, to this end I have included a number of summary charts at the end of the book.

Terrence Quested, in the Land of Smiles.   Hot season, 2004

To keep updated with any further books by the same author, monitor the web-site www.pattayabridge.com, where you will find loads of useful bridge information.

Acknowledgements

I would like to thank all members of the Pattaya Bridge Club (past, present and transient/visitors) for supplying me with the incentive and material to write this book. In particular I would like to thank Ian Barnes and Jim Wallington who proof read the book for me (no small task!).

I would also like to thank Trafford publishing, without whose help this book would never have been published.

When I refer to 'the club' I mean the Pattaya Bridge Club (I am the director/administrator) from where I have picked up much of the material in this book.

The Pattaya Bridge Club

The Pattaya Bridge Club, Thailand, is a friendly club meeting 3 afternoons a week with visitors always welcome. For details, visit the web site www.pattayabridge.com which also has a load of general bridge information, details of forthcoming books like this one, convention, news-sheets etc.

<u>Table of Contents</u>

Introduction

Why did I write a book on bidding after 1NT? Surely it's quite straightforward? Stayman and Transfers. Yes, but what happens after that? How many books have you picked up that answer all of these questions: -

- What does 3♦ mean in the sequence   1NT - 2♣ - 2♠ - 3♦?
  Is it forcing?
  Does responder have 4 ♥'s?

- What does 3♦ mean in the sequence   1NT - 2♣ - 2♦ - 3♦?
  Is it forcing?
  Is it a ♦ suit?
  Does responder promise a 4 card major?

- What does 2♠ mean in the sequence   1NT - 2♦ - 2♥ - 2♠?
  Is it forcing?

- How do you show a responding hand which is 5-4 (or 4-5) in the majors that is …
  Weak?
  Invitational?
  Game forcing?
  Do you use Stayman or Transfer?

- How do you show a responding hand which is 5-5 in the majors that is …
  Weak?
  Invitational?
  Game forcing?
  Do you use Stayman or Transfer?

- If you open 1NT with say 5 ♥'s and 2 ♠'s (so 2533) and partner transfers into ♠'s, how can you subsequently find a possible 5-3 ♥ fit if partner has game values and, say, 5332 shape? I bet you would be playing it in 3NT?

- Does responder guarantee a 4 card major in the sequence 1NT - 2♣ - 2♦ - 2NT?

And just have a look at all of the question marks on the next page. How many can you confidently answer - and be sure that your partner gives the same answer? How many gaps will you leave?

And it's not good enough to give an answer like 'weak' for 1NT - 2♣ - 2♦ - 2♠? How many ♥'s in responder's hand, and how many ♠'s?

It's high time that all of this was clearly defined.

So here it is, all in one book. And you will find the completed charts at the end of the book, so you know that everything is covered. And if you want to know what 3♦ means in the sequence 1NT - 1♣ - 2♦ - 3♦, just look it up in the bidding index.

Stayman Sequences

1NT - 2♣ - 2♦ - pass = ?
2♥ = ?
2♠ = ?
2NT = ?
3♣ = ?
3♦ = ?
3♥ = ?
3♠ = ?
3NT = ?
4♣ = ?
4♦ = ?
4♥ = ?
4♠ = ?
4NT = ?

1NT - 2♣ - 2♥ - pass = ?
2♠ = ?
2NT = ?
3♣ = ?
3♦ = ?
3♥ = ?
3♠ = ?
3NT = ?
4♣ = ?
4♦ = ?
4♥ = ?
4♠ = ?
4NT = ?

1NT - 2♣ - 2♠ - pass = ?
2NT = ?
3♣ = ?
3♦ = ?
3♥ = ?
3♠ = ?
3NT = ?
4♣ = ?
4♦ = ?
4♥ = ?
4♠ = ?
4NT = ?

Major Suit Transfer Sequences

1NT - 2♦ - 2♥ - pass = ?
2♠ = ?
2NT = ?
3♣ = ?
3♦ = ?
3♥ = ?
3♠ = ?
3NT = ?
4♣ = ?
4♦ = ?
4♥ = ?
4♠ = ?
4NT = ?

1NT - 2♥ - 2♠ - pass = ?
2NT = ?
3♣ = ?
3♦ = ?
3♥ = ?
3♠ = ?
3NT = ?
4♣ = ?
4♦ = ?
4♥ = ?
4♠ = ?
4NT = ?

And, of course, the same sort of thing after a minor suit transfer.

Terminology and Abbreviations

When indicating the shape of a hand, for example 3433, this means exactly in the order ♠♥♦♣. If I mean the suits in any order, then I say 4333 type hands.

A bid such as 2♣/♦ means either 2♣ or 2♦

ASID	=	Advanced Stayman In Doubt.
Blackwood	=	Easley Blackwood. Amongst his numerous achievements he is credited with the Blackwood convention which asks partner for aces.
BST	=	Broken Suit Transfers. The direct jumps to 3♦/♥ are used as transfers to the majors and indicate a broken suit with slam ambitions.
Captain (and Crew)	=	In most auctions one player usually limits his hand at some stage. His partner then knows the combined strength and is 'in charge'. He is called the captain and his partner is the crew. A player who bids Blackwood always becomes Captain.
Cue Bid	=	A bid in a suit in which the partnership does not wish to play. After trumps have been agreed such a bid is often a cue bid, usually showing 1st round control. Further bids (other than the trump suit) are also generally cue bids.
Crawling Stayman	=	A variation of Garbage Stayman that is meant to make it easier to find a fit. with very weak hands. We do not use it.
The Club	=	I am referring to the Pattaya Bridge Club.
DRKCB	=	Double (two-suit) Roman Key Card Blackwood.
EDRKCB	=	Exclusion Double Roman Key Card Blackwood.
ERKCB	=	Exclusion Roman Key Card Blackwood.
Four-way Transfers	=	In addition to the 2♦/♥ Jacoby Transfers to 2♥/♠ one can also play 2♠/NT. as transfers to 3♣/♦. This complete scheme is called 4-way transfers.
Garbage Stayman	=	Stayman after 1NT. The most common variation is when responder has no points requirement and it is sometimes referred to as Garbage Stayman.
HCPs	=	High Card Points
IMP	=	International Matchpoint. A form of scoring on a sliding scale used in team matches. Over tricks and the 10 extra for playing in NT as opposed to a major etc are insignificant. It is different to Matchpoint scoring.
Intermediates	=	10's, 9's and 8's. These have no point count but are often more important than lower cards.
Jacoby Transfers	=	After partner's 1NT opening, bids of 2♦/♥ are transfers to 2♥/♠. The same can be done one level higher after a 2NT opening. A further extension of the transfers over 1NT is using 2♠ and 2NT as transfers to 3♣/♦.
Key cards	=	These are defined as the 4 aces and the king of trumps. They are normally associated with RKCB but are also specific to some other conventions.
Kickback	=	A variation of RKCB whereby the suit above the trump suit (4NT in the case of ♠'s) is used as the key card ask.
The Law of Total Tricks	=	Often simply called 'The Law'. It states that the total number of tricks available to both sides is equal to the total number of trumps. So in its simple form, all things being equal, you can compete to the level of combined trumps that your side holds.
Limit Raise	=	The exact definition is a raise that specifies the point count, i.e. limits the hand. We usually use the term specifically for a limit raise of opener's suit to the 3 level (i.e. +- 11 points) or opener's 1NT to 2NT (i.e. 8-9 pts).

Matchpoints	=	The scoring method used in pairs competitions. It is different from IMP scoring in that overtricks are important and even the extra 10 points for making 3NT+1 as opposed to 4♥ exactly is very significant. I assume IMP scoring in this book.
Puppet	=	An artificial bid that demands that partner makes a specific bid (normally the next bid up). Lebensohl is the most well known example. A puppet is sometimes used in order to transfer captaincy so that the captain can become the crew and can describe his hand.
Puppet Stayman	=	Puppet Stayman asks for both 4 and 5 card majors. The most important version is 3♣ over a 2NT opening and this works extremely well. There are also variations over a 1NT opening (either 2♣ or 3♣) but none are really satisfactory. Note that with Puppet Stayman, the artificial 3♣ (or 2♣) bid is in fact a relay and not a puppet.
Quacks	=	Queens and Jacks.
Quest Transfers	=	A convention used after the sequence 1NT - 2♣ - 2♦ whereby a jump to 3♦ or 3♥ is a transfer to the suit above and shows 5 cards in the suit transferred into and 4 in the other major. This is an improvement on Smolen.
Relay	=	An artificial bid that seeks information about partner's hand. The most common examples are Blackwood and Stayman.
RKCB	=	Roman Key Card Blackwood. An improved form of Blackwood where the king of trumps is given equal importance to the four aces – thus giving five 'key cards'. Special significance is also allocated to the queen of trumps.
SARS	=	Shape Asking Relays after Stayman.
SID	=	Stayman in Doubt. A convention to check on shape duplication after a major suit fit has been discovered using Stayman. We use a considerably enhanced version (ASID – Advanced SID).
Smolen	=	A convention used after the sequence 1NT - 2♣ - 2♦ whereby a jump to 3♥ or 3♠ shows 4 cards in the major suit bid and 5 in the other major. We do not use it as it has been superseded by Quest Transfers.
South African Texas	=	A variation on Texas Transfers whereby 4♣/♦ are the transfer bids to 4♥/♠.
Splinter	=	A jump in a new suit to a level that is one more than the forcing bid is often a splinter, showing shortage (singleton or void). It usually agrees partner's last suit (normally a major) as trumps. We can splinter to the 3 level over a 1NT opening to offer one of the other 3 suits as trumps.
Stayman	=	Samuel Stayman. The convention named after him is a 2♣ bid after partner's 1NT opening (or 3♣ after a 2NT opening) which asks opener to clarify his major suit holdings. There are numerous variations of the convention.
Strong NT	=	15-17 HCPs.
Tenace	=	A holding such as Kx or AQ which is vulnerable to a lead from RHO.
Texas Transfer	=	After partner's 1NT opening, 4♦/♥ are transfers to 4♥/♠.
Transfer	=	An artificial bid that shows length in a specific suit. The most common example is Jacoby Transfers over NT.
Weak NT	=	12-14 HCPs.

About Kickback

'Everybody' these days plays Roman Keycard Blackwood (RKCB), and quite right too – it is far superior to the standard version and it is what we shall be using in this book. However, whenever you use Blackwood (whatever variety you choose) there is always a problem with the lower ranking suits as trumps because the reply may get you too high. In fact, you may even have a problem with RKCB when ♥'s are trumps: -

West	East	West	East		
♠ KQ62	♠ J	1NT	2♦		(1) RKCB ??
♥ KQ8	♥ AJ109765	2♥	4NT	(1)	(2) two key cards + ♥Q
♦ AJ54	♦ KQ	5♠ (2)	? (3)		
♣ 107	♣ KQJ				

Don't worry about the 2♦ transfer, we will cover that later. The point is that 4NT does not always work as RKCB when ♥'s are trumps. East justifiably had visions of slam but now 5NT at (3) would be asking for kings and we are too high! The problems are even worse with a minor suit and you may also get problems when asking for the trump queen. The only real way to solve this is to ensure that you have 4 steps between your Blackwood asking bid and the trump suit.

There are a few solutions; 4-of-the-minor as Blackwood for minor suits is one of them. But probably the best is Kickback; this uses the suit above trumps as the key card ask and it is what we shall be using in many situations.

Also, of course, because we have opened 1NT, we often need 4NT as a quantitative bid.

About Roman Key Card Blackwood (RKCB)

We use RKCB in this book as the keycard ask, but 4NT is not always the RKCB bid.

Because of the problems involved when a minor suit is trumps (and also when one of two suits may be trumps) we have various different methods for the key card ask. It is Kickback for ♥'s and ♠'s. But with a minor suit it may be 4 of the minor or Kickback, depending upon the sequence, and this is fully explained when it occurs.

Also I have assumed the 0314 variation of RKCB; it's up to you if you prefer 1430. The argument for using 1430 (more room for the queen ask) is not applicable when you use Kickback.

Note also that in a sequence such as   1NT - 2♦ - 2♥ - 4♣,   the 4♣ bid is often referred to as Gerber, or Roman Key Card Gerber. I think that this is misleading; when I refer to Gerber it is always an ace ask with no trump suit agreed. The 4♣ bid here is simply RKCB with 4♣ as the asking bid.

In many circumstances there are two suits that are very important and then we use Double (or two-suit) RKCB, or DRKCB. Sometimes asker may have a void, then it's Exclusion RKCB or ERKCB. And if there are two key suits and asker has a void then it's Exclusion Double RKCB or EDRKCB. These are all fully described later.

Matchpoint or Teams Scoring?

The type of scoring may affect the decision for your final contract. For example, a 75% 6NT may well actually score better than a 95% 6♥ at pairs (matchpoints). This is not 'real' bridge and I assume teams scoring (IMPs) or rubber bridge.

1   The 1NT Opener

The very first thing to be decided is the range of your 1NT opening. Of course there are numerous possible ranges but the most popular two are the strong NT (15-17) and the weak NT (12-14). Another aspect that is nowhere near as important is whether you play a 5 card major system or if you can open a 4 card major.

When I set about writing this book I had to decide which range to adopt, but since everything is applicable to both ranges I decided to write two parallel books. Virtually the same but one has all the examples for a strong NT and the other for a weak NT.

Since you are reading this book and not the weak NT one (<u>note</u> at this time, 2006, the weak NT version has not yet been published), I assume that your range is 15-17. Everything in this book is equally valid if you play a weak NT – in the examples, give responder 3 of opener's points. So no problem even if you play another range.

First of all, let's have a look at aspects of a hand that may influence your decision on whether or not to open 1NT.

Tenaces

Hand A	Hand B
♠ KJ9	♠ A97
♥ KJ9	♥ A65
♦ KJ9	♦ A87
♣ KJ92	♣ A932

You are playing a strong NT. What do you open? Hand A is a lovely 1NT opener, if you end up as declarer (often the case when you open 1NT because of Stayman, Transfers etc) then the opening lead is almost certain to help. With this Hand A you most certainly want to be declarer. What about Hand B? This is the complete opposite, it has no tenaces to protect. Most contracts will be better played by partner. So open 1♣? Unfortunately you cannot. What is your rebid? Partner will never place you with a balanced 16 count if you do not open 1NT.

It is usually best to be declarer with holdings such as AQx, KJx and Kx etc.

I also include Qx; let us consider this particular holding a little further, especially as regards a NT contract. If you hold Qx as declarer opposite Axx then the suit is immune from an opening lead without conceding 2 tricks to you. But what if partner has Kxx, surely it does not matter who plays the hand? Perhaps, but it is much better to have the three card holding on table and the two card holding in hand. If the suit is initially led, you duck in dummy and if your Q wins, you still have a stop if the ace is with LHO or is you can keep LHO from the lead. With the doubleton on table you have no such option. Obviously the same is true with Qxx opposite Kx, declarer should protect his doubleton. Ax is different; this is no problem in dummy as playing low does not leave a stiff K or Q to be felled next lead.

Hand Evaluation

Hand C	Hand D
♠ Q954	♠ AJ109
♥ AQ6	♥ QJ10
♦ AQ3	♦ KQJ10
♣ KJ2	♣ 98

I do not intend to write pages on this (well, not in this book), suffice it to say that the value of the hand is not simply the addition of the HCPs. I would open a strong 1NT with both of these hands.

When I state point counts, for example 8-9 for an invitational hand, I mean the value of the hand after evaluation.

I will generally deduct a point for 4333 type shape, add on for good 5 card suits, intermediates, etc.

Before we move onto some specific hand shapes, let's consider a few general examples of NT openings from the club which generated discussion: -

Hand E

♠ AQ109
♥ 92
♦ AQJ9
♣ QJ9

If you open 1 of a suit, you must always have a rebid. If you open 1NT you have said it all. Hand E was opened with 1♦, the opener being unhappy about the ♥'s. His partner considered 1NT the correct opening and I was asked for my considered opinion: -
If you open 1♦, then you would appear to have no rebid problem. If partner bids 1♥ then you bid 1♠ and if he bids 1♠ then you support. But what do you rebid if partner bids 2♣? The real problem is that you have not shown the strength or the balanced nature of the hand. No, open 1NT. We do not worry about a small doubleton if 1NT is the most descriptive bid.

Hand F

♠ 97
♥ AKQ104
♦ A73
♣ Q93

What about Hand F? Again a small doubleton, so do we open 1♥ or 1NT?
We have seen that a small doubleton does not deter us from opening 1NT but in this case if we open 1♥ we have a very comfortable rebid (2♥).
Contrary to some people's belief, this does not guarantee a 6 card suit when playing 5 card majors. So we open Hand F with 1♥, we come onto discussing hands with a 5 card major that should open 1NT shortly.

Hand G

♠ 96
♥ AKQ8
♦ 764
♣ AK75

And what about this Hand G. When this hand occurred in a club competition the holder opened 1♣ and the bidding went (a) 1♣ - 1♦ - 1♥ - 1♠ - 1NT ….
Obviously very silly as the 1NT bid here is the same as if it had gone
(b) 1♣ - 1♠ - 1NT …. and shows 12-14 points when playing a strong NT.
Now I asked around, and everybody out of a dozen or so said that they would open 1♣ as they would not open 1NT with two very weak suits.
Noble sentiments, but surely that is better than subsequently lying about your strength by two points? And you are no better off if you play 4 card majors and choose to open 1♥; you have the same problem over a 1♠ or 2♦ response.

Only one of those I questioned had even thought about the rebid; he said that he would reverse into 2♥ after partner's 1♠ response to the 1♣ opening. Reasonable, but there are a few flaws: -

(1) This hand is not really strong enough to reverse in the modern style.
(2) A reverse promises greater length in the first bid suit.
(3) You are still fixed if the bidding was as in sequence (a).

No, the only real solution is to open a strong NT. It's nice to have an honour in every suit, or in at least three suits, but it does not always turn out that way.

Shuffle Hand G around and it's a different story: -

Hand H	Hand J
♠ AKQ8	♠ AKQ8
♥ 96	♥ 96
♦ 764	♦ AK75
♣ AK75	♣ 764

With Hand H it's best to open 1♣ as you have an easy 1♠ rebid. But we have a problem with Hand J; if we open 1♦ and partner responds 2♣ then we have no sensible answer! 2NT would be 12-14 and 2♠ is played as a strong reverse by most players, promising more ♦'s than ♠'s. So with Hand J it's also best to open a strong NT.

Hand K	Hand L
♠ 96	♠ 96
♥ 764	♥ AK75
♦ AK75	♦ AKQ8
♣ AKQ8	♣ 764

And Hand K is also problematic. If you open 1♣ then a 1♦ or 1♥ response poses no problem (support), but what after 1♠? I guess 2♣? You could open 1♦ with a view to rebidding 2♣ over a 1♠ response, but that would imply longer ♦'s than ♣'s.
I would again prefer to open 1NT with this hand but I would agree that either 1♣ or 1♦ are quite reasonable.
It's the same sort of problem with Hand L. If you open 1♦ then a 2♦ rebid is best over 1♠. A 1NT opener may work out best.

Hand M	Hand N
♠ AKQ8	♠ AKQ8
♥ AK75	♥ AK75
♦ 96	♦ 764
♣ 764	♣ 96

With both majors it's often best to avoid opening 1NT. You always have a good rebid if you open 1♣ and the advantage is that you will always find a 4-4 fit that may be missed if you open Hand M with 1NT and partner is too weak to respond. My personal preference is the 'short ♣' system and I would also open 1♣ with Hand N. I realise that most would prefer 1♦ (but then you have a rebid problem over a 2♣ response).

So, it's nice not to have two wide open suits when you open 1NT, but it's not guaranteed! If you have a balanced hand within your 1NT opening range, then open 1NT unless you have a comfortable rebid over any non-jump response.

1.1   <u>Opening 1NT With a 5 Card Major?</u>

Most players accept opening 1NT with a balanced hand and a 5 card minor. However, one of the main considerations to be considered when opening 1NT is if you allow a 5 card major. Opinion is divided on this subject; some never open 1NT with a 5 card major, some will allow a weak suit such as J7543, while others will allow virtually any 5 card major suit. Which philosophy shall we adopt? All three probably have equal merit, but we shall adopt the last (providing the hand is balanced, i.e. the doubleton is Ax, Kx or Qx and the major is not top-heavy) for a number of reasons: -

1-   If you open 1♥/♠, then you will usually never be able to play in possibly the best contract of 1NT if you play a Forcing NT.
2-   It is usually best to limit your hand as soon a possible, especially if relatively flat.
3-   Once you open 1NT you never have a rebid problem. The hand is off your chest.
4-   1NT (and most other contracts) will be played from the strong hand. And a 1NT opening hand is the hand that is most likely to have tenaces that need protecting.
5-   The defenders do not have it so easy defending against a 1NT contract as they do not know if declarer has a 5 card major or not.
6-   Even if a 5-3 major suit exists, if partner is minimal 1NT is at a lower level.
7-   If the hand belongs to the opponents, they are less likely to compete over a strong NT opening.
8-   There is also the negative inference, that a major suit opening within our 1NT range is a good suit and/or unbalanced.

Let's just check on when we should open 1NT with a 5 card major and when not: -

Hand 1	Hand 2	Hand 3	Hand 4	Hand 5
♠ AJ9	♠ AJ9	♠ Q97	♠ AK9	♠ AKJ74
♥ AQ984	♥ Q10984	♥ AKQ104	♥ AQ984	♥ Q98
♦ K7	♦ AK7	♦ A7	♦ J7	♦ K73
♣ Q93	♣ Q3	♣ J93	♣ Q93	♣ K3

Hand 1:   Open 1NT.
Hand 2:   Open 1NT.
Hand 3:   Open 1♥, the ♥'s are top-heavy.
Hand 4:   Open 1♥, the doubleton is not good enough.
Hand 5:   Open 1NT, the short suits are just good enough and the tenaces may need protecting.

```
Dealer:          ♠ J752
West.            ♥ 10985
Love all         ♦ 97
                 ♣ A63

♠ KQ1043      N        ♠ A6
♥ AK6      W     E     ♥ J43
♦ J43         S        ♦ A10862
♣ 108                  ♣ K97
                 ♠ 98
                 ♥ Q72
                 ♦ KQ5
                 ♣ QJ542
```

So that's fine, and we know when to open 1NT with a 5 card major and when not to. But does everybody know this? And do they know the criteria needed for 1NT? 5 card majors are fine if they are not top-heavy, the hand should be balanced (in shape and high card distribution). Tenaces such as AQx, Kx, and Qx should encourage one to open 1NT and the lack of such tenaces should be discouraging. Consider this hand from a 2003 international competition. What do you open as West? At the first table, West chose 1♠ and eventually ended up in 3NT by East. This received a ♣ lead by south and the contract was made. I am ashamed to say that the English West opened a weak 1NT, and after the ♥10 opening lead from North, the final 3NT contract stood no chance.

Was West unlucky? Indeed he was! If this book had been published before this event, he would have known that absolutely everything about the West hand is wrong for an opening 1NT. The points are concentrated in two suits, the doubleton is weak, the ♦'s are also very weak and the hand contains absolutely no tenaces; if NT is the best contract (as in this case), then the hand has to be played by East.

Let's have a slightly more memorable example of an unsuitable 1NT opening. This time the hand is from the 1998 Macallan International Bridge pairs. You have to be a top class player to even be invited to this tournament, and these players were 4 of the world's top.

The N-S pair were playing a strong NT.

```
Dealer:          ♠ 1072
South            ♥ K2
Both vul         ♦ 875
                 ♣ 97654

♠ 6           N        ♠ J983
♥ 108      W     E     ♥ AQJ973
♦ AKQ1096     S        ♦ 2
♣ AJ103                ♣ 82
                 ♠ AKQ54
                 ♥ 654
                 ♦ J43
                 ♣ KQ
```

West	North	East	South
-	-	-	1NT (1)
dbl	pass	pass	pass

(1) 15-17

West cashed the first 6 ♦ tricks, followed by the ♣A and then 6 ♥ tricks took the remainder. 7 down in a 1 level contract! Perhaps rather a graphic example, but the South hand really is unsuitable for 1NT.

Opening 1NT With Two Doubletons?

Now we have seen that we allow both 5 card minors or 5 card majors in our opening 1NT, provided the hand is balanced. But what about semi-balanced hands, e.g. hands with 2 doubletons (so a 5 and 4 card suit within your opening NT range). The general rule is that if the 5 card suit is higher ranking than the 4 card suit, then open the 5-carder and rebid the 4-carder. If the 4-carder is higher ranking and the hand is not good enough for a reverse, then open 1NT.

Hand 6	Hand 7	Hand 8	Hand 9	Hand 10
♠ K9	♠ KJ104	♠ K9	♠ K9	♠ A9
♥ KJ104	♥ AK642	♥ Q7	♥ Q7	♥ Q7
♦ AQ642	♦ Q9	♦ KJ104	♦ AQ642	♦ AK1064
♣ K7	♣ Q7	♣ AQ642	♣ KJ104	♣ J1094

Hand 6:   Open 1NT. The hand is not good enough for a reverse and you will be fixed for a rebid if you open 1♦.

Hand 7:   The long suits are in the same order, but you should not open 1NT with 9 cards in the majors. Thus 1♥. If partner responds 2♣/♦ you can then bid 2♠, but only if you have agreed that a reverse after a two level response does not show extra values. With no such agreement the hand is difficult and 2♥ is probably the best bid. If partner responds with a forcing NT then this hand shape is difficult and 2♣ is probably best.

Hand 8:   Open 1NT, with these tenaces it's a much better bid than 1♣. The hand is not really strong enough for a reverse into 2♦ if you open 1♣.

Hand 9:   Now this hand has the suits in the 'easy' order and you can open 1♦ followed by 2♣. However, I still prefer 1NT with these tenaces.

Hand 10: 14 points, but look at that ♦ suit. And the ♣ suit is far better than just one point. With the ♥Qx which may need protecting NT is very likely to be the best contract and is best played by this hand. The hand easily has the values for a strong NT opener.

Incidentally, Hand 10 is from a club tournament and after it had occurred I did a poll at the club and found that about 75% would open the hand with 1♦ regardless of the NT range – interesting; but I still maintain that it is a strong NT opener.

Hand A

♠ J4
♥ AK102
♦ J6
♣ AQ1073

How about this hand? It comes from the Marty Bergen book 'Marty Sez... volume 2'. An opening of 1NT is recommended as the author maintains that you have a rebid problem after 1♠ from partner if you opened 1♣. Sure, a 1NT rebid would be an underbid and a reverse into 2♥ a slight overbid, but I see nothing wrong with rebidding this ♣ suit. A 1NT opening is, in my opinion, a distortion of this hand with two worthless doubletons and should be avoided if you have a reasonable rebid (as here). When you open 1NT you always run the risk of missing a 4-4 major suit fit; this is not so important if your hand is balanced but would be a disaster on this hand if partner had 4 ♥'s and was unable to respond to a 1NT opening. Be wary of opening 1NT on hands with a 5 card minor and a 4 card major; only consider it with decent doubletons (preferably tenaces).

Hand B	Let's change Hand A slightly, what do we open with this Hand B? Again we have to think about the rebid. If you open 1♣ then what is the rebid over partner's 1♠?			

Hand B

♠ K4
♥ AK102
♦ 76
♣ AJ1073

Let's change Hand A slightly, what do we open with this Hand B? Again we have to think about the rebid. If you open 1♣ then what is the rebid over partner's 1♠? A 2♣ rebid is perhaps acceptable, but if you open 1NT you get the strength of the hand off your chest immediately. Two doubletons is not ideal for a 1NT opening but you certainly have no further problems. This is a borderline case. My personal preference would be to open 1♣ because of the pathetic ♦'s and the risk of playing in 1NT with a 4-4 ♥ fit. But you can only do this if your partnership style allows you to occasionally rebid a decent 5 card ♣ suit (I have no problem with that).

Hand C   Hand D

♠ K4   ♠ AK102
♥ 76   ♥ K4
♦ AK104   ♦ 76
♣ AJ1073   ♣ AJ1073

Swap the red suits of Hand B to get Hand C then 1NT is a far better opening than 1♣ (or 1♦!).
But if you swap the major suits of Hand B to get Hand D you should open 1♣ as you always have an easy 1♠ rebid.

West	East	West	East	But make Hand D top-of-the-range such as our West hand here and there may be trouble.
♠ AK102	♠ QJ93	1♦	1♥	The problem is that West's 1♠ rebid shows anything from 12 to 17 points and game (or slam in this case) may be missed. So with 4225 shape there is a case for 1NT when max.
♥ A10	♥ KJ83	1♠	4♠	
♦ 76	♦ KQ43	pass		
♣ AJ1073	♣ K			

Let's have a summary of what you should open with 5422 type shape within your 1NT opening range. For argument's sake, let's assume that the doubletons are Kx and that the hand is a reasonable 15 count and not good enough for a reverse or jump rebid: -

5422	1♠. You have an easy 2♥ rebid. Do not open 1NT with 9 cards in the majors.
5242 **	1♠. Over 2♥ you will have to bid 2♠ unless 3♦ does not show extras in your style.
5224 **	1♠. Over 2♦/♥ you will have to bid 2♠ unless 3♣ does not show extras in your style.
4522	1♥. Your rebid may be tricky, but do not open 1NT with 9 cards in the majors.
4252 *	1NT or 1♦. You may have a problem if you open 1♦ and get a 2♣ response.
4225	1♣. You have a comfortable 1♠ rebid (unless maximum).
2542	1♥. You have a comfortable 2♦ rebid.
2524 **	1♥. Over 2♦ you will have to bid 2♥ unless 3♣ does not show extras in your style.
2452 *	1NT. If you open 1♦ you have no good rebid over 1♠/2♣.
2425 *	1NT. If you open 1♣ you have no good rebid over 1♠.
2254	1NT.
2245	1NT.

* note.   See previous page. Only open 1NT with good doubletons as you may miss a 4-4 major suit fit. If you do open the minor then you may have to rebid it.
** note.   1NT is a very reasonable option if the doubletons are tenaces.

You do not have to remember all of this and it is a general guideline. One simply has to think 'do I have a good rebid?' if I open 1 of a suit.
Some of the above may change depending upon the high card holdings and suit quality.

Not everybody will be happy with all of my suggestions; I'm used to that, no problem. Perhaps it's the 2254 shape? Let's have an example from the club: -

Hand E   I held this hand in a club competition, what would you open?

♠ 85   I opened 1NT. That lovely ♦ suit is worth way more than 5 points and the ♣ suit more
♥ K6   than 6. With two tenaces that may need protecting I chose a strong 1NT.
♦ KQ1098   Let's look at the complete deal: -
♣ AQ98

Dealer:	♠ QJ10732		Table A			
South	♥ 75		West	North	East	South (me)
Both vul	♦ A4		-	-	-	1NT
	♣ K105		pass	2♥ (1)	pass	2♠
			pass	4♠	pass	pass
♠ 96	N	♠ AK4	pass			
♥ J109832	W E	♥ AQ4				
♦ 632	S	♦ J75	Table B			
♣ 64		♣ J732	West	North	East	South
	♠ 85		-	-	-	1♦
	♥ K6		pass	1♠	pass	1NT (2)
	♦ KQ1098		pass	2♠	pass	pass
	♣ AQ98		pass			

2♥ at (1) was a Jacoby Transfer, if you play Texas Transfers then 4♥ (instructing partner to bid 4♠) is the bid. An easy 4♠ was missed at all the other tables, Table B was typical. The problem is that South does not have a decent rebid at (2). 2♣ is possible but 2♠ would again be the final contract.

I don't know how to continue at (2) after opening 1♦ with this hand when playing a strong NT. If you open 1♦ then what is your rebid over 1♥/♠? 2♣ is a bit feeble and a game forcing 3♣ is certainly too much. A 1NT rebid is 12-14 (this hand is too good) and 2NT is 18-19. That is why it's usually best to open 1NT when your hand is within your NT range and (semi) balanced.

Playing a weak NT then this Hand E is also a bit of a problem (maybe more so). It is too strong for a weak 1NT and so you open 1♦. If partner responds 1♠ then you obviously rebid 1NT (15-16), but if partner responds 1♥ then 1NT is not so nice with these ♠'s *.

Hand F   Hand G   If you play a weak NT and we change the hand to be in the 12-14 point
                            range then I would open 1NT with Hand F but1♦ with Hand G. But we
♠ Q5   ♠ 85   do not have the same problem as * (Hand E when playing a strong NT)
♥ K6   ♥ K6   as a 2♣ rebid here is fine.
♦ KJ987   ♦ KJ987   Basically, a 2♣ rebid with 12-14 is OK but with 15-17 it's not so nice.
♣ A985   ♣ AQ98

1.3   <u>Opening 1NT With a Six Card Minor?</u>

Hand A   So we may well elect to open 1NT with two doubletons, especially with 9 cards in the
                minors, but what about opening 1NT with a 6 card minor?
♠ KQ9   Not usually, but there are always exceptions. If you have a 6 card suit, then you have two
♥ Q5   doubletons (if balanced) and 1NT is not usually recommended. But with this hand,
♦ Q98643   surely it is the best shot? If game is on, it is probably in NT which must be best played
♣ AQ   from this hand. Tenaces need protecting and this hand should strive to be declarer.

Hand A was from a 2004 club competition: -

West	East	West	East	(1) Stayman
♠ KQ9	♠ 1053	1NT	2♣ (1)	
♥ Q5	♥ A963	2♦	3NT	
♦ Q98643	♦ AK72			
♣ AQ	♣ 32			

An excellent contract that is difficult to reach if you open 1♦. The board was played 6 times and
only this pair reached 3NT (the final contract at all of the other tables was 3♦ or 4♦).

Hand B   And how about this one? It comes from a 2003 club competition. There was
                considerable debate about this hand after the event. Let's have a look at the
♠ AK8   complete deal and the bidding at a couple of the tables: -
♥ 109
♦ KJ10943   Dealer   ♠ AK8
♣ A5   West   ♥ 109
                                                N-S vul   ♦ KJ10943
Table A   ♣ A5

West	North	East	South
pass	1♦	pass	1♥
pass	1NT (1)	all pass	

♠ 1097653	N	♠ J4
♥ 76	W E	♥ KJ42
♦ Q7	S	♦ A85
♣ K73		♣ QJ104

Table B

West	North	East	South
pass	1♦	pass	1♥
pass	3♦	pass	3♥ (2)
pass	4♥	all pass	

♠ Q2
♥ AQ853
♦ 62   (1) 12-14 !
♣ 9862   (2) forcing.

Now I am not arguing with the bidding at Table B, I think that the North hand is worth a 3♦ rebid.
And note that the 3♥ bid at (2) has to be played as forcing – otherwise it would be impossible to bid
this South hand sensibly. The experienced North player at Table A, however, maintained that the North
hand was not good enough for 3♦. Perhaps it's marginal, and in that case I said that North should open
1NT. North insisted that his bidding was correct (yes, he was playing a strong NT!). This 1NT rebid
shows 12-14 and is ludicrous of course. It really is so simple if you open 1NT (1NT - 2♦ - 2♥ - 2NT -
3NT), in my opinion this North Hand B is not minimum for a strong 1NT!

OK, so we've covered which hands warrant a 1NT opening. You don't have to agree with me about everything. The main point of this book is not the opening bid, but the continuations after 1NT has been opened. So it's time to consider the responses to this 1NT opening.

Before we go into everything in detail, let's have a general guideline as to what responder needs for weak, invitational or strong hands. This is a rough guide and everything is covered in detail later.

1.4   A Brief Overview of Responder's Options

This is a very brief summary and is by no means exhaustive of the options available – you get that in the rest of this book!

Responder's point range	Options available	Explanation
Weak hands **0-7**	2♣	Stayman. Only make this bid on weak hands if you have both majors and can cope with any (2♦/♥/♠) reply.
	2♦/♥	Transfer. With a weak hand and a 5+ card major suit you can transfer and pass the expected 2♥/♠ reply
	2♠/2NT	Transfer to 3♣/♦ respectively. With a weak hand you can transfer to a 6 card minor and play there.
	pass	With insufficient values to invite game and none of the above hand types, there is no other option but to pass
Invitational hands **8-9**	2♣	Stayman. With invitational values and a 4 card major, start with Stayman. If partner bids 2♦, rebid 2NT. Raise partner's 2♥ response to 3♥ if you have 4 ♥'s; otherwise rebid 2♠ with 4 ♠'s or 2NT with no 4 card major. Raise partner's 2♠ response to 3♠ if you have 4 ♠'s; otherwise rebid 2NT.
	2♣ and 2NT next	Since we play 4-way transfers, a natural 2NT invitation has to go via a 2♣ bid.
	2♣ and 3♦/♥ next	Over a 2♦ response, these bids show an invitational or better hand with 45 or 54 in the majors. They are fully described later.
	2♦/♥	Transfer. With a 5 card major you first transfer and then make an invitational bid. The only invitational rebids are 3 of the major (indicating a 6 card suit) or 2NT. All other bids are game forcing.
	2♠/2NT	Transfer to 3♣/♦ respectively. If you have a reasonable hand, you may wish to raise a super-accept from partner to 3NT.

Game hands i.e. hands that are not good enough to invite slam **10-15**	2♣	Stayman. With a 4 card major and no other suit of 5 cards or more, start with Stayman. There are numerous subsequent options available to discover fits etc.
	2♣ and 3♣ next	2♣ is initially Stayman. But a subsequent 3♣ bid asks about opener's shape and is game forcing.
	2♦/♥	Transfer. With a 5 card major you first transfer and then make a game forcing bid. You may bid game directly (4 of the major – showing a 6 card suit, or 3NT which shows a 5 carder). A new suit shows 4+ cards in the suit and is game forcing and often mildly slam invitational.
	2♠/NT	Transfer to 3♣/♦ respectively. A transfer to a minor followed by another bid is game forcing, showing 5+ in the minor and 4 in the other suit.
	3NT	(semi)balanced with no 4 card major.
	4♦/♥	Texas Transfers to 4♥/♠. Weaker than a Jacoby Transfer followed by 4 of the major.
Slam invitational **15-17**	2♣	Stayman to start, but may simply be a prelude to shape asking.
	2♦/♥	Transfer to 2♥/♠.
	2♠/NT	Transfer to 3♣/♦.
	4NT	This is traditionally slam invitational, denying a 4 card major. However, since we have shape asking sequences this bid will normally be preceded by one of the previous bids. A direct 4NT bid needs to be very specific and is discussed later.
	3♣/♦/♥/♠	Looking for slam. There are numerous options for these bids.
Definitely slamming **18+**	4♣	Gerber, asking for aces. 4♣ is RKCB or Gerber in most sequences that start with 1NT. Normally it is best to take things slowly and perhaps find out more about opener's shape, asking for aces later. With a flat hand one would typically start with 2♣ followed by 3♣ (SARS) in order to get shape information.
	5/6/7NT	Typically 5NT invites and 6NT/7NT says we have enough for the slam. I think it makes sense to check on aces first.

19

1.5   Passing Partner's 1NT Opening

Generally speaking we need about 25 combined points for game when both hands are relatively flat. If responder has 7 or less points then it's usually best to pass.

Hand A	Hand B	
♠ Q962	♠ 985	With Hand A there may be a 4-4 ♠ fit but we do not have a good enough hand to find out and have to pass 1NT
♥ J76	♥ 873	
♦ J982	♦ J2	And Hand B may well play better in 2♣, but we cannot bid that as it has a forcing conventional meaning (Stayman).
♣ 52	♣ AJ875	

But we do not always have to pass with very weak hands. I'll give a few examples here, it is all covered in much more detail later in this book.

Hand C	Hand D	
♠ Q962	♠ Q9632	With Hand C there may be a 4-4 ♥ or ♠ fit and with this shape we can actually look for a fit. We cover this later when we talk about Garbage Stayman.
♥ J762	♥ J762	
♦ J982	♦ J2	And we can also cope with Hand D. Again, this is covered in the Garbage Stayman section.
♣ 5	♣ 75	

Hand E	Hand F	
♠ Q9642	♠ 985	With Hand E 2♠ will almost certainly play better than 1NT, even if there is only a 5-2 ♠ fit. We will cover transfers to the majors later.
♥ J76	♥ 87	
♦ J982	♦ J2	We saw that we could not play in 2♣ with Hand B, but add an extra ♣ and we can transfer into 3♣. Again, it's covered later.
♣ 5	♣ AJ8752	

Hand G	Hand H	
♠ 982	♠ 98	Hand G will probably play better in a minor, but we have no way of finding a fit at a low level and we do not want to play at the 3 level with no fit when we could have been playing in 1NT.
♥ 7	♥ 7	
♦ J974	♦ J9742	There is a convention to show a hand that's weak and 5-5 in the minors like Hand H but we use the bid for another meaning. Anyway, the opposition has usually said something when they have the majors. So we pass 1NT with Hands G & H.
♣ QJ875	♣ QJ875	

1.6   **Raising to 2NT**

With a reasonably balanced hand and 8-9 points we can raise partner's 1NT opening to 2NT. This is an invitation for him to bid 3NT if he is maximum.

―――――

―――――――

―――――――――――――

> **Note:** As you will find out later, we play 4-way transfers and so we need the direct 2NT bid as a transfer to ♦'s. Thus, we have to go via a Stayman 2♣ bid and then bid 2NT with all of these hands. It's fully covered later in section 2.2.

―――――――――

―――――――

―――――

Hand A	Hand B	With Hand A we simply raise 1NT to 2NT.
♠ J76	♠ J76	With Hand B there may be a ♥ fit and so we investigate that
♥ A96	♥ A962	before bidding 2NT.
♦ K987	♦ K987	
♣ J92	♣ 105	

Hand C	Hand D	Hand C has a decent ♦ suit but we cannot mention it at an
♠ J76	♠ 1076	invitational level. So we simply raise to 2NT.
♥ A96	♥ A9	
♦ K9873	♦ K98763	And it's the same with a 6 card minor and invitational values,
♣ 98	♣ 98	raise 1NT to 2NT.

Hand E	Hand F	With the majors it's different, but minors suits are usually better
♠ J76	♠ 76	off in NT. Both of these hands should simply raise 1NT to 2NT.
♥ 9	♥ 9	
♦ K9873	♦ K9873	
♣ A985	♦ A9852	

2   <u>Stayman</u>

Stayman is a convention that uses 2♣ as an artificial bid to enquire about the 1NT opener's major suit holding. Opener's responses to Stayman 2♣ are: -

2♦ = no 4 card major
2♥ = 4 card ♥ suit, may have 4 ♠'s
2♠ = 4 card ♠ suit, denies 4 ♥'s

Higher bids (e.g. 2NT) are not generally used, but see section 2.7.

Note also that if you allow 5 card majors in your opening 1NT then obviously the 2♥/♠ response may be a 5 card suit.

The first thing that we have to consider when using Stayman is the high card points requirement. There are various versions of Stayman but the best (and most widely used – very important) is 'garbage' Stayman. So called because the Stayman bidder does not promise any points.

Once responder has bid 2♣, Stayman, he has various options after opener's reply and everything is covered in this Stayman section: -

1) pass or correct to 2♥/♠
2) invite to game in a major or NT
3) bid game in a major or NT
4) enquire further about opener's shape
5) ask about key cards/aces
6) look for slam via splinters, RKCB, Gerber and other means.

<u>Weak Hands</u>

Hand A	Hand B	How do you bid these hands if partner opens 1NT? If there was a

Hand A   Hand B

♠ Q963   ♠ Q9852
♥ J763   ♥ J763
♦ J9852   ♦ J2
♣ -   ♣ 74

How do you bid these hands if partner opens 1NT? If there was a points requirement then you would have to pass, even though you know that there is a better contract. Playing 'garbage' Stayman it is easy. With Hand A you bid 2♣ and pass any response from partner. And Hand B? You could transfer (transfers are defined in section 3) but if you transfer into ♠'s then you may miss a 4-4 ♥ fit. The way to bid weak hands that are 5-4 (or 4-5) in the majors is to use Stayman. You pass 2♥/♠ and convert a 2♦ response into your 5 card major.

Hand C   Hand D

♠ J6   ♠ 74
♥ Q963   ♥ J2
♦ J95   ♦ J763
♣ J874   ♣ J9852

These two hands are different. If you bid Stayman with Hand C then all is well if partner responds 2♥, but not if the reply is 2♦/♠. You cannot risk Stayman and so have to pass the 1NT opening. With Hand D it would be nice to be able to sign off in 2♣ but you cannot, 2♣ is Stayman. So again pass 1NT with this hand.

Invitational Hands

Hand E

♠ 975
♥ K973
♦ J2
♣ A974

Hand F

♠ K973
♥ A974
♦ J2
♣ 975

Hand G

♠ K973
♥ 975
♦ J2
♣ A974

Invitational hands present no problem. Here partner has opened 1NT. With Hand E you bid 2♣. If partner responds 2♥ then you invite game by bidding 3♥. If partner responds 2♦/♠ then you invite game by bidding 2NT. Hand F is similar; you bid 2NT over a 2♦ response and raise 2♥/♠ to 3♥/♠, invitational.

Hand G is slightly different. Again you bid 2♣ Stayman. If partner responds 2♦ you reply 2NT. If partner responds 2♠ then you invite with 3♠. But if partner responds 2♥ then he may also have 4 ♠'s. No problem, you can still invite with 2NT as partner knows that you must have a 4 card major (thus ♠'s) in order to bid Stayman. If he also has 4 ♠'s then he will correct to 3♠ or 4♠. Note, however, that playing 4-way transfers then this hand must bid 2♠ at the second turn (instead of 2NT). This is explained in the section 2.2.

Strong Hands

Hand H

♠ K975
♥ K973
♦ J2
♣ A97

Hand J

♠ KQ73
♥ A74
♦ J2
♣ K975

We also use Stayman with strong hands. These examples are good enough for game opposite a strong NT and we start off by looking for a 4-4 major suit fit, so 2♣. With Hand H if partner replies either 2♥ or 2♠ then we raise to game in that suit. With Hand J it is slightly more subtle. A 2♠ response is raised to 4♠ and 2♦ receives 3NT. If partner bids 2♥ then we bid 3NT; partner knows that we have 4 ♠'s as otherwise we would not have bid Stayman but bid 3NT directly, so he converts to 4♠ if he also has 4 ♠'s.

Very Strong Hands

Hand K

♠ K975
♥ K973
♦ AJ
♣ AJ7

Hand L

♠ AK3
♥ KJ73
♦ Q2
♣ KQ52

Here we are definitely looking for slam opposite a strong NT opener. Again we use Stayman as a tool to find a fit. With Hand K we bid a small slam in the major if partner replies 2♥/♠. After a 2♦ reply you could try 6NT; but 4NT (quantitative) is probably best, without a fit you need a maximum partner. Hand L is most certainly worth slam – perhaps a grand, we start with Stayman. If partner responds 2♦/♠ (denying 4 ♥'s) then we should investigate a ♣ slam. This Hand L is dealt with in section 2.5 (page 44).

No Major

Hand M

♠ K95
♥ 1093
♦ AJ7
♣ A976

Hand N

♠ Q32
♥ K73
♦ J2
♣ KQJ52

Hand M is balanced with no 4 card major. There are the values for 3NT – so bid it. This hand responds 3NT directly.
Hand N again has the values for 3NT but has a good ♣ suit. 2♣ is Stayman, 3♣ is defined in section 5.2 and is looking for slam. This is a good hand but not good enough to go slamming, so simply bid 3NT.

2.1 Denying a 4 Card Major

Many books will tell you that if partner opens 1NT and your shape is 4333 or 3433 then you should ignore Stayman and jump directly to 3NT if you have the values for game. **This is not one of those books!**

Hand A	Hand B	Hand C
♠ KQ53	♠ 74	♠ A107
♥ KJ74	♥ A1053	♥ A1053
♦ 64	♦ A1074	♦ J42
♣ 1094	♣ J94	♣ 1094

Partner opens a strong NT (15-17), what do you do? Obviously you have the values to try game, but Stayman or a direct 3NT? Now 'everybody' would bid Stayman with Hand A – if there is a fit in either major that will be preferable to 3NT with this small doubleton ♦. And Hand B? Again, use Stayman. If a 4-4 ♥ fit exists, then 4♥ will normally be a far superior contract to 3NT.

But what about Hand C? A direct 3NT on this flat hand or look for the 4-4 ♥ fit? This is from a club tournament and South opened 1NT, 15-17. North raised immediately to 3NT with Hand C. Is this the recommended bidding? I said no, the two players disagreed. Let's examine this all in a little more detail.

Now we all agree (I hope) that 4-4 major suit fits are usually better than 3NT, especially if one player has a weak doubleton. The argument for not bidding Stayman on Hand C is that it is totally flat – no ruffing values. I totally agree that there are no ruffing values in this hand – but what about partner? He has opened 1NT, promising a balanced 15-17. If he does not have a 4 (or 5!) card ♥ suit then there is no problem with bidding Stayman (you end up in 3NT anyway). So, let's consider the case where partner does have a 4 card ♥ suit, is 3NT best? – Very unlikely! The point is that although you do not have ruffing potential, partner may well have! Partner's most likely shape is (any order) 4432. If he shows 4 ♥'s then, with this shape, you almost certainly belong in 4♥, not 3NT. Partner will have a doubleton opposite one of your 3 card suits – when opponents have 8 cards in a suit then that spells trouble for a non-max 3NT. And what if partner also happens to be exactly 3433? Nowhere near so likely, but 4♥ is still probably the best spot! In this case you have three 6 card suits with the opponents on lead. It only needs one of them to be divided 5-2 (or worse) and 3NT is probably a disaster. The only case where it is preferable to play in 3NT rather than 4 of a major is when you have ample points (say 27+) and at least a double stop in every suit; even then, 4 of the major may be better. In this actual case you are nowhere near max for 3NT and both minor suits are suspect. Additionally, of course, if you are one of the enlightened pairs who may open 1NT with a 5 card major, then you will be the laughing stock of the club if you end up in 3NT missing a 5-4 ♥ fit!

Now if you change Hand C slightly, and swap the ♥A with the ♣4, thus having a very weak 4 card ♥ suit, then I would agree that there is a case for forgetting Stayman. With this actual hand (4½ points in ♥'s) the strong ♥ suit means that all the other suits cannot be adequately covered. Quite simply, a 4-4 fit will usually produce an extra trick and stops the rot of opponents running a suit.

The experts will continue to argue this for years to come (whether or not to bid Stayman when 4333 or 3433). Apart from all the arguments that I have put forward, two are undeniable: -
(1) Partner may have a 5 card major and
(2) Computer studies have shown that bidding Stayman has a higher success rate.

The bottom line: Never (or hardly ever) deny a 4 card major !

To satisfy the unbelievers, let's look at a possible bidding sequences a little more closely: -

West	East	Example 1
♠ KQ63	♠ A74	You are playing a strong NT. Obviously you open 1♣, partner replies
♥ KJ74	♥ AQ53	1♥, you support with 2♥ and partner raises to 4♥. But who was dealer?
♦ 65	♦ J74	Makes no difference, the bidding is the same. Actually, instead of the
♣ KJ5	♣ Q94	final 4♥, 3NT is a better bid just in case opener has supported on a
		3 card suit; either way, the correct 4♥ contract is easily reached.

Now what happens if you are playing a weak NT? You open 1NT, partner bids Stayman and you again reach the simple 4♥. If East opens the bidding that is certainly the case, but what if West is dealer? There are players out there who would not bid Stayman with 4333 type shape and just game values! 3NT is the wrong contract.

West	East	Example 2
♠ KQ63	♠ A74	Let's try a couple of strong NT openers. If you ignore Stayman then you
♥ KJ74	♥ AQ53	reach 3NT making +2 if ♠'s fail to break 3-3. You always make 12 tricks
♦ K5	♦ A74	in ♥'s. This shows (yet again) the power of a good 4-4 fit. Are there
♣ KJ5	♣ Q94	people out there who are trying to tell me that if East opens 1NT then
		they reach 4♥ but if West opens 1NT they play in 3NT?

West	East	Example 3
♠ KJ	♠ AQ4	So when does this policy of ignoring Stayman work? When you have an
♥ Q764	♥ 9532	abundance of points (28/29 is a good norm) and all the side suits well
♦ KQ63	♦ AJ4	covered. Often, the weakest suit is the 'trump' suit. Here, ten top tricks,
♣ AJ4	♣ KQ9	maybe also a ♥ trick in 3NT. And if ♥'s are trumps? Not so nice, you
		have to tackle ♥'s if they are trumps and it does not play so nicely.

There – 'I told you so' shout all the 3NT leapers in unison – 'East should not bid Stayman on his 4333 shape'. Hogwash – it has little to do with being 4333. Consider what happens if East opens the bidding with 1NT. Presumably West then bids Stayman?

Something is wrong – you reach 3NT if West is dealer but 4♥ when East is dealer? The answer is that deciding not to bid Stayman has little to do with being 4333, you must make the same decision if 4432! When the West hand opens 1NT in example 3, East could simply bid 3NT. And if East opens? - then West could simply bid 3NT. Being 4333 or 4432 is largely irrelevant to this decision to ignore Stayman, it is the quality of the 4-4 fit and having excellent cover in the outside suits that counts.

West	East	Example 4

West: ♠ KJ92 ♥ Q104 ♦ AJ3 ♣ A64

East: ♠ AQ84 ♥ KJ2 ♦ KQ4 ♣ 732

One more example, loads of points, so 3NT with 4333 shape? This deal illustrates what I have just said ideally. Partner (either!) opens 1NT. If you simply bid 3NT because you are 4333 then you will be in an inferior contract. Go for the 4-4 fit when you have decent trumps, especially if all outside suits are not well covered. The 4333 shape is a red herring.

East — Example 5

East: ♠ K62 ♥ J732 ♦ AKQ ♣ Q73

Partner opens a strong NT. Loads of points. Partner's 15-17 plus this 15 means 30-32. Worth looking for slam? NO. Even if there is a ♥ fit then there is no slam because of the poor quality of these ♥'s. With this abundance of points outside the major, bid 3NT. Another way of looking at it is that this hand is not worth 15 points!

West — **East**

West: ♠ AQ3 ♥ K8654 ♦ J8 ♣ AJ5

East: ♠ K62 ♥ J732 ♦ AKQ ♣ Q73

But partner's 1NT may include a 5 card major! True, but in that case his suit quality is not so great (we open the major with good suits) and so even with a 5-4 fit 3NT may be best. Note that this decision to bid 3NT with ample points outside the weak major applies to 4432 as well as 4333 type hands. Of course not if the other 4 carder is the other major!

West — **East** — Example 6

West: ♠ A1064 ♥ KQ84 ♦ AK4 ♣ 92

East: ♠ J952 ♥ A6 ♦ QJ2 ♣ AK64

Even with weak trumps it may still be best to play in the 4-4 fit, here 6♠ is a very reasonable contract but there are only 11 tricks in NT. Even if you replace the ♣4 with a small ♥ so that the East hand is 4333, 6♠ does not need ♥'s to behave and is the best spot.

West — **East** — Example 7

West: ♠ AQ3 ♥ KJ654 ♦ Q8 ♣ AJ5

East: ♠ KJ6 ♥ Q732 ♦ 1072 ♣ KQ3

And look at this example. Many (most) players would choose to open 1NT with the West hand. East really would look pretty silly if he bids 3NT when the opponents have 5 or 6 tricks off the top.

But there are always exceptions, and now we come onto something slightly different; we may have a 4-4 major suit fit but we have a long strong outside suit: -

West	East	Example 8
♠ A953	♠ J642	West opens 1NT, what should East do?
♥ A765	♥ 32	In these situations where the 4 card major is very weak and there is
♦ AJ7	♦ 8	a source of tricks elsewhere it is often best to go for the nine trick
♣ K9	♣ AQ8763	3NT game. I would raise 1NT directly to 3NT with this East hand.

West	East	Example 9
♠ A953	♠ J642	And if the 4 card major is very weak and we have 6 excellent cards in the
♥ K84	♥ AQJ1096	other major then that may well be the best strain. With this East hand
♦ AK4	♦ Q	you could transfer into ♥'s with 2♦ and then bid 4♥ but it's best to
♣ Q82	♣ 93	transfer to 4♥ directly via a Texas Transfer. Texas Transfers are covered
		in section 6.2).

I must emphasise here that ignoring the 4-4 major suit fit is very rarely a good decision. It only applies when: -

- the other three suits are well covered (with at least 27-29 combined pts and with no obvious weakness) and usually only when the 'trump' suit is very poor or
- the 4 card major is very weak and you have a strong 6 card suit elsewhere or
- we are not strong/shapely enough to bid over partner's 1NT.

OK, so we virtually always bid Stayman when we have a 4 card major. But does the 2♣ Stayman bid guarantee a 4 card major? And what are the continuations by opener and responder after

1NT - 2♣ - ?   that's what the next 80 or so pages are all about!

Stayman When Using 4-way Transfers

We have seen that when playing 'standard' Stayman then the 2♣ bid always promises at least one 4 card major. Later (in section 4) we will be discussing 4-way Jacoby Transfers and for the transfers to the minors we need, directly over a 1NT opening: -

   2♠ (transfer to ♣'s)   2NT (transfer to ♦'s)

There's no problem with the 2♠ bid (it is redundant) but using 2NT as a transfer means that it is no longer available as the limit raise (8-9 pts) (without a 4 card major). This means that all limit raises have to go via Stayman, regardless of whether they contain a 4 card major or not.

So we have to clear up how 2NT can be used as a transfer as it is normally used as an invitational (8-9 pts) raise in NT. Simple, we simply bid 2♣ and then bid 2NT after partner's response to 'Stayman'. Thus, when playing these 4-way transfers, a 2♣ 'Stayman' bid no longer guarantees a 4 card major. Does this lead to difficulties and a 4-4 major suit ever being missed? No, let's have some examples: -

Example 1		West	East	West	East
(1)	Stayman, may have no	♠ J863	♠ A97	1NT	2♣ (1)
	4 card major	♥ K64	♥ Q93	2♠	2NT (2)
(2)	invitational,	♦ AK63	♦ Q2	pass	
	3 or less ♠'s	♣ AJ	♣ 109764		

Example 2		West	East	West	East
(1)	Stayman, may have no	♠ J86	♠ A97	1NT	2♣ (1)
	4 card major	♥ K64	♥ Q93	2♦	2NT (2)
(2)	invitational, may have	♦ AK63	♦ Q2	pass	
	any major suit holding	♣ AJ3	♣ 109764		

So that all works fine, with no problems. The only area which needs some thought is when opener has both majors. In that case he responds 2♥, but a responder with 4 ♠'s cannot now simply bid 2NT as opener will not know if he has 4 ♠'s or not. A problem?

No, holding an invitational hand responder should bid 2NT if he does not have 4 ♠'s but bid 2♠ if he does. Thus: -

   In the sequence, 1NT - 2♣ - 2♥ - 2♠ ,   2♠ promises a 4 card ♠ suit and invitational values.
   In the sequence, 1NT - 2♣ - 2♥ - 2NT,   2NT is invitational with no 4 card ♠ suit.

Note: These invitational sequences are just one reason why opener should always respond 2♥ to Stayman when holding both majors. If he responds 2♠ and the bidding is 1NT - 2♣ - 2♠ - 2NT then opener has no idea if responder has 4 ♥'s or not.

Example 3

West	East	West	East
♠ AJ106	♠ K94	1NT	2♣
♥ AK64	♥ J97	2♥	2NT (1)
♦ Q63	♦ J975	pass	
♣ J3	♣ A105		

(1) In 'standard', this bid promises an invitational hand with 4 ♠'s and so opener may wish to retreat into 3♠. Playing 4-way transfers, this bid shows an invitational hand without a 4 card major. Opener passes the 2NT bid with this minimum. He would bid 3NT with a max whereas it would be 4♠ if not playing 4-way transfers.

Example 4

West	East	West	East
♠ AJ106	♠ K954	1NT	2♣
♥ AK64	♥ J97	2♥	2♠ (1)
♦ Q63	♦ J75	pass (2)	
♣ J3	♣ A105		

(1) In 'standard' this particular sequence is up to partnership understanding. When not using transfers, the bid is often used to show an invitational (or slightly less, say 7-8 pts) hand with 5 ♠'s. Since we can show that hand type using transfers we define a different meaning when using 4-way transfers: - Playing 4-way transfers this shows an invitational hand with 4 ♠'s. Opener will pass with a minimum and 4 ♠'s, correct to 2NT with a minimum without 4 ♠'s and bid the relevant game if holding a maximum.

(2) West has a minimum, so passes the invitational 2♠.

Being at the low level of 2♠ has other advantages. Sometimes a 4-3 fit may be preferable: -

Example 5

West	East	West	East
♠ AK6	♠ Q754	1NT	2♣
♥ Q9432	♥ 7	2♥	2♠
♦ Q63	♦ K75	pass	
♣ A3	♣ K9642		

In this example, 2♠ is better than 2NT

Example 6

West	East	West	East
♠ AJ86	♠ KQ54	1NT	2♣
♥ AK64	♥ J97	2♥	3NT (1)
♦ Q63	♦ A7	4♠	pass
♣ J3	♣ Q1092		

(1) This is the same if playing 4-way transfers or standard. The jump to 3NT shows game values with 4 ♠'s. If East did not have 4 ♠'s then he would have bid a direct 3NT.

Recap

Sequence A	1NT	-	2♣	-	2♦	-	2♠
Sequence B	1NT	-	2♣	-	2♥	-	2♠

Although seemingly similar, these sequences are totally different: -

With sequence A, 2♠ is to play. Responder has a weak hand containing 4 ♥'s and 5 ♠'s.
With sequence B, 2♠ is invitational. Responder has an invitational hand containing 4 ♠'s.

So the invitational sequences are: -

Sequence B	1NT	-	2♣	-	2♥	-	2♠	is invitational, with a four card ♠ suit
Sequence C	1NT	-	2♣	-	2♦	-	2NT	is invitational, may have 0, 1 or 2 four card majors
Sequence D	1NT	-	2♣	-	2♥	-	2NT	is invitational, no four card major
Sequence E	1NT	-	2♣	-	2♠	-	2NT	is invitational, may have a four card ♥ suit

And obviously the following sequences are weak: -

| Sequence F | 1NT | - | 2♣ | - | 2♦ | - | 2♥ | is weak, with 5 ♥'s and 4 ♠'s |
| Sequence A | 1NT | - | 2♣ | - | 2♦ | - | 2♠ | is weak, with 4 ♥'s and 5 ♠'s |

When we get on to discuss 5-5 major suited hands, we see that it is best to also use either sequence A or F with a very weak 5-5 hand. Basically, try Stayman and then bid the best 5 card major if there is no 5-4 fit.

Note   Playing traditional methods Sequence B, 1NT - 2♣ - 2♥ - 2♠, is redundant. It is sometimes used to show a hand with 5 ♠'s and 7-8 points which is not quite good enough to transfer and then invite. I guess that it's reasonable, but with no equivalent with a ♥ suit it really is a luxury that we cannot afford as we need the bid to show our invitational hand with 4 ♠'s.

Garbage or Crawling Stayman?

The Crawling Stayman convention seems to have some following these days so let's look at it: -

Crawling Stayman is an 'extension' of Garbage Stayman and is meant to be an improvement when responder has a weak hand containing both majors.

Hand A	Playing our Garbage Stayman you may have a problem with this particular hand type. You start off with 2♣ but if partner replies 2♦ then you are simply on a guess as to which major to retreat into. Crawling Stayman solved this dilemma.

Hand A

♠ Q8642
♥ Q8642
♦ 76
♣ 3

After partner's 2♦ bid you bid 2♥ which, when crawling, shows 5 cards in both majors and opener then chooses the best suit.

Excellent, so our weak 5-5 hand is solved. But is this really excellent?

Hand B   Hand C

♠ Q864   ♠ Q8642
♥ Q8642   ♥ Q864
♦ 763   ♦ 763
♣ 3   ♣ 3

No! This time consider one of these hands. We use our Garbage Stayman and bid 2♣ with both. If partner responds 2♦ then we bid our 5 card suit. Playing Crawling Stayman this is not possible as a 2♥ bid promises 5-5. So with Hand B a Crawling Stayman player would have to transfer to ♥'s and possibly miss a 4-4 (or 4-5) ♠ fit.

So neither convention is perfect, but since hand type B is more frequent than hand type A let's keep everything upright and forget all about crawling.

I won't bother to go into it, but there are further extensions to Crawling Stayman which enable 8 card minor suit fits to be located at the 3 level. As I said, let's forget all about it.

Opener's Bid After Responder's Invitational 2NT

In standard methods (playing a strong NT) responder raises 1NT to 2NT with 8-9 points and no four card major. Using 4-way transfers we go via Stayman, but we have seen that that's no problem. But what should opener do when responder has invited with 2NT? Clearly he usually bids 3NT or passes, but we can occasionally make use of the 3♥/♠ (or even 3♣/♦) bids: -

If opener is going to accept the game invitation then he can bid a 5 card major just in case there is a 5-3 fit there.

Suppose that you open 1NT and the bidding goes   1NT - 2♣ - 2♥ - 2NT - ? : -

Hand 1	Hand 2	Hand 3	Hand 4	Hand 5
♠ K86	♠ K86	♠ KJ6	♠ KJ64	♠ KJ64
♥ AJ1084	♥ AQ1094	♥ 108742	♥ AQ104	♥ AQ104
♦ KJ6	♦ KJ6	♦ AQ6	♦ Q96	♦ KJ9
♣ K3	♣ K3	♣ AQ	♣ K6	♣ K6

Hand 1:   Pass, you do not have enough to accept the invitation.

Hand 2:   Bid 3♥. You have enough to accept the game invitation and should show your decent 5 card suit.

Hand 3:   You could bid a forcing 3♥, but with all the honours outside the suit, I prefer 3NT.

Hand 4:   Pass, partner has denied 4 ♠'s.

Hand 5:   Bid 3NT. The sequences 1NT - 2♣ - 2♥ - 2NT - 3♠/4♠ do not exist when playing 4-way transfers as the 2NT bid here by responder denies 4 ♠'s.

And it's much the same if opener has a 5 card ♠ suit and the bidding starts 1NT - 2♣ - 2♠ - 2NT; where a 3♠ bid by opener shows a decent 5 card ♠ suit.

And a similar situation applies when responder has a 4 card ♠ suit and the bidding has gone 1NT - 2♣ - 2♥ - 2♠ - ?. But this time if opener has 4 ♠'s then there is a fit there: -

Hand 1:   Bid 2NT. Again, you do not have enough to accept the invitation. If the ♣'s were weaker then passing 2♠ and playing in the Moysian fit is a very real possibility.

Hand 2:   Bid 3♥. You again have enough to accept the game invitation and should show your decent 5 card suit. Partner's 4 card ♠ suit is irrelevant.

Hand 3:   Again, you could bid a forcing 3♥, but with all the honours outside the suit, I still prefer 3NT.

Hand 4:   Pass. You have a 4-4 ♠ fit but you are minimum.

Hand 5:   Bid 4♠, obviously.

And what would a 3♠ bid by opener in the sequence   1NT - 2♣ - 2♥ - 2♠ - 3♠   mean?

You could well use it as passing the buck, showing 4 card support but not sure whether to go to game or not. Quite plausible, but consider this hand: -

West	East	West	East
♠ AQ7	♠ KJ85	1NT	2♣
♥ AQJ8	♥ K95	2♥	2♠
♦ 95	♦ 6432	3♠ (1)	4♠
♣ KJ97	♣ Q8	pass	

With a weak doubleton minor, West uses the 3♠ bid at (1) to show decent 3 card ♠ support and offering 4♠ as an alternative contract to 3NT. Reverse East's minors and 4♠ is still best.

Now consider this one: -

West	West	East	
			Partner's 2NT bid is invitational and denies 4 ♠'s.
			We have game values but should we bid 3♥ to try to play
♠ 95	1NT	2♣	in a Moysian fit?
♥ AQJ8	2♥	2NT	No, a 3♥ bid here shows 5 ♥'s and the Moysian fit will not
♦ AQ7	?		play well as it is the long trump hand taking the ♠ ruff(s).
♣ KJ97			It's best to take your chances in 3NT.

So the sequence 1NT - 2♣ - 2♥ - 2NT - 3♥ promises a 5 card ♥ suit.

And what would a 3♠ bid by opener in the sequence   1NT - 2♣ - 2♥ - 2NT - 3♠   mean?

Could it be a hand 4-4 in the majors with a weak minor and suggesting the ♠ Moysian fit?

West	West	East	
			Partner's 2NT bid is again invitational and denies 4 ♠'s.
			We have game values but should we bid 3♠ to try to play in a
♠ KJ97	1NT	2♣	Moysian fit there?
♥ AQJ8	2♥	2NT	No. If there is a ♦ problem it will be the hand long in trumps
♦ 95	?		that will be forced. It's best to take your chances in 3NT and
♣ AQ7			if you keep quiet about the ♠'s you may well get a not
			unwelcome ♠ lead.

So the sequence 1NT - 2♣ - 2♥ - 2NT - 3♠ is undefined.

33

Now again consider   1NT - 2♣ - 2♥ - 2NT   what would 3♣ or 3♦ mean?

Hand 5	Hand 6	
♠ 86	♠ 86	Partner has an invitational hand with no 4 card major.
♥ AK64	♥ AK64	With Hand 5 it seems prudent to bid 3♣, to play. This will almost certainly be a safer contract than 2NT unless partner is
♦ K9	♦ AQ873	exactly 3352. Hand 6 is similar and should bid 3♦ to play.
♣ AQ873	♣ K9	

And after   1NT - 2♣ - 2♦ - 2NT   what would 3♣ or 3♦ mean?

Hand 7	Hand 8	
♠ 86	♠ Q6	Partner again has an invitational hand and may or may not have a 4 card major. With Hand 7 it may be best to bid 3♣, to play.
♥ AQ6	♥ K6	With Hand 7 it's not clear, but with Hand 8 it's best to bid 3♦
♦ K97	♦ AQ8743	now having opened 1NT.
♣ AQ873	♣ K97	

But after   1NT - 2♣ - 2♠ - 2NT   things are different.

Hand 9	Hand 10	
♠ AQ64	♠ AQ64	Partner again has an invitational hand but we do not know if he has a 4 card ♥ suit or not. Bidding 3♣ with Hand 9 would
♥ 86	♥ 86	be silly if partner has 3442 shape. And it's much the same with
♦ K9	♦ AQ873	Hand 10. It's best to pass 2NT with these hands.
♣ AQ873	♣ K9	

Summary: 1NT - 2♣ - 2♥ - 2NT - 3♥,
                        1NT - 2♣ - 2♠ - 2NT - 3♠   and
                        1NT - 2♣ - 2♥ - 2♠ - 3♥   show a decent 5 card suit and offer responder the choice of games.

And   1NT - 2♣ - 2♥ - 2♠ - 3♠   is showing decent 3 card support
but   1NT - 2♣ - 2♥ - 2NT - 3♠   is not required and is undefined.

And   1NT - 2♣ - 2♥ - 2NT - 3♣,
                1NT - 2♣ - 2♥ - 2NT - 3♦,
                1NT - 2♣ - 2♦ - 2NT - 3♣   and
                1NT - 2♣ - 2♦ - 2NT - 3♦   are all weak, to play.
But   1NT - 2♣ - 2♠ - 2NT - 3♣   and
                1NT - 2♣ - 2♠ - 2NT - 3♦   are not required and are undefined.

In this section we discuss the situation where opener replies to Stayman with a major suit bid and responder then bids a minor at the 3 level. So the four sequences: -

1NT - 2♣ - 2♥ - 3♣   1NT - 2♣ - 2♠ - 3♣
1NT - 2♣ - 2♥ - 3♦   1NT - 2♣ - 2♠ - 3♦

Four fairly similar sequences, a 3 level minor suit bid after Stayman had received a major suit reply. But what does this 3♣/♦ bid mean? If you ask around then you will probably get any or all of the following: -

1) The 3♣/♦ bid is to play, saying nothing about majors.
2) The 3♣/♦ bid is natural, looking for slam, saying nothing about majors
3) Natural, 4 card major & 5 card minor, game forcing.
4) Natural, 4 card major & 5 card minor, forcing for one round.
5) Natural, 4 card major & 4 card minor, seeking a 4-4 fit for slam.
6) Natural, invitational.
7) Natural, weak, 4 card major & 6 card minor.
8) 3♦ is Stayman in Doubt (SID).
9) 3♣ is Spring Stayman.
10) A more sophisticated idea for both 3♣ and 3♦.

Many non-steady partnerships will have never discussed this, so let's look at all the sensible alternatives (assume a strong NT throughout): -

1)   The 3♣/♦ bids are to play

Back in the days before transfers (to minors) it was not easy to play in a ♣ contract with a very weak hand because 2♣ is Stayman and 3♣ a slam try. The solution was to first bid 2♣ and then 3♣ over any response. The 3♣ bid simply showed 6 ♣'s (probably no 4 card major) and was to play. These days we have transfers to the minors and so this meaning is redundant. Now that transfers to the majors are common (so 2♦ is used as a transfer to ♥'s), the same situation applies in ♦'s.

So, no sensible use for our 4 sequences yet. Let's continue the search: -

2)   The 3♣/♦ bid is natural, looking for slam, saying nothing about majors.

This scheme is favoured by players who do not play 4-way transfers and who would like to play direct jumps to 3♣/♦ as something special. The direct jumps to 3♣/♦ are discussed in detail later in section 5. Anyway, we play transfers to the minors and so do not need these bids to show good minor suits.

3)   Natural, 4 card major & 5 card minor, game forcing

This is the most popular use of the bids, but it is totally unsatisfactory!

Hand A	Hand B	
♠ 2	♠ AK98	Partner opens a strong NT. So bid Stayman and then your long minor if no major suit fit is immediately found? Certainly a plausible use for these sequences. But wait a minute, we will learn later (sections 3 & 4) that a transfer followed by a new suit is game forcing. So we can bid both of these hands by transferring to the minor and then bidding the major. Game forcing.
♥ K984	♥ 8	
♦ J3	♦ KQJ83	
♣ AQJ763	♣ 872	

Now bidding Stayman with these hand types is a popular treatment, but there are drawbacks. If LHO sticks his oar in and the opponents compete, then opener is left in the dark. You have bid 2♣ and that really means nothing – you could be weak, invitational, have a 4 card major or not etc. At least if you transfer to the minor partner knows something about your hand, and LHO is less likely to interfere over 2♠/2NT. If you bid Stayman first then you have little chance of showing both suits if opponents intervene.

But my main objection to this treatment is that opener does not know which 4-card major responder has if opener responds 2♦. Consider these examples: -

Example 1

West	East 1	East 2	West	East
♠ A4	♠ 75	♠ Q1087	1NT	2♣
♥ KJ9	♥ Q1087	♥ 75	2♦	3♣
♦ A962	♦ K7	♦ K7	? (1)	
♣ KJ76	♣ AQ543	♣ AQ543		

So what does West bid at (1)? If East has Hand 2 then 3NT is fine, if East has Hand 1 then West wants to play in the Moysian ♥ fit.

Example 2

West	East 3	East 4	West	East
♠ A4	♠ K5	♠ Q1087	1NT	2♣
♥ KJ9	♥ Q1087	♥ 7	2♦	3♣
♦ A962	♦ 7	♦ K5	3NT (1)	4♣
♣ KJ76	♣ AQ10543	♣ AQ10543	?	

Let's suppose that West tosses a coin and it comes down 3NT, so he bids 3NT at (1). This happens to be no problem as partner has a stronger hand this time and is looking for slam anyway. So East bids 4♣, looking for a ♣ slam; West would be delighted to accept if he knew that his ♥'s were working (East 3) but not opposite East 4.

Bidding Stayman unnecessarily gives the defence knowledge about opener's hand. If opener responds 2♦ or with the 'wrong' major then the defence has additional information about his hand. And you are no better off if you bid Stayman and a 4-4 major suit fit is found immediately. If opener also has a fit for responder's minor then there may well be a slam which is easier to find if responder had bid both of his suits: -

Example 3

West	East	West	East
♠ Q743	♠ K8	1NT	2♣
♥ AQ74	♥ K963	2♥	4♥
♦ A3	♦ 84	pass	
♣ KJ8	♣ AQ764		

The ♥ fit is found immediately but East has no idea about the superb ♣ fit and so quite reasonably simply bids game. An easy 6♥ missed.

Example 4

West	East	West		East	
♠ AQ74	♠ K963	1NT		2♣	
♥ Q743	♥ K8	2♥		3♣	
♦ A3	♦ 84	3♠	(1)	4♠	(2)
♣ KJ8	♣ AQ764	pass			

This time West knows about East's two suits at (1) so he shows his ♠ support, he cannot realistically do anything else as he has no idea if East is interested in slam or not. And at (2) East does not know about the great ♣ fit and again quite reasonably just bids game. Slam again missed.

We will see how easy it is to bid these last four example hands correctly when we come onto minor suit transfers, and in particular minor-major two suiters, in section 4.2

♠ K963
♥ Q8
♦ Q4
♣ AQ764

And one further point. Consider this East hand from example 4 but slightly stronger. Suppose that partner opens 1♥ (or 1♦), what do you respond? This is an analogous situation; you have a game forcing two suiter opposite partner's opener. The recommended bid is 2♣ followed by a forcing ♠ bid.

So why on earth would you want to do it the other way round when partner opens 1NT? And, what's more, partner does not even know that it's a ♠ suit when you bid Stayman! No, these types of hands must be bid by transferring to the minor and then bidding the major, opener then knows both of responder's suits. Simple.

4)   <u>Natural, 4 card major & 5 card minor, forcing for one round.</u>

This is one answer that I got when I was asking about the sequence. I guess an invitational sequence?

Since the 3♣/♦ bid is at the three level it is difficult to see how this is not game forcing. Makes no sense to me. We use the transfer to a minor sequence with strong hands and so this meaning does not exist. Let's look further for a **useful** purpose for these sequences: -

5)   <u>Natural, 4 card major & 4 card minor, seeking a 4-4 fit for slam.</u>

Hand A	Hand B	
		Partner opens a strong NT and the hand is worth slam if (and probably only if) there is a 4-4 fit. So obviously start with Stayman and if no major
♠ K92	♠ KJ52	fit materialises then bid your 4 card minor looking for the fit there. This
♥ KJ52	♥ K92	obviously is the best use so far and is very sensible. But actually there are
♦ AJ83	♦ K3	a couple of drawbacks.
♣ K3	♣ AJ83	Firstly, could this 3♣/♦ bid be a 5 card suit?

Hand C	
	Secondly, how does responder bid if he has no 4 card major but one or two 4 card minors, say Hand C? The problem is that responder has started off by being the captain
♠ K92	and finding something out about opener's shape, but by then bidding naturally he is
♥ K3	passing some of the captaincy back to opener. As you will see later (SARS, section 2.5),
♦ AJ83	we have a far better scheme whereby responder can establish if opener has a 4 (or 5!)
♣ KJ52	card minor(s) even after having tried Stayman and found no fit there.

6)   <u>Natural and invitational</u>

Why not transfer? If responder does not have a 4 card major but has a minor suit, then he can transfer into the minor or simply invite with 2NT (via 2♣ playing 4-way transfers). As we see later when we discuss 4-way transfers (specifically transfers to a minor, section 4) opener can show game interest when responder transfers to a minor.

Hand A	Hand B	
		With Hand A we simply invite with 2NT (via 2♣).
♠ K106	♠ 976	
♥ 87	♥ J4	Hand B is similar, but with no real possibility of an entry outside ♦'s it
♦ K9876	♦ KQ8764	is best to transfer into ♦'s. If opener has the ♦Axx required to make
♣ Q42	♣ J2	3NT then he will super-accept.
		We go through all of this later in section 4.1.

7)   Natural, weak, 4 card major and 6 card minor

Hand A	Hand B	Partner opens a strong NT. Seems simple, look for the 4-4 fit and if it
♠ 2	♠ Q984	does not materialise then settle for 3 of the minor. Let's look a little deeper. With Hand A we have no problem, if partner bids 2♦/♠ then we
♥ Q984	♥ 2	bid 3♣; works fine if partner is on the same wavelength. But then what
♦ J3	♦ J3	about Hand B? You may miss a 4-4 ♠ fit. Now this scheme works fine
♣ Q87642	♣ Q87642	(you may occasionally miss a 4-4 ♠ fit) and is what I would recommend if these sequences were not needed elsewhere.

Oops, I've given it away – there is a really good use for both the 3♣ and the 3♦ bids in these sequences and we come onto it in next chapters. So with these hand types, simply transfer into the minor.

8)   3♣ is Spring Stayman

With this convention, popular in France, the 3♣ bid is artificial and asks opener to define his hand; in particular the minor suits. This convention is, in fact, very similar to what we shall be using but has the disadvantage that the bidding may go above 3NT when there is no fit.

So what do we use these sequences for? The 3♣ bid is used to find out about opener's minor suit distribution, fully covered in section 2.5. The 3♦ bid agrees the major suit as trumps and enquires: -

9)   3♦ is Stayman in Doubt (SID)

Stayman in Doubt (SID) is a convention designed to ignore 4-4 major suit fits when both hands are 4333 (or 3433). When responder has one of these flat hands with game values and partner opens 1NT then responder bids 2♣ Stayman. If opener replies in responder's 4 card major then responder bids an artificial 3♦ that says 'I am totally flat with 4 of your major, if you are also totally flat then bid 3NT'. This enables the contract to be 3NT when there is total duplication of shape. Now you need only to refer back to section 2.1 to see what I think of this philosophy. Even with total duplication in shape 4 of the major is usually best unless there are 28+ points with all three outside suits very well covered. However, this philosophy of 3♦ to ask about opener's shape can be extended such that it is a really useful conventional bid; especially when investigating slam.

Let's call it Advanced Stayman in Doubt (ASID). It's fully described next.

10)   A more sophisticated idea for both 3♣ and 3♦

We have just decided to use 3♦ as a shape/strength enquiry (ASID) when the major suit is 'agreed' as trumps. But what about that 3♣ bid? We shall use 3♣ to enquire more about opener's distribution, normally specifically looking for a minor suit fit. This is our form of minor suit Stayman. It is widely used in Holland and is superior to the French equivalent, Spring Stayman. More about it later in section 2.5.

2.4   **3♦ (After Stayman) - Advanced SID (ASID)**

So finally we are really going to define a meaning for the sequences

1NT - 2♣ - 2♥ - 3♦   and   1NT - 2♣ - 2♠ - 3♦.

The 3♦ bid agrees trumps (but does not rule out 3NT as a final contract) and asks opener to further define his hand. Responder has 4 trumps but may be any shape (unlike the original SID convention). Responder is the captain. Opener's replies are: -

After 1NT - 2♣ - 2♥ - 3♦ : -   after 1NT - 2♣ - 2♠ - 3♦ : -

3♥   =   3433, min   3♥   =   doubleton ♥
3♠   =   doubleton ♠   3♠   =   4333, min
3NT =   3433, non min   3NT =   4333, non min
4♣   =   doubleton ♣   4♣   =   doubleton ♣
4♦   =   doubleton ♦   4♦   =   doubleton ♦
4♥   =   5 card ♥ suit
                               4♠   =   5 card ♠ suit

Responder may then sign off in the appropriate contract or investigate slam. It is fairly logical to use a subsequent 4♠ as RKCB in the ♥ sequence (Kickback) and 4NT in the ♠ sequence.

Obviously we need to elaborate on a few of the aspects. Let's start with the totally flat hand that is shown by 3 of the major or 3NT. All examples assume a strong NT: -

Example 1

West   East   West   East

♠ K87   ♠ A92   1NT   2♣   (1) ASID enquiry
♥ AJ43   ♥ K952   2♥   3♦   (1)   (2) 3433, min
♦ K74   ♦ Q95   3♥   (2) pass (3)   (3) good judgement
♣ AJ4   ♣ 963

East establishes that West is minimum with totally duplicated distribution, so he stays out of game (neither 3NT nor 4♥ is likely to be a success). Note that both East and West evaluate their hands as a minimum because of the flat shape.

———————————————

Example 2

West	East	West	East		
♠ KQ8	♠ A92	1NT	2♣		(1) ASID enquiry
♥ K743	♥ J952	2♥	3♦	(1)	(2) 3433, max
♦ A74	♦ QJ5	3NT	pass	(2) (3)	(3) With ample points and poor trumps,
♣ AJ4	♣ KQ6				East elects to go for the NT game.

Example 3

West	East	West	East		
♠ Q8	♠ 962	1NT	2♣		(1) ASID enquiry
♥ A10743	♥ Q952	2♥	3♦	(1)	(2) 5 ♥'s
♦ A74	♦ KQ5	4♥	pass	(2)	
♣ AJ2	♣ KQ6				

It really would be pretty silly to be in 3NT on this deal.

Example 4

West	East	West	East		
♠ KQ8	♠ AJ6	1NT	2♣		(1) ASID enquiry
♥ AJ74	♥ Q952	2♥	3♦	(1)	(2) doubleton ♦
♦ Q4	♦ 852	4♦	4♥	(2)	
♣ A942	♣ KQ6	pass			

ASID is not only used for looking for the best possible game; if responder bids on over game, he is looking for slam (or he may simply bid slam): -

Example 5

West	East	West	East		
♠ KQ85	♠ A6	1NT	2♣		(1) ASID enquiry
♥ KQ74	♥ AJ92	2♥	3♦	(1)	(2) doubleton ♣
♦ QJ4	♦ K1063	4♣	6♥	(2)	
♣ Q2	♣ A73	pass			

A reasonable slam on minimal values. Excellent on a non-♣ lead.

2.5   <u>3♣ (After Stayman) - Shape Asking Relays after Stayman (SARS)</u>

So this time we are really going to define a meaning for the sequences

1NT - 2♣ - 2♥ - 3♣   and   1NT - 2♣ - 2♠ - 3♣

and, in addition, the hitherto unmentioned sequence   1NT - 2♣ - 2♦ - 3♣

2.5.1   <u>Minor Suit Shape Asking Relays</u>

We shall cover the latter sequence first, where opener has denied a 4 card major.

Hand A   Partner opens a strong NT. Obviously we try 2♣, Stayman, and opener replies 2♦.
                So no major suit fit but you are still interested in slam, especially if there is a 4-4 ♦ fit.
♠ AJ108   You could try 4NT, quantitative. Partner would then bid any minor suit that he has, but
♥ K3   the problem is that he may pass with a minimum 15-16 points and you still want to try
♦ KQJ4   slam. We need an asking bid to enquire about partner's minor suit holdings.
♣ KJ8

   After 1NT - 2♣ - 2♦ ,   3♣ asks: -

3♦ = 5 card minor (either ♣'s or ♦'s), no 4 card minor.
3♥ = 4 card ♣'s but not ♦'s, so 3334
3♠ = 4 card ♦'s but not ♣'s, so 3343
3NT = 4 card ♣'s and 4 card ♦'s, so 2344 or 3244. (2245 or 2254 is also possible if you open 1NT
       with these distributions, but see below).

With this 3♣ ask partner is looking for a minor suit slam if there is a fit. So, actually, there is no
problem with extending these replies when you have 9 cards in the minors. A possible extension is: -

4♣ = 5 card ♣'s and 4 card ♦'s, so 2245
4♦ = 5 card ♦'s and 4 card ♣'s, so 2254

If you allow 6 card minors in your opening 1NT, then there is no way to show this. Bidding above
3NT is too dangerous as partner may only be interested in the other minor, so you have to treat a 6 card
minor as a 5 carder in these replies.
   Note that after a 3♥ or 3♠ reply, responder knows that opener is exactly 3334 or 3343 respectively.
   With the 3♦ response, asker needs another relay to establish the 5 (maybe 6?) card suit: -

   After 1NT - 2♣ - 2♦ - 3♣ - 3♦ ,   3♥ asks: -

3♠ = 5 card ♣'s
3NT = 5 card ♦'s

Example 1

West	East	West	East		
♠ KQ7	♠ AJ108	1NT	2♣		(1) minor suit shape?
♥ A42	♥ K83	2♦	3♣ (1)		(2) 4 ♦'s
♦ A765	♦ KQJ4	3♠ (2)	etc (3)		(3) East knows West is 3343
♣ K94	♣ Q8				and bids on to 6♦.

Example 2

West	East	West	East		
♠ KQ4	♠ AJ108	1NT	2♣		(1) minor suit shape?
♥ A42	♥ K83	2♦	3♣ (1)		(2) a 5 card minor
♦ A7652	♦ KQJ4	3♦ (2)	3♥ (3)		(3) which?
♣ KJ	♣ Q8	3NT (4)	etc (5)		(4) ♦'s
					(5) East bids on to 6♦ or 6NT.

Example 3

Sometimes there is no minor suit fit: -

West	East	West	East		
♠ KQ4	♠ AJ108	1NT	2♣		(1) minor suit shape?
♥ A42	♥ K83	2♦	3♣ (1)		(2) a 5 card minor
♦ A2	♦ KQJ4	3♦ (2)	3♥ (3)		(3) which?
♣ K7652	♣ Q8	3♠ (4)	3NT (5)		(4) ♣'s
		pass			(5) wrong one

After the minor suit shape ask, a bid of 4 of a minor sets the trump suit. Since it is preferable to use something lower that 4NT as the key card ask with a minor suit, we use this bid to double up as RKCB. You could play Kickback or cue bid if you prefer but that would leave less room for quantitative bids as explained in the next couple of pages.

Example 4

West	East	West	East		
♠ KQ	♠ AJ108	1NT	2♣		(1) minor suit shape?
♥ A62	♥ K83	2♦	3♣ (1)		(2) two 4 card minors
♦ A982	♦ KQJ4	3NT (2)	4♦ (3)		(3) ♦'s are trumps, RKCB
♣ A652	♣ K8	4♥ (4)	etc to 7♦		(4) 3 key cards

Example 5

As promised, East Hand L from the beginning of section 2.

West	East (L)	West	East		
♠ 976	♠ AK3	1NT	2♣		(1) shape?
♥ AQ	♥ KJ73	2♦	3♣ (1)		(2) two 4 card minors
♦ AJ52	♦ Q3	3NT (2)	4♣ (3)		(3) setting trumps, RKCB
♣ AJ107	♣ KQ52	4♦ (4)	etc to 6♣ or 6NT		(4) 3 key cards

As I said in the previous example, playing 4 of a minor at (3) to set trumps and as RKCB is very sensible.

Fit Showing Quantitatives

We have seen that it is advantageous to use 4 of the minor as RKCB. Then 4NT is obviously quantitative, but is there a minor suit fit or not? Responder knows this but opener may well need to know, especially if he fancies a minor suit slam if there is a fit.

The answer is to reserve a 4♠ bid (and sometimes 4♥) as further quantitative bids, similar to 4NT but stating that there is a fit. This is no problem as the bids would be cue bids otherwise. With a minor suit as trumps it is better to have the RKCB bid at a low level and it really is not a good idea to have to start cue bidding at a level above Blackwood.

So, basically, 4NT is quantitative with no fit and 4♠ is quantitative but acknowledges a fit. In the situations, where opener has shown both minors, then 4♥ is used to indicate the ♣ fit and 4♠ for the ♦ fit. We can also extend the principle to indicate to opener what sort of fit (4-4, 5-4, 5-3) we have. The complete scheme is as follows, where the spare bids may be used as cue bids or anything else you wish: -

1NT - 2♣ - 2♦ - 3♣ - 3♥	3♠	is
	3NT	is to play, no fit
(4 ♣'s)	4♣	is RKCB for ♣'s
	4♦	is
	4♥	is quantitative, indicating a 4-4 ♣ fit
	4♠	is quantitative, indicating a 4-5 ♣ fit
	4NT	is quantitative, no fit.

1NT - 2♣ - 2♦ - 3♣ - 3♠	3NT	is to play, no fit
	4♣	is
(4 ♦'s)	4♦	is RKCB for ♦'s
	4♥	is quantitative, indicating a 4-4 ♦ fit
	4♠	is quantitative, indicating a 4-5 ♦ fit
	4NT	is quantitative, no fit.

1NT - 2♣ - 2♦ - 3♣ - 3NT	4♣	is RKCB for ♣'s
	4♦	is RKCB for ♦'s
(4 ♣'s + 4 ♦'s)	4♥	is quantitative, indicating a ♣ fit
	4♠	is quantitative, indicating a ♦ fit
	4NT	is quantitative, no fit.

1NT - 2♣ - 2♦ - 3♣ - 3♦ - 3♥ - 3♠	3NT	is to play, no fit
	4♣	is RKCB for ♣'s
(5 ♣'s)	4♦	is
	4♥	is quantitative, indicating a 5-3 ♣ fit
	4♠	is quantitative, indicating a 5-4 ♣ fit
	4NT	is quantitative, no fit.

1NT - 2♣ - 2♦ - 3♣ - 3♦ - 3♥ - 3NT	4♣	is
	4♦	is RKCB for ♦'s
(5 ♦'s)	4♥	is quantitative, indicating a 5-3 ♦ fit
	4♠	is quantitative, indicating a 5-4 ♦ fit
	4NT	is quantitative, no fit.

Example 6

West	East	West	East	
♠ KQ7	♠ AJ108	1NT	2♣	(1) shape?
♥ A42	♥ K83	2♦	3♣ (1)	(2) 4 ♦'s
♦ A765	♦ KQJ4	3♠ (2)	4♥ (3)	(3) quantitative, 4-4 ♦ fit
♣ K94	♣ J8	4NT (4)	pass	(4) With a flat minimum, West elects to play in 4NT.

Example 7

West	East	West	East	
♠ KQ7	♠ AJ108	1NT	2♣	(1) shape?
♥ AJ2	♥ K83	2♦	3♣ (1)	(2) 4 ♦'s
♦ A765	♦ Q8	3♠ (2)	4NT (3)	(3) quantitative, no fit
♣ K94	♣ AQJ8	6NT (4)	pass	

Note that East needs a better hand to invite than he had in example 6 because there is no fit. West knows there is no fit, so East must have around 17 points to invite (with a lesser hand he would sign off with 3NT at (3)). With his max and top cards, West accepts at (4).

Example 8

West	East	West		East		
♠ Q72	♠ K984	1NT		2♣		(1) shape?
♥ A72	♥ KJ	2♦		3♣	(1)	(2) a 5 card minor
♦ AQJ65	♦ K103	3♦	(2)	3♥	(3)	(3) which?
♣ K9	♣ AQ84	3NT	(4)	4♥	(5)	(4) ♦'s
		6♦		pass		(5) quantitative, 5-3 fit

With just a 5-3 fit, East needs a good hand (good 16 or 17) to invite slam at (5). West has values to accept and the 5-3 fit is probably superior to 6NT. The mere fact that East has invited (rather than bid slam/RKCB) means that there are not points to spare and a decent fit is usually safer. Also, of course, West knows a great deal about East's shape. He has 3 ♦'s and at least 4 ♣'s; it is quite likely that he is short in one major and there may be a ruff available.

Incidentally, West does not know that East has a 4 card major for sure. As we will see shortly responder also has to use similar SARS sequences starting with 2♣ when he is just interested in opener's minors.

Since the fit-showing quantitative bids are forcing, responder may use them to indicate the fit and then bid on over opener's reply. I won't bother to elaborate on this possible extension. Most of the time responder will either wish to use RKCB or to invite using a quantitative bid.

2.5.2   <u>**Shape Asking Relays after Stayman (SARS) – After a Positive Stayman Response.**</u>

Here we cover the sequences when opener does have a 4 (perhaps 5) card major, i.e. : -

1NT - 2♣ - 2♥ - 3♣   and   1NT - 2♣ - 2♠ - 3♣

After 1NT - 2♣ - 2♥ , 3♣ asks: -   After 1NT - 2♣ - 2♠ , 3♣ asks: -

3♦	=	a 4 card ♣ or ♦ suit	(1)	3♦	=	a 4 card ♦ suit	(1)
3♥	=	a 5 card ♥ suit		3♥	=	a 4 card ♣ suit	(1)
3♠	=	a 4 card ♠ suit		3♠	=	a 5 card ♠ suit	
3NT	=	3433		3NT	=	4333	

(1) If you have opened 1NT on something like 4252 shape, then you can only indicate the long minor as a 4 card suit. Note that the responses in the ♠ sequence are out of order; this is a slightly better method as an eventual ♦ contract will be played by the 1NT opener.

The ♥ sequence is not totally explicit and so we need another relay to establish the 4 card minor after a 3♦ reply: -

After 1NT - 2♣ - 2♥ - 3♣ - 3♦ , 3♥ asks: -

3♠   =   4 ♣'s or possibly 2425
3NT =   4 ♦'s or possibly 2452

Example 1

West	East	West	East			
♠ K76	♠ AJ98	1NT	2♣		(1)	shape?
♥ A962	♥ K8	2♥	3♣	(1)	(2)	a 4 card minor
♦ A9	♦ KQ74	3♦	(2)	3♥	(3)	(3) which?
♣ KQ42	♣ A83	3♠	(4)	3NT		(4) ♣'s
		pass				

With a ♠ or ♦ fit, East would be looking for slam.

Example 2

West	East	West	East			
♠ A962	♠ K8	1NT	2♣		(1)	shape?
♥ K76	♥ AJ98	2♠	3♣	(1)	(2)	4 ♣'s
♦ A9	♦ KQ74	3♥	(2)	3NT		
♣ KQ42	♣ A83	pass				

Again, no slam with no fit.

A Word About Kickback etc.

We have seen that there are times when it is advisable to use another bid other than 4NT as RKCB. Kickback uses the suit above trumps as the key card ask, so 4NT when ♠'s are trumps and 4♠ when ♥'s are trumps etc. In our situation here we often want 4NT (and other bids) as quantitative, so we use Kickback for the majors and, in this situation, 4 of the minor as RKCB for the minor.

More Fit Showing Quantitatives

Again we have to define our RKCB and quantitative (with and without fit) bids.

Let's assume that we play 4 of the minor as RKCB and Kickback as RKCB for the majors. 4NT, if available, is quantitative without a fit and the next free bid(s) below is (are) quantitative with a fit: -

1NT - 2♣ - 2♥ - 3♣ - 3♥	3♠	is
	3NT	is to play, no fit
(5 ♥'s)	4♣	is
	4♦	is quantitative, indicating a 5-3 ♥ fit
	4♥	is to play
	4♠	is RKCB (Kickback)
	4NT	is quantitative, no fit.

1NT - 2♣ - 2♥ - 3♣ - 3♠	3NT	is to play, no fit
	4♣	is quantitative, 4-4 ♠ fit
(4 ♠'s)	4♦	is quantitative, no fit
	4♥	is to play (probably a 4-3 fit)
	4♠	is to play
	4NT	is RKCB for ♠'s

Now the above may seem strange, why would responder use SARS if he has a 4 card ♠ suit? The answer probably is that he also has a 4 card minor suit and is looking for a fit in either.

1NT - 2♣ - 2♥ - 3♣ - 3NT	pass	is to play, no fit
	4♣	is RKCB for ♣'s (3-5 fit)
(3433)	4♦	is RKCB for ♦'s (3-5 fit)
	4♥	is quantitative, indicating a 3-5 ♣ fit
	4♠	is quantitative, indicating a 3-5 ♦ fit
	4NT	is quantitative, no fit

1NT - 2♣ - 2♥ - 3♣ - 3♦ - 3♥ - 3♠	3NT	is to play, no fit
	4♣	is RKCB for ♣'s
(4 ♣'s)	4♦	is
	4♥	is to play (probably a 4-3 fit)
	4♠	is quantitative, indicating a ♣ fit
	4NT	is quantitative, no fit

48

1NT - 2♣ - 2♥ - 3♣ - 3♦ - 3♥ - 3NT	pass	is to play, no fit
	4♣	is
(4 ♦'s)	4♦	is RKCB for ♦'s
	4♥	is to play (probably a 4-3 fit)
	4♠	is quantitative, indicating a ♦ fit
	4NT	is quantitative, no fit

1NT - 2♣ - 2♠ - 3♣ - 3♦	3♥	is
	3♠	is
(4 ♦'s)	3NT	is to play, no fit
	4♣	is
	4♦	is RKCB for ♦'s
	4♥	is quantitative, indicating a ♦ fit
	4♠	is to play (probably a 4-3 fit)
	4NT	is quantitative, no fit

1NT - 2♣ - 2♠ - 3♣ - 3♥	3♠	is
	3NT	is to play, no fit
(4 ♣'s)	4♣	is RKCB for ♣'s
	4♦	is
	4♥	is quantitative, indicating a ♣ fit
	4♠	is to play (probably a 4-3 fit)
	4NT	is quantitative, no fit

1NT - 2♣ - 2♠ - 3♣ - 3♠	3NT	is to play, no fit
	4♣	is
(5 ♠'s)	4♦	is quantitative, indicating a 5-3 ♠ fit
	4♥	is quantitative, no fit
	4♠	is to play
	4NT	is RKCB for ♠'s

1NT - 2♣ - 2♠ - 3♣ - 3NT	pass	is to play, no fit
	4♣	is RKCB for ♣'s (3-5 fit)
(4333)	4♦	is RKCB for ♦'s (3-5 fit)
	4♥	is quantitative, indicating a 3-5 ♣ fit
	4♠	is quantitative, indicating a 3-5 ♦ fit
	4NT	is quantitative, no fit

Example 3

West	East	West	East	
♠ KQ76	♠ AJ108	1NT	2♣	(1) shape?
♥ A962	♥ K8	2♥	3♣	(1) (2) 4 ♠'s
♦ A92	♦ KQJ4	3♠ (2)	4NT (3) etc	(3) RKCB
♣ K2	♣ A83	etc to 7♠		

Example 4

West	East	West	East	
♠ KQ6	♠ AJ108	1NT	2♣	(1) shape?
♥ A962	♥ K8	2♥	3♣ (1)	(2) a 4 card minor
♦ A962	♦ KQJ4	3♦ (2)	3♥ (3)	(3) which?
♣ K2	♣ A83	3NT (4)	4♦ (5)	(4) ♦'s
		etc to 7♦.		(5) RKCB

Sometimes you may not be looking for slam, but just the best game: -

Example 5

West	East	West	East	
♠ KQ6	♠ AJ108	1NT	2♣	(1) shape?
♥ AQ962	♥ KJ3	2♥	3♣ (1)	(2) 5 ♥'s
♦ Q62	♦ KJ94	3♥ (2)	4♥	
♣ Q7	♣ 98	pass		

SARS is not just used to establish a fit, it is also uncovers possible weakness (shortage) in a potential NT contract: -

Example 6

West	East	West	East	
				(1) shape?
♠ KQ6	♠ AJ108	1NT	2♣	(2) a 4 card minor
♥ AQ96	♥ KJ3	2♥	3♣ (1)	(3) which?
♦ Q652	♦ KJ94	3♦ (2)	3♥ (3)	(4) ♦'s
♣ Q7	♣ 98	3NT (4)	4♥ (5)	(5) with a ♣ weakness, East
		pass		goes for the Moysian fit.

Note that East cannot use 4♥ as a quantitative bid here as it is needed to sign off.

The following example is from a (2004) club competition. A hopeless 6NT was reached at 7 of the 9 tables where it was played. Let's have a look at how we handle it using SARS: -

Example 7

West	East	West	East		
♠ AJ92	♠ Q8	1NT	2♣		(1) shape?
♥ AK103	♥ J7	2♥	3♣ (1)		(2) 4 ♠'s
♦ A93	♦ KQJ42	3♠ (2)	3NT (3)		
♣ 109	♣ AQ42	pass			

East has a slam invitational hand, and would investigate slam if a 5-4 or 4-4 minor suit fit was found. With no such fit there is no slam (5-3 is probably not good enough, but if East did decide to go for a pushy slam then 6♦ is far better than 6NT), so a quiet 3NT at (3) is very prudent. An invitational 4NT (4♦ in our system) would be an overbid at (3) with no fit. Even if East did overbid with a quantitative 4NT (4♦), West, with no fit and little in the way of minor suit honours, should pass (bid 4NT).

Another way of bidding this hand is to transfer into ♦'s and then bid ♣'s (we cover this later in section 4.3) but you are then at the 4♣ level and I would prefer a stronger and more shapely hand. I would only look for slam if there is a 4-4 ♣ or 5-4 ♦ fit, and the way to discover that is via SARS.

So, we don't actually need a 4 card major to bid SARS. More of this in the next section.

Summary

It is fairly plain that SARS and the fit Showing quantitatives work very well. We keep the RKCB bid at or below the Kickback level and the Fit Showing quantitatives fill up most of the remaining bids admirably, but are there any drawbacks?

The Down Side?

Just one really. We frequently use 4-of-the-minor as RKCB and that is very sensible as it is just one bid below the safe Kickback threshold, but occasionally we will thus be bidding RKCB with an outside weak suit (not a recommended practice).

This certainly is a negative factor, but most of the time it will work out OK and there is no guarantee that an alternative approach (cue bidding) will work out any better as you are already rather high. I believe that the gains made by using RKCB at a low level and the gains from using Fit Showing Quantitatives more than outweigh any negative results form occasionally using Blackwood with a weak suit. And remember, the Blackwood bidder is usually responder and partner has opened a strong NT and so usually has a holding in the weak suit.

Basically, you cannot have everything. If you wish your RKCB bids to be at or below the Kickback level then you may occasionally have to bid RKCB with a weak suit outside.

2.5.3   Minor Suit Stayman.

There are various versions of minor suit Stayman. Perhaps the most common is 2♠ as this bid is redundant when you play major suit Jacoby Transfers. Let's just have a look at this 2♠ as minor suit Stayman; opener responds 2NT with no 4 card minor and 3♣/♦ holding a 4 card minor (if both, he bids his best one?). Woefully inadequate! There is no mechanism to show both minors and what if opener has a 5 card minor? Yet this is the choice of many experts! I think that we can certainly find something far better! Read on.

Another, somewhat antiquated, but more accurate version is the Sharples 4♣/♦ after Stayman. We, however, wish to retain the traditional 4♣ Gerber bid and so we utilise our 3♣ asking after Stayman (SARS) as a substitute for Minor Suit Stayman. Thus our original 2♣ bid may not contain a 4 card major if we subsequently bid 3♣.

Actually, our SARS scheme is a definite improvement on 2♠ Minor Suit Stayman as it allows us to find minor suit fits after trying (and failing) to find a major suit fit. Also, SARS enables us to establish partner's shape much more closely.

Bidding Stayman and Subsequent Shape Asking Relays Without a 4 Card Major.

Hand A	Partner opens a strong NT. You want to be in slam, preferably in a minor suit if there is a fit. 4NT, quantitative, would find the fit; but only if partner does not pass. With this
♠ AJ8	slam forcing hand we need to have some form of Minor Suit Stayman. The solution?
♥ K3	Bid 2♣ anyway and then ask about partner's shape by bidding 3♣ next turn.
♦ KQJ4	
♣ KJ84	

Example A.1

West	East	West	East			
♠ KQ7	♠ AJ8	1NT	2♣		(1)	minor suit shape?
♥ A42	♥ K3	2♦	3♣	(1)	(2)	4 ♦'s, so 3343
♦ A1065	♦ KQJ4	3♠	(2) etc.	(3)	(3)	and onwards to 6♦.
♣ A95	♣ KJ84					

No problem. There is also no problem if opener does have a 4 card major, we simply employ the Shape Asking Relay. Partner may assume that we have the other major, but that does not matter, we are the Captain: -

Example A.2

West	East	West	East			
♠ K1072	♠ AJ8	1NT	2♣		(1)	shape?
♥ A42	♥ K3	2♠	3♣	(1)	(2)	4 ♦'s
♦ A1065	♦ KQJ4	3♦	(2) etc	(3)	(3)	with the fit established,
♣ A9	♣ KJ84					East bids on to 6♦.

After a 3♣ shape ask, asker often finds a fit; and if there is or is not a minor suit fit this is always established below the level of 3NT (a big advantage over Sharples 4♣/♦). When no fit is found, then asker can always sign off in 3NT. A bid of the minor shown agrees trumps and is best used as RKCB. 4NT is invitational, and we have our Fit Showing Quantitatives to indicate if there is a fit or not.

Obviously this knowledge of whether there is a fit is extremely useful for opener in deciding if he should push on or not.

Now quite a lot of new stuff here and it certainly needs clarifying with examples.

Hand B	I came across this hand in a British magazine's bidding quiz. You were asked the correct bid after partner had opened 1NT. Now actually the problem involved a weak NT opening (12-14) and so I have adjusted this hand slightly by 3 points (the ♠J was the ♠A) so that now partner opens a strong NT (15-17). What do you do?
♠ J4	
♥ K73	
♦ AQ42	The recommended bid was 3NT. The author stating that '*You have a balanced hand with no four card major, and therefore little prospect of playing in anything other than a no-trump contract.*
♣ KQ76	*You are very strong, but do you have enough for slam?*'.
	I have adjusted the author's comments for a strong NT opening: -

To be fair, the system used was not sophisticated, with no mechanism for finding a 4-4 minor suit other than a quantitative 4NT, which may be too high. We, however, can do much better than the recommended 3NT bid as we can establish any minor suit fit below 3NT.

West	East	
		This was the complete hand shown in the solutions (♠J & ♠A changed). The recommended bidding being 1NT – 3NT – pass.
♠ A7	♠ J4	The author went on to say '*With balanced hands you should aim for 33 points to*
♥ AQJ2	♥ K73	*be able to make a small slam. You have 15 and your partner's maximum is 17, so*
♦ KJ105	♦ AQ42	*your maximum combined total is 32: not usually enough for a slam. Settle for 3NT.*'
♣ J105	♣ KQ76	

As I said, the bidding quiz scenario had a limited bidding system, so this statement may be true in context; but it is not true if you have our more sophisticated system to find 4-4 minor suit fits below the level of 3NT.

Finally, the author adds '*In general, if you have a balanced hand you need 16 points to have a real chance to make slam in no-trumps after your partner has opened a strong NT. On this hand, your limit is surprisingly just 9 tricks after the ♠ lead*'. Probably true, but why not investigate a minor suit slam if you have the tools! 6♦ is an excellent contract, requiring only a 3-2 trump break (plus additional chances even if they are 4-1).

Let's use this Hand B in all of the following examples and see if we can get to the correct contract depending upon opener's shape and strength.

We start with the actual hand (the ♠J and ♠A are interchanged from the original weak NT deal): -

Example B.1

West	East	West		East	
♠ A7	♠ J4	1NT	(1)	2♣	
♥ AQJ2	♥ K73	2♥		3♣	(2)
♦ KJ105	♦ AQ42	3♦	(3)	3♥	(4)
♣ J105	♣ KQ76	3NT	(5)	4♠	(6)
		6♦	(7)	pass	

(1) 15-17
(2) shape?
(3) 4 card ♣ or ♦
(4) which?
(5) ♦'s
(6) quantitative, ♦ fit

(7) With a near maximum, superb trumps, decent shape and good intermediates; West has no problem in accepting the invitation.

Example B.2

West	East	West		East	
♠ A7	♠ J4	1NT	(1)	2♣	
♥ AQ92	♥ K73	2♥		3♣	(2)
♦ KJ85	♦ AQ42	3♦	(3)	3♥	(4)
♣ J52	♣ KQ76	3NT	(5)	4♠	(6)
		5♦	(7)	pass	

(1) 15-17
(2) shape?
(3) 4 card ♣ or ♦
(4) which?
(5) ♦'s
(6) quantitative, ♦ fit

(7) With a bare minimum, West cannot accept the slam invitation. Because of his poor holding in both black suits, he elects for 5♦ instead of 4NT.

Note that 3NT probably will not even make if the ♥'s fail to split.

Example B.3

West	East	West		East	
♠ A987	♠ J4	1NT	(1)	2♣	
♥ AQJ2	♥ K73	2♥		3♣	(2)
♦ KJ5	♦ AQ42	3♠	(3)	3NT	(4)
♣ J5	♣ KQ76	pass			

(1) 15-17
(2) shape?
(3) 4 card ♠
(4) With no fit, the East hand is not worth an invitation.

Perhaps a ♥ game is the best contract: -

Example B.4

West	East	West		East	
♠ A7	♠ J4	1NT	(1)	2♣	
♥ AQ982	♥ K73	2♥		3♣	(2)
♦ KJ5	♦ AQ42	3♥	(3)	4♦	(4)
♣ J85	♣ KQ76	4♥		pass	

(1) 15-17
(2) shape?
(3) 5 ♥'s
(4) quantitative, 5-3 ♥ fit

And there may be a slam in ♥'s: -

Example B.5

West	East	West		East	
♠ A7	♠ J4	1NT	(1)	2♣	
♥ AQJ82	♥ K73	2♥		3♣	(2)
♦ KJ5	♦ AQ42	3♥	(3)	4♦	(4)
♣ J105	♣ KQ76	6♥		pass	

(1) 15-17
(2) shape?
(3) 5 ♥'s
(4) quantitative, 5-3 ♥ fit

And ♣'s may be just as good a suit for slam: -

Example B.6

West	East	West		East	
♠ A72	♠ J4	1NT	(1)	2♣	
♥ AQ82	♥ K73	2♥		3♣	(2)
♦ K7	♦ AQ42	3♦	(3)	3♥	(4)
♣ A1052	♣ KQ76	3♠	(5)	4♠	(6)
		6♣		pass	

(1) 15-17
(2) shape?
(3) a 4 card minor
(4) which
(5) ♣'s
(6) quantitative, ♣ fit

All in all, I think that there is more to this East hand than just selling out in 3NT (which may not even make). Don't you agree? So don't believe everything that you read in the magazines.

The bottom lines: -

Look for a fit. We really do need a good mechanism for finding slams with a fit and this concept of the Fit Showing Quantitatives really does improve slam bidding, especially with slam invitational hands.

Invitational slam bidding is an area that is grossly overlooked in modern bidding theory. One is more likely to hold a slam invitational hand than one that definitely wants to go slamming – think about it.

Minor suit slams are often overlooked in favour of less secure 6NT contracts. Perhaps a negative effect of matchpoint (pairs) scoring? It's usually best to go for the safer contract.

Points are important, of course, but the value of a fit is underestimated. The following example shows that even an excellent 17 count is not good enough opposite a respectable strong No Trump opener if there is no fit.

For this final example, we'll improve the East hand slightly so that it's certainly looking for slam, but have a West hand with no fit.

Example B.7

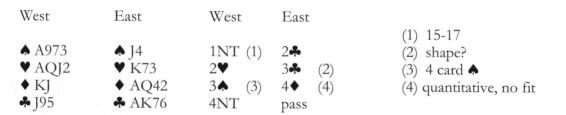

West	East	West	East		
				(1)	15-17
♠ A973	♠ J4	1NT (1)	2♣	(2)	shape?
♥ AQJ2	♥ K73	2♥	3♣ (2)	(3)	4 card ♠
♦ KJ	♦ AQ42	3♠ (3)	4♦ (4)	(4)	quantitative, no fit
♣ J95	♣ AK76	4NT	pass		

East has a maximal invitation (some would jump straight in). West has a decent hand, but with no fit there is no slam.

Responder Has 5-4, 4-5, 6-4 or 4-6 In The Majors.

And now for something completely different. Partner opens 1NT and we have 9 cards in the majors (5-4 or 4-5) or 10 cards (6-4 or 4-6).

Hand A   We have covered the weak 5-4 (or 4-5) hands already, just to recap: -

With this 'garbage' hand you just want to play in a better spot than 1NT. So transfer and get partner playing in 2♠? That would often be fine, but it may just be that partner has 4 (or even 5) ♥'s and you miss a 4-4 ♥ fit. So it's best to bid 2♣ and then pass a 2♥ or 2♠ response but convert 2♦ to 2♠. Thus the Stayman sequence: -

♠ Q9652
♥ Q854
♦ 93
♣ 76

1NT - 2♣ - 2♦ - 2♥   shows a weak hand with 5 ♥'s & 4 ♠'s and is drop dead.
1NT - 2♣ - 2♦ - 2♠   shows a weak hand with 5 ♠'s & 4 ♥'s and is drop dead.

And how about if you are 64 or 46 in the majors and weak? There are two options here; you can bid Stayman and then the 6-carder if opener replies 2♦. The other, perhaps preferable, option is to simply transfer into the 6 card suit.

Hand B	Hand C	
♠ K842	♠ KJ8542	Partner opens 1NT.
♥ Q98542	♥ J982	
♦ 105	♦ 105	
♣ 2	♣ 2	

Some would bid 2♣ with both of these hands. Others would transfer into the 6 card suit. Yet others would bid Stayman with Hand B and transfer with Hand C because of the weaker ♥'s.

And me? I would always look for the 4-4 fit, but that is my 'thing'. However, transferring may well work out best as the strong NT hand will always be declarer. It's up to you and does not really matter too much.

Example

Dealer:	♠ K842		West	North	East	South
South	♥ Q98542					
Both vul	♦ 105		-	-	-	1NT
	♣ 2		pass	2♣	pass	2♠
			pass	pass	pass	

♠ J73	N	♠ 96
♥ K3	W E	♥ AJ10
♦ K98	S	♦ Q763
♣ Q10543		♣ K876

          ♠ AQ105
          ♥ 76
          ♦ AJ42   2♠ probably plays better than 2♥, but then I guess that
          ♣ AJ9   it's just as easy to construct hands where 2♥ plays better.

Hand D

♠ QJ10852
♥ J872
♦ 74
♣ 9

Take this example, with very weak ♥'s and a robust ♠ suit it is surely best to transfer into ♠'s and pass. We cover transfers later in section 3.

Hand E

♠ KQ10852
♥ J872
♦ J4
♣ 9

It's similar with an invitational hand. Here the ♠'s are far better than the ♥'s and so it will normally work out best to transfer into ♠'s and then invite with 3♠.

Hand F

♠ KQ10852
♥ J872
♦ K4
♣ 9

And the same with a game going hand. This hand should simply transfer into ♠'s. We can transfer into 4♠ directly with a Texas Transfer when we have no slam interest and we'll cover it later in section 6.2.

Hand G

♠ QJ852
♥ AJ87
♦ K4
♣ 74

OK, but what about hands with a decent 4 card major? You could transfer into the 5/6 card major and then bid the 4 carder (so 1NT - 2♥ - 2♠ - 3♥ here). This sequence is normally considered as game forcing. However, the recommended modern practice is to reserve the transfer sequences for 5-5 hands and to bid Stayman on all major suit 5-4's and 6-4's (no matter what strength).

With this example bid Stayman and raise any major suit response to game. If opener responds 2♦ then jump to 3♠, game forcing, offering partner the choice of 4♠ or 3NT.

A possible slight improvement on this scheme is to jump in the 4 card major, thus ensuring that the NT opener is declarer (the Smolen Convention – we cover it in detail, for what it's worth, in section2.6.1). So that's fine with Hand G, but what about invitational hands? …

Smolen At The Two Level

I'll mention this but it's perhaps a somewhat unwieldy convention that I don't like at all. When opener replies 2♦ to our Stayman enquiry this convention uses both 2♥ and 2♠ as artificial bids: -

2♥   is a puppet to 2♠ which may be a weak hand (5-4, responder passes the 2♠ bid) or any number of other meanings (responder bids on).

2♠   asks opener to define his hand.

Amongst all of these complex sequences it is possible for responder to hit upon the correct contract when he is 5-4 or 4-5 in the majors but there are drawbacks: -

1)   We lose our fundamental 'Garbage Stayman' possibility of playing in 2♥ with a weak 4-5 hand.
2)   It is rather complex.
3)   It goes against the general Smolen philosophy in that responder is usually declarer in an eventual 3♠ or 4♠ contract.
4)   Nobody (or very few) plays it.

So you don't like 'Smolen at the two level'? Then there is no established method to handle invitational 5-4's & 4-5's – tough luck?! The scheme I outlined for game forcing hands (Smolen 3♥/♠ or natural 3♥/♠ over partner's 2♦ response to Stayman) is pretty well universally used but there is no simple invitational bid if opener responds 2♦ to your Stayman enquiry! Your options are a game force (Smolen 3♥/♠ or natural 3♥/♠), an offbeat 2NT or pass. This is, however, what the majority of experienced players play and so I'll cover it in detail in the next section.

But don't despair! There is a simple solution to the invitational 5-4 / 4-5 (and 6-4 / 4-6) problem (Quest Transfers) and we will meet them later in section 2.6.2 and they have the advantages that: -

1)   We retain our fundamental 'Garbage Stayman' possibilities with all weak hands.
2)   They are simple.
3)   Opener becomes declarer in virtually all ♥,♠ or NT contracts
4)   Everybody will be playing them in the future!

But first, let's look at what most people do at present: -

2.6.1   The Traditional Method – Smolen etc.

Smolen is game forcing and is basically a command for partner to bid 4♥/♠ so that he becomes declarer in that contract (or perhaps a slam). Declaring from the NT opener's hand very often has its advantages: -

Example

Dealer:	♠ AK9		West	North	East	South
North	♥ Q3					
Both vul	♦ KQ75		-	1NT (1)	pass	2♣
	♣ K863		pass	2♦	pass	3♠ (2)
			pass	4♠	all pass	

♠ 105	N	♠ 742
♥ 10872	W E	♥ J95
♦ J964	S	♦ A1082
♣ QJ10		♣ A42

    ♠ QJ863
    ♥ AK64
    ♦ 3
    ♣ 975

(1) 15-17
(2) natural and forcing, not playing Smolen.

West leads the obvious ♣Q, down one. Clearly the wrong hand is declarer. Let's see how we can solve this problem (by playing Smolen): -

Smolen

We will be covering transfers later in section 3 and we will see that game going two suiters are easy. The traditional method using Jacoby Transfers is to transfer into the 5 card suit and then bid your 4 card suit (game forcing). This is certainly the recommended method with a 5 card major and a 4 or 5 card minor. However, with 5-4 (or 4-5) in the majors, most serious players these days employ Stayman (they use the transfer and bid sequences in the majors only when 5-5). So, with a game forcing 5-4 (or 4-5) in the majors opposite a 1NT opening you bid Stayman. If partner replies in a major then raise to game. And what if partner replies 2♦? Normally you the bid 3 of your 5 card major (game forcing) and give partner the choice between 4 of the major or 3NT. A slight improvement on this (when playing a strong NT) is the Smolen convention, whereby you bid 3 of your 4 card major, thus giving opener the same options but ensuring that the 1NT opener is declarer.

So when playing Smolen we have: -

Hand A

♠ QJ852
♥ AK87
♦ J4
♣ 74

1NT - 2♣ - 2♦ - 3♥   shows 5 ♠'s, 4 ♥'s game forcing.

Opener normally completes this Smolen transfer by bidding 4♠. 3NT is an allowable but not common alternative. It notes that responder is 5-4 but suggesting that 3NT is preferable.

Hand B

♠ KJ52
♥ AJ872
♦ J4
♣ 74

1NT - 2♣ - 2♦ - 3♠   shows 5 ♥'s, 4 ♠'s game forcing.

Opener normally completes this Smolen transfer by bidding 4♥. Again 3NT is an allowable but not common alternative, noting that responder is 4-5 but suggesting that 3NT is preferable.

Example

Dealer: South Both vul	♠ AQ104 ♥ 108543 ♦ A3 ♣ 62		West	North	East	South
			-	-	-	1NT
			pass	2♣	pass	2♦
			pass	3♠ (1)	pass	4♥
♠ 652 ♥ AQJ ♦ K764 ♣ 543	N W E S	♠ 9873 ♥ 76 ♦ J109 ♣ Q1087	all pass			

♠ KJ
♥ K92
♦ Q852
♣ AKJ9

(1) Smolen. 5 ♥'s and 4 ♠'s

If North was declarer, then ♦J lead would kill the contract. With South as declarer, careful play will see the contract home despite the bad trump position.

So, all very nice and simple. But hang on! If after   1NT - 2♣ - 2♦ - 3♥   opener is expected to bid 4♠, then what the hell does 3♠ mean? And come to think of it, what do 4♣, 4♦ and 4♥ mean? And the similar bids in the 3♠ sequence?

Explicitly, after	1NT - 2♣ - 2♦ - 3♥ …	what are 3♠, 4♣, 4♦ and 4♥ ?
and after	1NT - 2♣ - 2♦ - 3♠ …	what are 4♣ and 4♦ ?

Responder has shown 5-4 (or 4-5) shape and game-going values (but no more – although he may have of course). Opener has denied a 4 card major. Why on earth would he want to break the Smolen transfer? Simple, he has a max, good 3 card support for responder's 5 card suit and shape that indicates that slam may be on if partner is interested.

But what should these bids mean? A cue bid? A 2nd suit? A (weak) doubleton? I guess that you could choose it to be any of these, but I prefer the cue bid option. So let's state that these bids are cue bids, showing the ace of the suit bid (or ♥A in the case of 3♠) and good three card support (slam interest).

Thus we could have: -

After 1NT - 2♣ - 2♦ - 3♥	and after	1NT - 2♣ - 2♦ - 3♠
3♠ = three ♠'s + ♥A		4♣ = three ♥'s + ♣A ?
4♣ = three ♠'s + ♣A		4♦ = three ♥'s + ♦A ? *
4♦ = three ♠'s + ♦A		4♥ = normal transfer completion
4♥ = slam interest but no ace to cue *		
4♠ = normal transfer completion		

We could call these bids Smolen super-accepts.

It's unfortunate that there is not so much room in the sequence with ♥'s as trumps; I guess that you could decide not to play Smolen … ?

Example

West	East	West	East	
♠ KJ7	♠ AQ954	1NT	2♣	(1) Smolen, 5 ♠'s & 4 ♥'s
♥ K103	♥ AQ42	2♦	3♥ (1)	(2) 3 ♠'s, ♦A, slam interest
♦ AKJ8	♦ Q105	4♦ (2)	4NT (3)	
♣ Q95	♣ 2	etc to 6♠		

With excellent support for both majors, West cues his ♦ ace. East could re-transfer with 4♥ at (3) but it is hardly important who declarer is. RKCB finds the excellent ♠ slam.

So they can work well, but Smolen super-accepts are by no means established – you are already in a game forcing situation and so it has less sense. Combined with the fact that it's awkward with ♥'s as trumps and that you perhaps wish to leave the suit below trumps * available for a re-transfer, the Smolen transfer will normally be simply completed on most occasions. So we'll stick with straightforward Smolen (if you play a strong NT – see next page for the weak NT) and not bother with super-accepts.

Smolen Playing a Weak NT?

At the start of this Smolen section I gave an example of the advantage of playing Smolen (the lead coming up to the strong balanced hand). Playing a weak NT, however, the advantages are not so obvious. Responder has an equally strong (perhaps stronger) hand. If you play a weak NT and like the idea of the 'Smolen super-accepts' then it may be preferable to forget all about Smolen and go back to the natural method (responder bids 3 of his 5-carder, game forcing). Opener then has straightforward super-accepts available: -

So then we have: -

After   1NT - 2♣ - 2♦ - 3♥   and after   1NT - 2♣ - 2♦ - 3♠

3♠ =	three ♥'s + ♠A		4♣ =	three ♠'s + ♣A
4♣ =	three ♥'s + ♣A		4♦ =	three ♠'s + ♦A
4♦ =	three ♥'s + ♦A		4♥ =	three ♠'s + ♥A
4♥ =	no slam interest		4♠ =	no slam interest
	(or no ace to cue)			(or no ace to cue)

Much simpler, and nearly complete (no distinction between no ace and no interest is a problem – we solve this later in section 2.6.2 with Quest Transfers). Playing a weak NT you have to weigh up the possible advantage of the NT bidder being declarer against the advantage that these super-accepts have to offer. Up to you, but I do like to keep things simple!

Example (playing a Weak NT)

Dealer:	♠ AQ975	West	North	East	South
South	♥ AQ104				
Both vul	♦ K3	-	-	-	1NT (1)
	♣ K2	pass	2♣	pass	2♦
		pass	3♠ (2)	pass	4♣ (3)
♠ J3	N ♠ 642	pass	4NT (4)	pass	5♥ (5)
♥ 975	W E ♥ 8632	pass	6♠	all pass	
♦ QJ102	S ♦ A97				
♣ J976	♣ 1083				

♠ K108	(1) 12-14
♥ KJ	(2) 5-4, forcing, not playing Smolen
♦ 8654	(3) ♣A, super-accept
♣ AQ54	(4) RKCB
	(5) 2 key cards

An excellent contract if played by North, I guess it's swings and roundabouts if you play a weak NT; but not playing Smolen is simpler and seems superior, especially in light of these super-accepts. Anyway, for the next couple of sections on 5-4's and 6-4's I'll assume that we play a strong NT and Smolen without super-accepts.

And it's all academic anyway, when we come onto Quest Transfers we will see that Smolen (or the natural 3♥/♠ jump) is redundant whichever strength of NT you play.

We have covered weak hands and there are 4 more basic hand types to be covered. They are as follows, with both 5-4's and 6-4's being covered for each type.

2.6.1.1	invitational	5-4's, where we want to invite game.
2.6.1.2	invitational	6-4's, where we want to invite game.
2.6.1.3	game going	5-4's, where we want to play in just 3NT or 4♥/♠.
2.6.1.4	game going	6-4's, where we want to play in just 4♥ or 4♠.
2.6.1.5	game going	5-4's, but with slam interest.
2.6.1.6	game going	6-4's, but with slam interest.
2.6.1.7	slam going	5-4's, how to investigate slam.
2.6.1.8	slam going	6-4's, how to investigate slam.

You will discover that everything is not perfect, however. And I have kept the same order, section titles, example numbers etc. in the next chapter (Quest Transfers) where all the loose ends are tidied up – and more.

2.6.1.1   <u>Invitational 5-4's, Where We Want to Invite Game.</u>

I guess that there are two options here: You could transfer into the 5-carder and then invite with 2NT – the problem is that you may miss a 4-4 fit. The more sensible alternative is to bid Stayman and then 2NT if no fit is uncovered (but you may miss a 5-3 fit). We can't have everything, and a 5-3 fit will often play just as well in NT but a 4-4 fit should not be missed. So, Stayman.

Hand A	Hand B	Partner opens 1NT.
♠ K842	♠ KJ854	With Hand A we bid 2♣. If partner responds 2♦ then we bid 2NT.
♥ KJ854	♥ KJ82	If partner responds 2♠ then we invite with 3♠. If partner responds 2♥
♦ J52	♦ 105	then it's worth game with a 5-4 fit, so 4♥.
♣ 2	♣ 32	And much the same with Hand B although some conservative players may prefer to just invite over a 2♥/♠ response.

Example 1

West	East	West	East	
♠ AQ3	♠ K842	1NT	2♣	
♥ Q9	♥ KJ854	2♦	2NT (1)	(1) invitational.
♦ K964	♦ J52	pass		
♣ A753	♣ 2			

A poor contract, but with limited tools …?

64

Example 2

West	East	West	East	
♠ AJ3	♠ K842	1NT	2♣	
♥ AQ3	♥ KJ854	2♦	2NT (1)	(1) invitational
♦ KQ64	♦ J52	3NT	pass	
♣ J53	♣ 2			

I would much prefer to be in 4♥.

Example 3

West	East	West	East	
♠ AKJ	♠ Q1042	1NT	2♣	
♥ KQ	♥ AJ854	2♦	2NT (1)	(1) invitational
♦ A864	♦ 532	3NT	pass	
♣ 9853	♣ 2			

It is debatable if the East hand is really worth an invitation at (1). West obviously accepts and 3NT will make if the ♣'s split. But how do you reach the good 4♥ contract?

Example 4

West	East	West	East	
♠ 96	♠ KJ842	1NT	2♣	
♥ A54	♥ KJ82	2♦	2NT (1)	(1) invitational
♦ AK64	♦ 105	3NT	pass	
♣ AQ85	♣ 32			

It's a poor game that West would have avoided had he known that the hand was a misfit. Note that West has no idea that the hand is a misfit, we play 4-way transfers and so 2♣ followed by 2NT may be any shape.

2.6.1.2　　Invitational 6-4's, Where We Want to Invite Game.

So, Smolen/traditional methods do not work too well with invitational 5-4's, but how about 6-4's?

It's even worse! Suppose that we start with Stayman, if a fit is uncovered then you can invite or perhaps just go for the game. But what if opener responds 2♦ and we still feel that there may be a game in a possible 6-3 fit? In the similar situation when we were 5-4 (or 4-5) we had to settle for a not completely satisfactory 2NT (we may miss a superior 5-3 fit). We cannot afford to miss a 6-3 fit (either partscore or game), so what's the solution?

Hand A	Hand B	Partner opens 1NT (strong).
♠ Q1042	♠ KJ9542	These hands are probably too strong to sign off at the two level.
♥ KJ8542	♥ Q942	If we bid Smolen then that is game forcing. How can we show that we
♦ 105	♦ 105	have invitational values and a 6 card suit when partner responds 2♦ to
♣ 2	♣ 2	our initial Stayman? 2NT is the only invitational bid. We have the same
		dilemma when playing a weak NT (3 points different).

Example 5

West	East	West	East	
♠ AQ3	♠ KJ9542	1NT	2♣	
♥ AK3	♥ Q942	2♦	2NT (1)	(1) invitational
♦ K64	♦ 105	pass		
♣ 9753	♣ 2			

Obviously bidding 2NT as invitational is silly.

So should you transfer into the 6-carder with these hand types? You then have an invitational bid (3 of the 6-carder) if partner simply completes the transfer. Often fine, but not if you miss a 4-4 fit in the other major (you cannot bid the 4 card major as that is played as 5-5 by most players, or else as forcing):

Example 6

West	East	West	East		
♠ 63	♠ KJ9542	1NT	2♥ (1)	(1) transfer to ♠'s	
♥ AK103	♥ Q942	2♠	3♠ (2)	(2) invitational, 6 ♠'s	
♦ KQJ4	♦ 105	3NT	pass		
♣ A73	♣ 2				

A poor contract, ♥'s never got a mention! 4♠ may be preferable to 3NT, but 4♥ is the best contract. You may sometimes get away with inviting with 2NT with the 5-4's but the 6-4's are impossible.

Basically, you cannot sensibly bid these invitational hands unless you employ Quest Transfers!

2.6.1.3   Game Going 5-4's, Where We Want To Play In Just 3NT or 4♥/♠.

Here we use Smolen. We start with the 5-4's again.

Hand C	Hand D	Partner opens 1NT (strong).
♠ AQ42	♠ KJ954	Having failed to find a 4-4 or better fit with Stayman, these hands now
♥ K9854	♥ AJ42	want to play in game in a 5-3 fit or else 3NT. So we start with Stayman
♦ J52	♦ Q5	and if there is no immediate fit we bid 3 of the 4-carder – Smolen.
♣ 5	♣ 52	Partner knows our major suit distribution is 5(or 6)-4 and bids either
		3NT of 4 of the major if there's a 5-3 fit.

Example 7

West	East	West	East		
♠ Q3	♠ KJ954	1NT	2♣		
♥ K103	♥ AJ42	2♦	3♥	(1)	(1) Smolen, 5+ ♠'s
♦ K984	♦ Q5	3NT	pass		
♣ AKJ3	♣ 52				

Looks good to me.

_____

Example 8

The 5-3 fit is usually best if opener has a weak suit: -

West	East	West	East		
♠ A83	♠ KJ954	1NT	2♣		
♥ K103	♥ AJ42	2♦	3♥	(1)	(1) Smolen, 5+ ♠'s
♦ AKJ3	♦ Q5	4♠	pass		
♣ J84	♣ 52				

_____

So no problems here. If you simply want to play in game then Smolen gets you to the correct spot played by the correct hand. And so it should – that is what it was designed to do!

2.6.1.4   <u>Game Going 6-4's, Where We Want To Play In Just 4♥ or 4♠.</u>

Again, we have responded 2♣ to partner's 1NT opening and he replied 2♦. Here we shall consider hands that are certainly worth game (in the 6-3 or 6-2 fit) but where we really do not wish partner to make a move towards slam.

In the corresponding situation with 5-4 (or 4-5) in the majors we informed partner that we had these 9 cards in the majors and left it up to him to play in a 5-3 fit or in 3NT. In this situation with a 6 card suit we want (partner) to play in the 6-3 or 6-2 fit.

Hand E	Hand F	Partner opens 1NT (strong).
♠ AQ42	♠ KJ9542	Having failed to find a 4-4 or better fit with Stayman, these
♥ K98542	♥ AJ42	hands now simply want to play in the long major suit game.
♦ 85	♦ 105	We do not want to encourage partner, and so we bid 4♦/♥.
♣ 5	♣ 2	This is a Texas Transfer (known as Extended Texas) and shows a desire to play in 4 of the major without inviting partner to bid on.

So we have   1NT - 2♣ - 2♦ - 4♦ - transfer to 4♥
and   1NT - 2♣ - 2♦ - 4♥ - transfer to 4♠   as Extended Texas Transfers.

Example

West	East	West	East		
♠ A63	♠ KJ9542	1NT	2♣		
♥ K75	♥ AJ42	2♦	4♥ (1)	(1) Extended Texas	
♦ AQ74	♦ 105	4♠	pass		
♣ K63	♣ 2				

This works fine (provided partner does not forget and leave you in 4♥!). Anyway, an excellent scheme and we use it for this hand type even when we move on to Quest Transfers.

2.6.1.5   Game Going 5-4's With Some Slam Interest

Here we are concerned with hand types that are not adverse to a slam suggestion from partner or may wish to make a mild try themselves. We start with Stayman of course and then Smolen 3♥/♠. Smolen does not lend itself to super-accepts and so opener normally either bids 3NT or bids 4 of our 5 card major. We are then at the level of 3NT or 4 of the 5-3 fit and it's up to us to take the next step.

Hand G	Hand H	
♠ AK854	♠ AK42	We begin with Stayman, if partner responds in a major then we are definitely in slam mode. It's best to use 4♣ as RKCB for the major.
♥ AQJ2	♥ AJ954	If there is no immediate fit then there may still be slam if there is a 5-3 fit. So Smolen. If partner denies a 5-3 fit with 3NT (or prefers 3NT) then
♦ J52	♦ K5	you can either give up or try a quantitative 4NT. If partner confirms a 5-3
♣ 5	♣ J2	fit then you are at the level of 4 of the major. It's up to you if you cue bid, Blackwood or whatever next.

Example 9

West	East	West	East		
♠ J73	♠ AK42	1NT	2♣		
♥ K3	♥ AJ954	2♦	3♠ (1)	(1)	Smolen, 5+ ♥'s
♦ AQ84	♦ K5	3NT	4NT (2)	(2)	quantitative
♣ AK93	♣ J2	6♥	pass		

West is max here and so bids slam. It's not a very good one (neither is 6NT); I guess that if West does not confirm a 5-3 fit then East needs more to go slamming?

With a fit, East should have a go: -

Example 10

West	East	West	East		
♠ Q7	♠ AK42	1NT	2♣	(1)	Smolen, 5+ ♥'s
♥ KQ3	♥ AJ954	2♦	3♠ (1)	(2)	3 ♥'s
♦ QJ42	♦ K5	4♥ (2)	4♠ (3)	(3)	RKCB (Kickback)
♣ AQ93	♣ J2	5♥ (4)	6♥	(4)	2 key cards + ♥Q
		pass			

Good show. It looks like East's bidding works fine, but ....

… but is it (a good show)? Luckily West had the right cards but it is not usually a good idea to bid Blackwood when you have a weak doubleton and don't know about partner's overall strength or holding in the weak suit: -

Example 11

West	East	West	East		
♠ Q7	♠ AK42	1NT	2♣		(1) Smolen, 5+ ♥'s
♥ KQ3	♥ AJ954	2♦	3♠ (1)		(2) 3 ♥'s
♦ AQJ84	♦ K5	4♥ (2)	4♠ (3)		(3) RKCB (Kickback)
♣ Q93	♣ J2	5♥ (4)	6♥		(4) 2 key cards + ♥Q
		pass			

East has got uncomfortably high and only knows that one key card is missing. There is no space to find out if the missing card is the ♥K or the ♣A, or if partner has the ♣K; and so he takes a chance and plays the percentages – it worked last time, so just unlucky? Perhaps, but see how we handle this example later playing Quest Transfers (section 2.6.2).

We also have a similar problem if West's trumps are rather poor: -

Example 12

West	East	West	East		
♠ J87	♠ AK42	1NT	2♣		(1) Smolen, 5+ ♥'s
♥ Q63	♥ AJ954	2♦	3♠ (1)		(2) 3 ♥'s
♦ AQJ	♦ K5	4♥ (2)	4♠ (3)		(3) RKCB (Kickback)
♣ AQ83	♣ J2	5♥ (4)	6♥		(4) 2 key cards + ♥Q
		pass			

West had no chance to inform East that he was minimum and so the poor slam was reached with exactly the same sequence as the good one (good slam, that is, not good sequence!) in example 10.

Now I realise that you want to know how these hands should be bid. Be patient. All good things come to those who wait. We'll finish all the examples using Smolen before we move on to the superior scheme (Quest Transfers).

70

2.6.1.6   Game Going 6-4's With Some Slam Interest

And how about 6-4's where we would not be adverse to partner's advances towards slam with a 6-3 fit?

Hand F	Hand G	Partner opens 1NT (strong).

Hand F	Hand G	
♠ AQJ2	♠ AK9542	Having failed to find a 4-4 or better fit with Stayman, there is still a
♥ KQ8542	♥ AQ42	chance of slam if partner has 3 of our long major and the right cards.
♦ 105	♦ 105	This time we go through our Smolen sequence right up to the point
♣ 2	♣ 2	where we have transferred into our longer suit. If partner bids 3NT

(usually showing a doubleton or perhaps a weak triplet) then we re-transfer (with 4♦/♥) into our 6-carder to show this good hand. Opener will normally simply accept this transfer. Note that some players state that opener must accept the re-transfer. I'm not so sure, there are most certainly hands where responder would not go past 4 of the major without a push from opener where slam is on. Remember, the fact that responder did not use Extended Texas is a mild slam invitation and responder may feel that he cannot move on without a nudge from opener.

Example 13

West	East	West	East		
♠ 107	♠ AK9542	1NT	2♣		(1) Smolen, 5 ♠'s & 4 ♥'s
♥ KJ3	♥ AQ42	2♦	3♥	(1)	(2) I prefer NT
♦ AK83	♦ 105	3NT	(2)	4♥	(3)	(3) re-transfer, slam interest
♣ KQ53	♣ 2	4♠	(4)	pass		(4) no slam interest

If partner had responded to our original Smolen bid by bidding 4 of our major (showing three card support), then we could agree to cue bid our singleton/void. This would show slam ambitions but could be either a 5-4 or 6-4 type hand.

Example 14

West	East	West	East		
♠ QJ7	♠ AK9542	1NT	2♣		(1) Smolen, 5 ♠'s & 4 ♥'s
♥ KJ3	♥ AQ42	2♦	3♥ (1)		(2) 3 ♠'s
♦ QJ8	♦ 105	4♠ (2)	5♣ (3)		(3) ♣ shortage, slam interest
♣ KQJ3	♣ 2	5♠	pass		

East had options here. Instead of cueing the shortage he could have tried RKCB, but I believe that indicating the shortage is better. This was indeed valuable information to West as he then knew that ♣KQ were not pulling their full weight.

So it's one too many, whether you cue or bid RKCB. But surely East should try for slam, shouldn't he? Just tough that 5♠ has 3 top losers? Playing Quest Transfers it's easy to stop low (4♠), as we will see later.

When opener has just a doubleton, slam may still be on. After responder's Smolen transfer opener bid 3NT, but when responder re-transfers to show a 6 card suit, opener may break the transfer with a suitable hand: -

Example 15

West	East	West	East		
♠ QJ	♠ AK9542	1NT	2♣		(1) Smolen, 5 ♠'s & 4 ♥'s
♥ KJ3	♥ AQ42	2♦	3♥ (1)		(2) 2 ♠'s
♦ AJ87	♦ 105	3NT (2)	4♥ (3)		(3) 6 ♠'s, slam interest
♣ AJ53	♣ 2	4NT (4) etc to 6♠			(4) RKCB

West has a near max hand, but is 2-3 in partner's majors; thus 3NT at (2) is correct. However, East's subsequent 4♥ (3) bid shows slam interest - otherwise he would use Extended Texas at (1) - and West's hand becomes enormous. Excellent major suit holdings (for what he has shown) and controls in the minors must make slam an excellent proposition. West must break the transfer at (4) to show slam ambitions. A 5♣ cue bid would be equally effective.

Contrast this West hand with the previous example; first round controls in the minors are all-important. Quacks in the minors are useless and even a king may be worthless opposite a singleton/void.

2.6.1.7   Slam Going 5-4's, How To Investigate Slam.

Hand H	Hand J	Partner opens 1NT (strong).
♠ AQJ2	♠ AK954	We are obviously going to slam here, preferably in a major suit and
♥ KQ854	♥ AQ42	possibly a grand. So we start with Stayman.
♦ K52	♦ 1052	After a 2♦ response we bid Smolen and partner completes the transfer.
♣ 2	♣ A	What now?

A 5♣ cue bid is obviously a good move with Hand J, but what about Hand H? …

1NT	2♣	You hold Hand H and the bidding has started like this. What now?
2♦	3♠	A key card ask looks like a good idea, but it's going to be difficult to establish if
4♥	?	partner has the ♠K rather than the ♣K. There are ways to establish specific kings after RKCB but generally only if all key cards are present. Agreeing to cue bid the shortage is also a very playable method.

Anyway, we have established our fit and you can choose your favourite slam seeking methods. I'll cover the best slam seeking method when we move on to discuss these hands using Quest Transfers.

2.6.1.8   Slam Going 6-4's, How To Investigate Slam.

Hand K	Hand L	Partner opens 1NT (strong).
♠ AKJ542	♠ AQJ2	Clearly going to slam again. So obviously Stayman and Smolen. If partner
♥ AQJ2	♥ KQ8542	completes the Smolen transfer then we go into our preferred slam mode.
♦ A5	♦ -	Should partner bid 3NT (usually showing just 2 card support for our
♣ 2	♣ KQ2	6-carder) then we bid 4♦/♥ - a re-transfer and promising a 6 card suit.

Partner may simply accept this re-transfer or perhaps super-accept with a very good doubleton. Either way we then go into slam mode. I will again cover the method for investigating the best slam when we cover these hands using Quest Transfers.

_____

Well, that's covered the commonly used Smolen approach. Not totally satisfactory, eh? So let's see if we can come up with something better …

2.6.2   A New Approach To 5-4, 6-4 etc.

So as we have seen, the invitational hands (and others) pose a huge problem using traditional or Smolen methods. I'll come onto the solution shortly but first we need to establish that a bidding sequence that we need is free.

When opener has replied 2♦ to Stayman, there is one sequence that has not yet been defined: -

1NT - 2♣ - 2♦ - 3♦

So what are the possible uses for this sequence? It cannot be a weak hand with a 4 card major and a ♦ suit (pass 2♦). It's not an invitational ♦ hand - we would transfer into ♦'s or simply invite with 2NT (via 2♣). But there are ½ a dozen or so quite plausible uses in current practice: -

1)	3♦ is Extended Stayman	a weak (or forcing) 5-5 in the majors
2)	3♦ is invitational	5+ ♦'s and a 4 card major
3)	3♦ is forcing for one round	5+ ♦'s and a 4 card major
4)	3♦ is game forcing	5+ ♦'s and a 4 card major
5)	3♦ is looking for slam	4♦'s and a 4 card major
6)	3♦ is Weissberger	an invitational (or forcing) 5-5 or 5-4 in the majors

Let's look at these possibilities: -

1)   <u>3♦ is Extended Stayman?</u>

Hand A	Hand B	
		Partner opens a strong NT. You could start off with 2♣, when a 2♥/♠ reply would be music to your ears. Of course partner will usually reply
♠ Q9876	♠ KQ984	2♦. 3♦ by you is then the Extended Stayman convention, showing 5-5 in
♥ Q8432	♥ QJ842	the majors and asking partner to bid a 3 card major. You then pass with
♦ 93	♦ J3	Hand A and raise to game with Hand B. Looks OK?
♣ 2	♣ 2	But what do you do with an invitational hand? And isn't the two level safer with hand A?

No, Extended Stayman does not really work. Transfers have solved all the problems, and we see how to handle invitational, game forcing and slam seeking 5-5's later in section 3.1.4.

---

2)   <u>3♦ is invitational, 5+ ♦'s and a 4 card major?</u>

Hand C	Hand D	
		Partner opens a strong NT. You obviously try Stayman but get a 2♦ response. You have invitational values, so try 3♦ with Hand C?
♠ 43	♠ 43	I don't like it. First of all, there is no similar bid when you have a ♣ suit
♥ K987	♥ K987	(Hand D) - 3♣ is SARS. So you have to rebid 2NT with Hand D (fine).
♦ AJ873	♦ 82	But in any case I would prefer to rebid 2NT with Hand C – if partner is
♣ 82	♣ AJ873	minimum and does not like ♦'s you are at the 3 level and fixed; the 2NT rebid is far better.

3)   <u>3♦ is forcing for one round, 5+ ♦'s and a 4 card major?</u>

Hand E	Hand F	
♠ Q3	♠ 43	
♥ K987	♥ K987	
♦ AJ8743	♦ AJ874	
♣ 8	♣ 98	

I got this answer from two leading players at the club. But I don't really understand it! Forcing for one round? Since you are already at the 3♦ level I guess that you may subside in 4♦? It makes little sense to me. With hands like this you have to decide where you are going. With Hand E I would transfer into ♦'s and then bid 3♥ - game forcing. With Hand F I would try Stayman and then an invitational 2NT if there is no ♥ fit (or 3NT if you are in desperate need of a swing).

4)   <u>3♦ is game forcing, 5+ ♦'s and a 4 card major?</u>

Hand G	Hand H	
♠ J3	♠ 43	
♥ K987	♥ K987	
♦ AQ8743	♦ AQJ74	
♣ 8	♣ J8	

Now this is more like it! No pussyfooting around. So you try Stayman and get a 2♦ response. A 3♦ bid is then game forcing. But what have you achieved? You are at the 3♦ level and have shown an undisclosed major and a ♦ suit. Consider the alternative approach, transfer to ♦'s and then bid 3 of the major. We cover how to transfer to minors in section 4. This latter approach has some major advantages: -

(a) Opener has a mechanism to tell you if he likes your ♦ suit (a super-accept - we cover this later in section 4.1).

(b) Opener knows which major suit you have.

(c) Opener will usually be declarer however you bid the hand. If you start with Stayman and opener bids the major that you don't have and you bid 3♦, 3NT is quite likely to be the final resting place. Why give the defence the gratuitous information about opener's 4 card major?

Not convinced? No problem! Suppose that you do elect to bid Stayman with Hands G and H and get a 2♦ response. There is little point in attempting to describe your hand to partner with a natural 3♦ (he does not know which major you hold, if you have 5 or 6 ♦'s, or even if you have slam ambitions!). You know partner's point range and something about his distribution. It's far better to bid 3♣, SARS, and find out more about opener's shape.

One more point. We have established that a sequence like 1NT - 2♣ - 2♥ - 3♦ is ASID and not ♠'s and ♦'s. It would thus be inconsistent to have our sequence showing a major and ♦'s.

So, whether you elect to transfer to the minor or to bid Stayman followed by SARS with these hand types does not really matter, the sequence 1NT - 2♣ - 2♦ - 3♦ is not needed in a natural sense. We most certainly do not need three options of bidding for the same hand type.

5)   <u>3♦ is looking for slam, 4♦'s and a 4 card major.</u>

We discussed this option in section 2.3. It obviously works OK but as I said we have SARS which copes equally well (better).

---

6)   <u>3♦ is the Weissberger Convention, an invitational (or forcing) 5-5 or 5-4 in the majors</u>

Now here we do have something that caters for invitational hands. With this scheme the sequences 1NT - 2♣ - 2♦ - 3♥   and   1NT - 2♣ - 2♦ - 3♠ are invitational, showing 4-5 and 5-4 respectively (a treatment used by some British players).

The 3♦ bid in the sequence 1NT - 2♣ - 2♦ - 3♦ is then used to show either: -

(a) 5 ♠'s and 4 ♥'s,   game forcing or
(b) 5 ♠'s and 5 ♥'s,   game forcing or
(c) 5 ♠'s and 5 ♥'s,   invitational

Now this works (I suppose) but the responses to the 3♦ bid are somewhat convoluted. Also, a game forcing 4-5 is not catered for and there is no mention of 6-4's or 4-6's. In addition, most players are used to having the jumps to 3♥/♠ as game forcing and using Jacoby Transfers with invitational and game forcing 5-5's. Yet another drawback is that responder will be declarer much of the time.

No, we have a far simpler solution which covers everything: -

A New Approach To 5-4, 6-4 etc. - Quest Transfers

So what is the solution to our invitational sequences? We just need a little lateral thinking and to forget about gadgets such as Smolen and Weissberger.

The 3♦ bid is not needed. Thus we use it (and 3♥) as transfers — simple.

After 1NT - 2♣ - 2♦,

3♦ = transfer to ♥'s
3♥ = transfer to ♠'s

This is now so straightforward that I hardly need to write any more (but I will). This initial transfer may be game invitational or stronger, 5-4 or 6-4 types. Unlike Smolen (which is game forcing), Quest Transfers are invitational or better (unlimited).

After a Quest Transfer opener has the obvious super-accepts available whichever suit is trumps. What's more, you can choose whatever type of super-accept suits your partnership style — perhaps similar to what you do over a Jacoby Transfer? But, as responder is known to be short in both minor suits, I prefer to show an ace. Let's assume that we use super-accepts to show an ace, then we have: -

After   1NT - 2♣ - 2♦ - 3♦   and after   1NT - 2♣ - 2♦ - 3♥

3♥   =   normal accept   3♠   =   normal accept

where a normal accept is a minimal hand with two card support or perhaps three. And we have the super-accepts: -

3♠	=	three ♥'s + ♠A	3NT	=	natural, non-min, normally 2-3 in the majors
3NT	=	natural, non-min, normally 3-2 in the majors	4♣	=	three ♠'s + ♣A
4♣	=	three ♥'s + ♣A	4♦	=	three ♠'s + ♦A
4♦	=	three ♥'s + ♦A *	4♥	=	three ♠'s + ♥A *
4♥	=	three ♥'s (no ace to cue)	4♠	=	three ♠'s (no ace to cue)

* <u>Note</u> Some players prefer not to use the bid below the agreed suit as a super-accept as they want to reserve it for partner's use as the re-transfer. In that case the 4-of-the-major super-accept may have the ace of the re-transfer suit. I much prefer to have the complete set of super-accepts and assume this in the examples.

After a super-accept responder will normally re-transfer if possible, and then either pass or investigate slam.

This all works fine, but we still have no bid to explicitly show the invitational hand if you opt for these simpler Quest Transfers rather than Smolen or natural. No problem, it is up to opener to super-accept with a suitable hand: -

Quest Transfers Are Defined As Invitational Or Better.

They can be treated in a similar way to Jacoby Transfers but there is one very big (and very important) difference – super-accepts. When playing Jacoby Transfers super-accepts are often very useful, but they are usually not essential as responder can invite after a normal accept. With Quest transfers it is different, you are at the 3 level and there is no room for a polite 2nd invitation. Quest Transfers are defined as invitational or better and opener **must** super-accept with a suitable hand. This also makes slam bidding much easier of course.

First of all, let's look at a typical hand that's difficult without Quest Transfers: -

Hand A	Partner opens a strong NT. You start with Stayman but get a 2♦ response. What now?
	2NT is reasonable, but there may be a better 5-3 ♥ fit (either partscore or game).
♠ K1042	3♥/♠ is forcing (whether you play Smolen or not).
♥ KJ752	So you simply have to give up on a possible fit and bid 2NT?
♦ 75	
♣ 52	

Playing Quest Transfers it's easy. Stayman to start and then transfer over a 2♦ response. Partner simply accepts the transfer with an unsuitable hand and will super-accept if game is on. Occasionally you will end up in 3♥ or 3♠ with a 5-2 fit, but that's probably just as good (often better) than 2NT.

Example A

West	East (A)	West	East		
				(1)	Quest Transfer
♠ A73	♠ K1042	1NT	2♣	(2)	normal accept
♥ 983	♥ KJ752	2♦	3♦ (1)	(3)	with no more than an
♦ KQ6	♦ 75	3♥ (2)	pass (3)		invitational hand, East passes
♣ AQJ7	♣ 52				

With a minimum (a flat hand) West correctly does not super-accept.

_____

Example B

West	East (A)	West	East		
				(1)	Quest Transfer
♠ Q3	♠ KJ102	1NT	2♣	(2)	Super-accept, ♣A
♥ Q93	♥ KJ752	2♦	3♦ (1)	(3)	re-transfer
♦ KQ64	♦ 75	4♣ (2)	4♦ (3)		
♣ AK76	♣ 52	4♥	pass		

This West has good trumps and reasonable shape, so he super-accepts.

_____

So clearly Quest Transfers work in this otherwise difficult scenario. We now have to look at all the cases that we covered earlier, but this time using Quest Transfers: -

2.6.2.1   invitational   5-4's, where we want to invite game.
2.6.2.2   invitational   6-4's, where we want to invite game.
2.6.2.3   game going   5-4's, where we want to play in just 3NT or 4♥/♠.
2.6.2.4   game going   6-4's, where we want to play in just 4♥ or 4♠.
2.6.2.5   game going   5-4's, but with slam interest.
2.6.2.6   game going   6-4's, but with slam interest.
2.6.2.7   slam going   5-4's, how to investigate slam.
2.6.2.8   slam going   6-4's, how to investigate slam.

Now Quest Transfers, although straightforward, are new! There are most certainly die-hards out there who have always played Smolen or natural methods, and so I accommodated them in the previous sections. I will now cover Quest Transfers in the same detail. And to make it easy for everybody I will use the same examples and chapter titles for the Quest and Smolen sections. Just see which you think works best!

2.6.2.1   Invitational 5-4's, Where We Want To Invite Game.

Simple. We start with Stayman and if we get a 2♦ response we make a Quest Transfer.

Example 1

West	East	West	East		
♠ AQ3	♠ K842	1NT	2♣		(1) Quest Transfer
♥ Q9	♥ KJ854	2♦	3♦ (1)		(2) normal accept
♦ K964	♦ J52	3♥ (2)	pass (3)		(3) only invitational, so pass
♣ A753	♣ 2				

A good contract, better than 2NT which is what we reached earlier when not playing Quest Transfers (1NT - 2♣ - 2♦ - 2NT - pass). A 5-2 fit will often play better than NT, as in this case.

Example 2

West	East	West	East		
♠ AJ3	♠ K842	1NT	2♣		(1) Quest Transfer
♥ AQ3	♥ KJ854	2♦	3♦ (1)		(2) Super-accept, ♠A
♦ KQ64	♦ J52	3♠ (2)	4♦ (3)		(3) re-transfer
♣ J53	♣ 2	4♥	pass		

Playing standard methods we landed up in the inferior 3NT.

Example 3

Occasionally opener may super-accept with just two trumps – when he has top cards in both the majors: -

West	East	West		East			
♠ AKJ	♠ Q1042	1NT		2♣		(1)	Quest Transfer
♥ KQ	♥ AJ854	2♦		3♦	(1)	(2)	super-accept. ♠A
♦ A864	♦ 532	3♠	(2)	4♦	(3)	(3)	re-transfer
♣ 9853	♣ 2	4♥		pass			

West knows that East has a maximum of 4 cards in the minors and so there are at most 3 losers there.

Playing traditional methods we end up in 3NT if East invites with 2NT. And East may not even elect to invite, but simply bid 2♥.

Example 4

East has a clear invitation in this example, but the knowledge of responder's shape may mean that poor games are avoided on misfits: -

West	East	West		East			
♠ 96	♠ KJ842	1NT		2♣		(1)	Quest Transfer
♥ A54	♥ KJ82	2♦		3♥	(1)	(2)	an excellent bid with the
♦ AK64	♦ 105	3♠	(2)	pass			knowledge of the misfit
♣ AQ85	♣ 32						

A combined 25 points, so most pairs will reach 3NT. The poor 3NT game was reached earlier with the sequence 1NT - 2♣ - 2♦ - 2NT - 3NT. 3♠ may not make but it's better than 3NT which stands very little chance. Playing the invitational Quest Transfer is superior to the invitational 2NT, as West knows it's a misfit and can avoid 3NT.

2.6.2.2   Invitational 6-4's, Where We Want To Invite Game.

We handle 6-4 invitational hands in the same way and can use the re-transfer if necessary.

Example 5

West	East	West	East		
♠ AQ3	♠ KJ9542	1NT	2♣	(1)	Quest Transfer
♥ AK3	♥ Q942	2♦	3♥ (1)	(2)	Super-accept, ♥A
♦ K64	♦ 105	4♥ (2)	4♠		
♣ 9753	♣ 2	pass			

With great major suit cards, west should accept. We floundered in a silly 2NT when we had no Quest Transfer and East bid an invitational 2NT. Note that as we play 4-way transfers West has no way of knowing that East even has a 4 card major and so does not know how good his major suit holdings are if East bids 2NT.

This 4♠ contract is played from the 'wrong' hand. But it's better to play in the correct contract than to play in a poor one from the 'right' hand. Even if South does lead a ♦ and you lose the first 3 tricks, 4♠ is still odds-on to make.

With the following example playing Smolen etc. we were fed up with being in the wrong contract using Stayman and 2NT, so we used a Jacoby Transfer. Needless to say, that did not work either. It's no problem playing Quest Transfers as the original Stayman always finds the 4-4 fit: -

Example 6

West	East	West	East		
♠ 63	♠ KJ9542	1NT	2♣	(1)	with great shape, worth an invitation
♥ AK103	♥ Q942	2♥	3♥ (1)		
♦ KQJ4	♦ 105	4♥	pass		
♣ A73	♣ 2				

We managed to land in a poor 3NT (or 4♠) when we bid this example via a Jacoby Transfer.

2.6.2.3   <u>**Game 5-4's Where We Want To Play In Just 3NT or 4♥/♠.**</u>

This is quite simple, and the best contract should be reached whether you play Smolen or Quest. We've seen these before, but let's just check that Quest Transfers work equally well: -

Example 7

West	East	West	East		
♠ Q3	♠ KJ954	1NT	2♣	(1)	Quest, 5+ ♠'s
♥ K103	♥ AJ42	2♦	3♥ (1)	(2)	min
♦ K984	♦ Q5	3♠ (2)	3NT (3)	(3)	offering the choice of 3NT or 4♠.
♣ AKJ3	♣ 52	pass			

Looks good to me. Same final contract as before.

_____

Example 8

West	East	West	East		
♠ A83	♠ KJ954	1NT	2♣	(1)	Quest, 5+ ♠'s
♥ K103	♥ AJ42	2♦	3♥ (1)	(2)	super-accept, ♦A.
♦ AKJ3	♦ Q5	4♦ (2)	4♥ (3)	(3)	re-transfer
♣ J84	♣ 52	4♠	pass		

The super-accept at (2) is marginal (West is minimum but does have good top cards and trumps) but 4♠ would be reached either way.

_____

2.6.2.4   <u>**Game Going 6-4's, Where We Want To Play In Just 4♥ or 4♠.**</u>

This is exactly the same whatever scheme you use. Stayman followed by Extended Texas jumps to 4♦/♥ if no fit is found. Quest or Smolen do not feature.

1NT - 2♣ - 2♦ - 4♦, transfer to 4♥   and
1NT - 2♣ - 2♦ - 4♥, transfer to 4♠   are Extended Texas Transfers.

2.6.2.5   <u>Game Going 5-4's With Some Slam Interest</u>

Here we are concerned with hand types that are not adverse to a slam suggestion from partner or may wish to make a mild try themselves. We start with Stayman of course and then a Quest Transfer.

Example 9

West	East	West	East	
♠ J73	♠ AK42	1NT	2♣	(1) Quest, 5+ ♥'s
♥ K3	♥ AJ954	2♦	3♦ (1)	(2) non-min
♦ AQ84	♦ K5	3NT (2)	4NT (3)	(3) quantitative
♣ AK93	♣ J2	pass (4)		

Note that 4NT is quantitative after a 3NT bid from opener, so what does responder do when he had 5 or 6 ♠'s and wants to bid Blackwood? The answer is that with just 5 ♠'s he normally would not, and with 6 ♠'s he can re-transfer, we come onto that shortly when we discuss the 6-4 type hands

When we bid this hand using Smolen we ended up in a poor 6♥ after East bid the quantitative 4NT at (3). It was perhaps debatable if West should have accepted the slam invitation with a misfit, but he is max. Playing Quest Transfers it's slightly different. West's 3NT bid has already promised a maximum (otherwise he would simply accept the transfer) and so East's quantitative bid ask for something extra – this can only mean good ♥'s and/or ♠'s.

      West's ♥Kx is good, but the poor ♠'s are not good enough. Aware of the misfit, he
♠ QJ3   correctly declines the invitation at (4). But exchange the ♠7 and ♦Q to get this hand
♥ K3   and opener should accept by bidding 6NT. Points in partner's suits are all important
♦ A874   – it's what you need when you have already shown a maximum.
♣ AK93

Example 10

West	East	West	East	
♠ Q7	♠ AK42	1NT	2♣	(1) Quest, 5+ ♥'s
♥ KQ3	♥ AJ954	2♦	3♦ (1)	(2) max, 3 ♥'s + ♣A
♦ QJ42	♦ K5	4♣ (2)	4♠ (3)	(3) RKCB (Kickback)*
♣ AQ93	♣ J2	5♥ (4)	6♥	(4) 2 key cards + ♥Q
		pass		

We reached the same good slam playing Smolen but that sequence really was not a good one because East launched into Blackwood with a small doubleton (♣) – not good practice. Here it's fine as West has cue bid the ♣A.

   * Now I said that 4♠ at (3) is RKCB, but is simple RKCB really the best meaning? Should both majors be key suits? We will discuss it shortly, but let's first do the examples 11 & 12 that we saw earlier.

Example 11

When we bid this one earlier East bid the poor slam because he knew nothing much other than that there was a key card missing.

West	East	West		East			
♠ QJ	♠ AK42	1NT		2♣		(1)	Quest, 5+ ♥'s
♥ KQ3	♥ AJ954	2♦		3♦	(1)	(2)	3 ♥'s + ♦A
♦ AQJ84	♦ K5	4♦	(2)	4NT	(3)	(3)	♠ cue bid
♣ Q93	♣ J2	5♥	(4)	pass			

West super-accepted and so East is certainly in slam mode. But he knows to be very careful as West has denied the ♣A. Blackwood is not a good idea with a weak doubleton and so he cue bids instead. Note that when you play Kickback then 4NT is the ♠ cue bid. West's 5♥ at (4) denies the ♣K and so the poor slam is avoided. If West did have the ♣K then he had two options – he could cue it, in which case East would bid 6♦ to transfer the 6♥ contract to West. West could also simply bid 6♥.

Example 12

West	East	West		East			
♠ J87	♠ AK42	1NT		2♣		(1)	Quest, 5+ ♥'s
♥ Q63	♥ AJ954	2♦		3♦	(1)	(2)	min
♦ AQJ	♦ K5	3♥	(2)	3NT	(3)		
♣ AQ83	♣ J2	4♥		pass			

When we bid this example earlier West had no chance to inform East that he was minimum and so the poor ♥ slam was reached. Here East knows that West is minimum and so elects not to go slamming. Very wise. He bids 3NT at (3) to give opener the choice of 3NT or 4♥.

Note that the West hand is certainly minimum here as the queens in partner's short suits (the minors) may not be worth much. Since responder is known to hold 4 ♠'s West might consider passing 3NT at pairs scoring.

2.6.2.6 Game Going 6-4's With Some Slam Interest

Let's look at 6-4's where we would not be adverse to partner's advances towards slam with a 6-3 fit. If opener responds 3NT to our Quest Transfer then we can re-transfer. This shows slam interest as we did not use Extended Texas.

Example 13

West	East	West		East		
♠ 107	♠ AK9542	1NT		2♣		(1) Quest, 5 ♠'s & 4 ♥'s
♥ KJ3	♥ AQ42	2♦		3♥	(1)	(2) I prefer NT, non min.
♦ AK83	♦ 105	3NT	(2)	4♥	(3)	(3) re-transfer, slam interest
♣ KQ53	♣ 2	4♠	(4)	pass		(4) no slam interest

As it happens, exactly the same as the Smolen sequence. Fine.

In the next example we got too high (5♠) playing Smolen.

Example 14

West	East	West		East		
♠ QJ7	♠ AK9542	1NT		2♣		(1) Quest, 5 ♠'s & 4 ♥'s
♥ KJ3	♥ AQ42	2♦		3♥	(1)	(2) 3 ♠'s, non-min, no ace to cue
♦ QJ8	♦ 105	4♠	(2)	pass		
♣ KQJ3	♣ 2					

Playing Quest Transfers it's easy to stop low (4♠).

When opener has just a doubleton trump, slam may still be on. After responder's Quest Transfer opener bid 3NT showing a non-min, when responder re-transfers to show a 6 card suit and slam interest (no Texas), opener breaks the transfer with a suitable hand: -

Example 15

West	East	West		East		
♠ QJ	♠ AK9542	1NT		2♣		(1) Quest, 5 ♠'s & 4 ♥'s
♥ KJ3	♥ AQ42	2♦		3♥	(1)	(2) 2 ♠'s, non-min
♦ AJ87	♦ 105	3NT	(2)	4♥	(3)	(3) 6 ♠'s, slam interest
♣ AJ53	♣ 2	4NT	(4)	etc to 6♠ or 6NT		(4) *(D)RKCB for ♠'s

* The same as the previous Smolen auction except that the 4NT at (4) is to be discussed shortly.

2.6.2.7   <u>Slam Going 5-4's, How To Investigate Slam.</u>

Hand H	Hand J	Partner opens 1NT (strong).
♠ AQJ2	♠ AK954	Much the same as when using Smolen. We are obviously looking for a
♥ KQ854	♥ AQ42	slam here, preferably in a major suit. So we start with Stayman. After a
♦ K52	♦ 1052	2♦ response we bid Quest and then whatever your favourite slam seeking
♣ 2	♣ A	method is.

Of course you do have a big advantage when using Quest in that opener will cue bid an ace in response to Quest if he has 3 trumps and is non-min. It certainly would be handy to know if partner has the ♣A or not with Hand H.

So what is the best method to investigate slam with these types of hand? A 5♣ cue bid is possibly a good move with Hand J, but what about Hand H? …

1NT	2♣	You hold Hand H and the bidding has started like this. What now?
2♦	3♦	Note that we are already way ahead of the previous Smolen auction in that the
4♣	? (1)	level is just 4♣, opener has cue bid indicating the ♣A, 3 trumps and a non-min.

Playing Smolen the auction would be at 4♥ with responder in the dark.

A key card ask looks like a good idea, but it's going to be difficult to establish if partner has the ♠K rather than the ♣K. There are ways to establish specific kings after RKCB but generally only if all key cards are present.

The answer is that responder should employ Double Roman Key Card Blackwood – DRKCB. With these major 2-suited hands the kings (and queens) in the major suits are very important and minor suit kings are often insignificant.

The trump suit has been established but East really also needs to know about key cards in the other major as well. So East uses two suit, or Double RKCB (DRKCB); there are thus 6 key cards.

DRKCB After A Quest Transfer

When responder has shown at least 9 cards in the majors then the king (and sometimes queen – as we shall see in the next few pages) in both major suits are important. So our RKCB (Kickback) bid is now DRKCB, with both major suit kings counted as key cards. The responses are: -

Next step	=	0 or 3 key cards
Next step + 1	=	1 or 4 key cards
Next step + 2	=	2 or 5 key cards
Next step + 3	=	2 or 5 key cards + the 'trump' queen

Where, by 'trump' queen I mean the queen of responder's longer suit.

Example 16

West	East	West	East		
♠ K9	♠ AQJ2	1NT	2♣		(1) Quest, 5 ♥'s & 4 ♠'s
♥ AJ3	♥ KQ854	2♦	3♦	(1)	(2) 3 ♥'s, non-min +♣A
♦ QJ87	♦ K52	4♣	(2)	4♠ (3)	(3) DRKCB (Kickback)
♣ AJ53	♣ 2	4NT	(4)	6♥ (5)	(4) 3 key cards
		pass			

(5) As long as the ♠K is included along with the key cards then 3 key cards is all East needs. If the ♠K was not included then a 2 key card response would leave slam dubious.

If the DRKCB reply was 0/3 or 1/4 and so gave no information about the trump queen, asker may enquire about both queens with the next free bid, the responses are: -

Next step	=	no queen
Next step + 1	=	♥Q
Next step + 2	=	♠Q
Next step + 3	=	♥Q & ♠Q

And if the response was 2/5 and thus indicated the presence or absence of the trump queen, asker may enquire about the other queen. The responses are up to you but best is that you simply use the same procedure as you do with your normal RKCB trump queen ask. Here I assume that the next bid up denies the major suit queen and that any other bid acknowledges it – show a king or else return to the trump suit, so: -

Next step	=	denies the other major suit queen
Return to the trump suit	=	shows the other queen but denies ♣K or ♦K.
any other bid	=	shows the other queen and the king of the suit bid.

Note that a queen ask does not necessarily guarantee that all key cards are present, asker may simply be looking for the small slam.

2.6.2.8   <u>**Slam Going 6-4's, How To Investigate Slam.**</u>

Hand K	Hand L	Partner opens 1NT (strong).
♠ AKJ542	♠ AQJ2	And the same here. Stayman, Quest and then onto slam; either
♥ AQJ2	♥ KQ8542	small or grand. Again you have more to go on using Quest
♦ A5	♦ -	because of the possible super-accept response (or lack of it).
♣ 2	♣ KQ2	

Now you could choose to use either RKCB or DRKCB with 5-4's but with 6-4's responder really should use DRKCB. The problem is that opener will not always know if responder is 5-4 or 6-4 and so it's best to always use DRKCB with these two-suited (5-4 or 6-4 type) hands.

Example 17

West	East		West	East			
			1NT	2♣		(1)	Quest, 5 ♠'s & 4 ♥'s
				2♦	3♥ (1)	(2)	min, 2 or 3 ♠'s
♠ Q9	♠ AKJ542		3♠ (2)	4♥ (3)		(3)	6 ♠'s, slam interest
♥ 953	♥ AQJ2		4♠ (4)	4NT (5)		(4)	nothing extra
♦ KQJ3	♦ A5		5♦ (6)	6♠		(5)	DRKCB
♣ AQJ6	♣ 2		pass			(6)	1 key card

West has a good doubleton ♠, but with poor ♥'s he really can do nothing more than complete the re-transfer at (4). However, the East hand is still looking for slam, possibly even a grand, but when West's response at (6) revealed that either the ♣A or ♥K was missing he gave up on the grand.

There is another interesting point in this auction; the re-transfer at (3) is not really a re-transfer of course, as West has already bid ♠'s. Thus East can bid either 4♥ or 4♠ at (3). It's best to play 4♠ as a sign off and 4♥ as looking for slam with a 6 card suit. A subsequent Blackwood bid by either opener or responder is then DRKCB.

But with this Hand K it is certainly worth looking for the grand. Consider the situation where West has a more suitable hand. This one's the same strength but the king in responder's 2nd suit is worth more than 3 points elsewhere: -

Example 18

West	East		West	East			
						(1)	Quest, 5 ♠'s & 4 ♥'s
						(2)	min, 2 or 3 ♠'s
West	East		1NT	2♣		(3)	6 ♠'s, slam interest
				2♦	3♥ (1)	(4)	completing the re-transfer
♠ Q9	♠ AKJ542		3♠ (2)	4♥ (3)		(5)	DRKCB
♥ K83	♥ AQJ2		4♠ (4)	4NT (5)		(6)	2 key cards + ♠Q
♦ KJ83	♦ A5		5♠ (6)	6♣ (7)		(7)	minor suit kings?
♣ AQ65	♣ 2		6♠ (8)	7NT		(8)	♦K only
			pass				

5NT at (7) would have been queen clarification, so 6♣ is the (♣/♦) king ask. 6♠ at (8) is next step + 2.

So that's fine, but what if the DRKCB reply shows 0/3 or 1/4 keycards and says nothing about the trump queen? Then the next bid up then asks about queens: -

Let's change the ♦ suit in example 18 very slightly: -

Example 19		West	East		(1) Quest, 5 ♠'s & 4 ♥'s
					(2) min, 2 or 3 ♠'s
West	East	1NT	2♣		(3) 6 ♠'s, slam interest
		2♦	3♥	(1)	(4) completing the re-transfer
♠ Q9	♠ AKJ542	3♠	(2) 4♥	(3)	(5) DRKCB
♥ K83	♥ AQJ2	4♠	(4) 4NT	(5)	(6) 3 key cards
♦ AJ83	♦ K5	5♣	(6) 5♦	(7)	(7) queens?
♣ AQ65	♣ 2	5NT	(8) 7NT		(8) ♠Q
		pass			

And sometimes the information about the other major suit queen is useful: -

Example 20		West	East		(1) Quest, 5 ♠'s & 4 ♥'s
					(2) min, 2 or 3 ♠'s
West	East	1NT	2♣		(3) 6 ♠'s, slam interest
		2♦	3♥	(1)	(4) completing the re-transfer
♠ Q9	♠ AKJ542	3♠	(2) 4♥	(3)	(5) DRKCB
♥ Q93	♥ AKJ2	4♠	(4) 4NT	(5)	(6) 2 key card + ♠Q
♦ AJ83	♦ K4	5♠	(6) 5NT	(7)	(7) ♥ queen?
♣ AQ65	♣ 2	6♠	(8) 7NT		(8) yes, no king.
		Pass			

♠ Q9   If West had denied the ♥Q, say with this hand, then the grand is not a good bet.
♥ 983   Note that the ♥Q is more important than the ♣K.
♦ AJ83
♣ AKJ5

So DRKCB works like a treat with Hand K and similar hands, but what about Hand L?

Exclusion Double Roman Keycard Blackwood (EDRKCB)

Hand L is not interested in the ♦A and so should use Exclusion DRKCB = EDRKCB.

A rare beast, but there are situations where we are only interested in the kings (and perhaps queens) of two suits and have a void. Exclusion RKCB (ERKCB) would enable us to ask for key cards outside the exclusion suit and Double RKCB (DRKCB) would enable us to locate the king in the other major directly but responder would not know about our void (and thus include that ace in his reply). So when our partner does not know about our void and we are in a situation where DRKCB is the Blackwood bid, then a bid of 5 of a minor is EDRKCB. So with EDRKCB we have 5 key cards; the three aces outside the exclusion suit and the two key kings. The step responses are the obvious 0/3, 1/4, 2.

Example 21

West	East (L)	West	East		
♠ K9	♠ AQJ2	1NT	2♣		(1) Quest, 5 ♥'s & 4 ♠'s
♥ AJ3	♥ KQ8542	2♦	3♦	(1)	(2) 3 ♠'s, non-min +♣A
♦ KJ853	♦ -	4♣ (2)	4♦	(3)	(3) re-transfer, 6 ♥'s
♣ A87	♣ KQ2	4♥	5♦	(4)	(4) EDRKCB
		5♥ (5)	7♥		(5) 3 key cards
		pass			

But if opener did not have the ♠K it's different: -

Example 22

West	East (L)	West	East		
♠ 98	♠ AQJ2	1NT	2♣		(1) Quest, 5 ♥'s & 4 ♠'s
♥ AJ3	♥ KQ8542	2♦	3♦	(1)	(2) 3 ♠'s, non-min +♣A
♦ AQ853	♦ -	4♣ (2)	4♦	(3)	(3) re-transfer, 6 ♥'s
♣ AJ7	♣ KQ2	4♥	5♦	(4)	(4) EDRKCB
		5NT (5)	6♥		(5) 2 key cards
		pass			

So DRKCB and EDRKCB work fine in this scenario, whether opener has super-accepted or not. It's up to you if you wish to include them in your armoury, and we come upon then again in section 3.1.4 when we discuss hands that are 5-5 in the majors (where I believe that they are even more important). Let's move on to something different: -

2.6.2.9   The 3♠ Bid Using Quest Transfers

Now that we are using Quest Transfers, the previous Smolen/natural sequence

1NT - 2♣ - 2♦ - 3♠ is a spare bid.

I guess that you could use it for whatever you like, but it needs to be a hand type that can cope with a 2♥/♠ response to Stayman. There are a few possibilities, but my favourite is strong 4-4 (game forcing) in the majors with both minor suits weak: -

Hand M	Hand N	Partner opens 1NT (strong).
♠ AQ92	♠ AK94	You try Stayman but get a 2♦ response. Now 3NT is the standard bid
♥ KQJ5	♥ AQ102	and will often be fine. But a Moysian fit may be best if partner has good
♦ J85	♦ 105	3 card support for one major and a weak minor.
♣ 72	♣ 743	

Example 1

West	East	West	East		
♠ KJ7	♠ AQ92	1NT	2♣		(1) both majors, weak minors
♥ A3	♥ KQJ5	2♦	3♠	(1)	(2) With very weak ♣'s, West elects to play in
♦ AK973	♦ J85	4♠	pass	(2)	the Moysian fit.
♣ J53	♣ 72				

Example 2

Sometimes 3NT would be a very poor contract: -

West	East	West	East		
♠ QJ6	♠ AK94	1NT	2♣		(1) both majors, weak minors
♥ K73	♥ AQ102	2♦	3♠	(1)	(2) West knows that the opponents have
♦ 73	♦ 105	4♥	pass	(2)	4 or 5 ♦ tricks off the top.
♣ AKQ102	♣ 743				

Example 3

And nothing is lost if West has both minors well covered: -

West	East	West	East		
♠ Q7	♠ AK94	1NT	2♣		(1) both majors, weak minors
♥ J73	♥ AQ102	2♦	3♠	(1)	(2) let then lead a minor, see if I care.
♦ AK973	♦ 105	3NT	pass	(2)	
♣ AQ10	♣ 743				

2.6.3   <u>Summary Of All 5-4's And 6-4's (assuming no fit is found)</u>

(a) when using Smolen

Weak 5-4 *	Stayman and correct, or transfer if you prefer.
Weak 6-4 *	Transfer, or Stayman and correct if you prefer.
Invitational 5-4	Stayman. There is no invitational bid other than 2NT if Stayman gets a 2♦ response (Smolen is game forcing).
Invitational 6-4	Stayman or transfer? There is no invitational bid (except 2NT) if Stayman gets a 2♦ response so it's probably best to use a Jacoby Transfer? It's no problem using Quest Transfers of course.
Game going 5-4	Stayman and Smolen 3♠/♥.
Game going 6-4 *	Stayman and Extended Texas 4♦/♥
Slam interest 5-4	Stayman and Smolen. If partner replies 3NT to Smolen then a quantitative 4NT is the slam try.
Slam interest 6-4	Stayman, Smolen and Smolen re-transfer.

(b) when using Quest Transfers

Weak 5-4 *	Stayman and correct, or transfer if you prefer.
Weak 6-4 *	Transfer, or Stayman and correct if you prefer.
Invitational 5-4	Stayman and Quest Transfer 3♦/♥. Partner is expected to super-accept if game is on. If the shape and quality of the majors is poor then 2NT is a remote alternative to the Quest Transfer.
Invitational 6-4	Stayman and Quest Transfer. Partner is expected to super-accept if game is on.
Game going 5-4	Stayman and Quest Transfer. If opener simply completes the Quest Transfer then bid 3NT, partner will pass or correct to a 5-3 fit.
Game going 6-4 *	Stayman and Extended Texas 4♦/♥.
Slam interest 5-4	Stayman and Quest Transfer. If partner has a hand such that slam makes then he will presumably super-accept. If opener responded 3NT to the Quest Transfer then there probably is no slam, you could try a quantitative 4NT with a really good invitational hand.
Slam interest 6-4	Stayman, Quest Transfer and Quest Re-transfer.

The * sequences are the same whether you play Smolen (or natural) or Quest Transfers.

The Advantages of Quest Transfers

- They are simple.
- The super-accept structure is complete (a bid for each suit + one over).
- The straightforward super-accepts mean that invitational hands are easy.
- Responder does not have to stretch with a hand that possibly has slam potential (opener will super-accept).
- Slam bidding is easier as opener has indicated if he is min or not and has had a chance to cue bid.
- The 3♠ bid (after 1NT - 2♣ - 2♦) is free for use to show 4-4 in the majors and weak minors.

2.7   <u>Stayman Super-accepts</u>

The original Stayman concept incorporated a 2NT response to show a maximum hand. Now this is acceptable if your style is to guarantee invitational values with your Stayman enquiry. These days, most people play Garbage Stayman and so this response is unsound if partner has a weak hand and there is no major suit fit.

Another idea which has some followers is that 2NT shows both majors. Again, unsound because if opener is minimum then the 3 level may be too high, even with a fit. Let's hear the general expert view: -

Quoting Marty Bergen, '*never, Never, NEVER respond* 2NT *to Stayman*'.
Ron Klinger states '*the* 2NT *response doesn't exist. The idea that it should be to show both majors is totally unsound*'.

Excellent advise, unless you and your partner **really** know what you are doing.

When we get onto transfers (Section 3) you will see that opener super-accepting when he likes responder's suit is widely accepted (even though responder's transfer bid promises zero points). This philosophy can be extended to the situation where responder has bid Stayman.

If you are maximum, and like the fact that responder probably has a major suit, then a super-accept is in order. Let's start of with the basic idea: -

1)   1NT - 2♣ - 3♦   =   maximum, both majors
2)   1NT - 2♣ - 3♥   =   maximum, 5 ♥'s
3)   1NT - 2♣ - 3♠   =   maximum, 5 ♠'s

Why are these responses sound? First consider 2 & 3, partner (responder) has either invitational values or both majors (or a better hand). If it is the weak hand with two 4 card majors then this 3 level bid is sound according to the law of total tricks. If responder's hand does not contain this major, then he must have invitational values and can bid 3NT (or 4 of the major to play in a 5-3 fit) as you are max. And how about sequence 1? No problem if partner has any invitational hand, he just chooses the correct game contract. If partner is very weak with both majors then you usually have a 9 card fit and always a double fit, so settling in 3 of a major is OK. But why do we use 3♦ for the 'both majors' bid when 2NT is available? We have 3 available bids (2NT, 3♣ or 3♦). We need the 2NT/3♣ bids as described later in this section, so 3♦ shows this max with both majors hand.

So, after 1NT - 2♣ - 3♦ (max, both majors) we have: -

3♥	=	sign off
3♠	=	sign off
3NT	=	to play
4♣	=	Gerber
4♦	=	transfer to ♥'s
4♥	=	transfer to ♠'s

Example 1

West	East	West		East	
♠ AQ64	♠ K852	1NT		2♣	
♥ AJ106	♥ Q9853	3♦	(1)	4♥	(2)
♦ Q53	♦ 2	4♠		pass	(3)
♣ A8	♣ 972				

(1) Max, both majors
(2) Transfer, the double fit and a max partner make 4♠ a good bet.

An excellent contract. Very difficult to bid if West had simply replied 2♥ to the Stayman enquiry. Note that East elects to play in the 4-4 fit. The 4-4 fit will often provide an extra trick over the 5-4 fit. If you don't agree (I have a 'thing' about 4-4 fits), then transfer into the 5-4 fit at (2) by bidding 4♦. No problem. Either way you reach a very reasonable game.

Example 2

West	East	West		East	
♠ AJ106	♠ 98532	1NT		2♣	
♥ AQ64	♥ J852	3♦	(1)	3♠	(2)
♦ Q53	♦ 72	pass			
♣ A8	♣ 92				

(1) Max, both majors
(2) It is perhaps a matter of style if you want to play in the 4-4 or 5-4 fit in a partial. Without game-going values the 5-4 fit is probably safer.

Example 3

West	East	West		East
♠ AQ6	♠ K9852	1NT		2♣
♥ A9864	♥ K852	3♥	(1)	4♥
♦ Q53	♦ 7	pass		
♣ A8	♣ 932			

(1) Max, 5 ♥'s

An excellent game that would be difficult to bid if West had responded 2♥.

Example 4   Sometimes a 5-3 fit may be located and a thin but respectable game bid: -

West	East	West	East		
♠ AQ754	♠ K86	1NT	2♣ (1)	(1)	Intending to pass 2♦/♠
♥ KQ4	♥ A852	3♠ (2)	4♠	(2)	Max, 5 ♠'s
♦ A4	♦ 87632				
♣ J54	♣ 7				

4♠ is a very respectable contract, the bidding would normally go 1NT - 2♣ - 2♠ - pass.

Example 5   And it does not go wrong if East has a heap: -

West	East	West	East		
♠ AQ754	♠ 9862	1NT	2♣	(1)	Max, 5 ♠'s
♥ KQ4	♥ J852	3♠ (1)	pass		
♦ A54	♦ 8762				
♣ J5	♣ Q				

The opponents would surely find 3♣ if West bid just 2♠.

Example 6   And nothing is lost when there is no fit: -

West	East	West	East		
♠ AQ75	♠ K8	1NT	2♣ (1)	(1)	intending to invite with 2NT next.
♥ KQ94	♥ J8	3♦ (2)	3NT (3)	(2)	Max, both majors.
♦ Q53	♦ J764			(3)	Max is good enough, let's try 3NT
♣ A8	♣ KJ842				

This concept of showing your maximum hand (when 4-4 or with a 5 card major) is also used if there is intervention: -

Example 7

West	East	West	North	East	South
♠ AQ754	♠ K862	1NT	pass	2♣	3♣
♥ KQ4	♥ J852	3♠	pass	4♠	all pass
♦ Q53	♦ K762				
♣ A8	♣ 2				

Example 8   Usually after intervention there is still room to show both majors (using 3♦): -

West	East	West	North	East	South
♠ AQ75	♠ K862	1NT	pass	2♣	3♣
♥ KQ43	♥ J852	3♦ (1)	pass	4♠	all pass
♦ Q53	♦ K762				
♣ A8	♣ 2	(1) Max, both majors			

Example 9   And how about after a 3♦ intervention? : -

West	East	West	North	East	South
♠ AQ75	♠ K862	1NT	pass	2♣	3♦
♥ KQ43	♥ J852	? (1)			
♦ A8	♦ 2				
♣ Q53	♣ K762				

(1) What would a double show here? Standard would be penalties. Showing a ♦ holding such as ♦AJ1085. But realistically, unlikely. You could well apply the 'stolen bid' principle here and use the double to show a 3♦ bid – i.e. max with both majors.

So far we have only considered situations where responder is weak. When responder is strong the knowledge that opener is maximum with both majors does no harm at all: -

Example 10

West	East	West	East	
♠ AQ75	♠ KJ102	1NT	2♣	(1) Max, both majors
♥ KQ43	♥ AJ982	3♦ (1)	4♥ (2)	(2) transfer
♦ A83	♦ K62	4♠	4NT (3)	(3) RKCB
♣ Q5	♣ 8	etc to 6♠		

Note that without this convention, the poorer 6♥ contract may be reached (but East should use SARS to find the 4-4 ♠ fit).

So, an old concept (the 2NT response) rejuvenated (except that we use 3♦). Something to think about? And the down side? Defenders know more about declarer's shape.

One Step Further – The 2NT/3♣ Bids

Well then, do these 3♦/3♥/3♠ bids make sense? Presumably so if you have got this far in this section. But what about those bypassed bids of 2NT/3♣? Can anything be done with these? The obvious hand type to consider is a 6 card minor suit: -

♠ AQ	You choose to open this hand with a strong 1NT. Partner bids 2♣. Is this a hand where
♥ Q43	a 3♣ response is called for? No. The knowledge that partner probably has a 4 card major
♦ K5	has not improved your hand. You elected to open this hand with 1NT and you have to
♣ KQ9865	be consistent, so 2♦ now.

Thus these jump bids after Stayman only make sense if our hand has improved after partner's Stayman bid, i.e. we have a 4 card major: -

West	East	
		A matter of style. Would you open a strong 1NT with this West hand? (I would). If yes, then read on.
♠ QJ54	♠ K973	You open 1NT, partner bids 2♣, you reply 2♠ and partner passes.
♥ K4	♥ Q1052	A combined 22 count so seems OK. So 4♠ makes, maybe with an
♦ AQ953	♦ J842	overtrick, but it's impossible to bid?
♣ A8	♣ 6	

Now consider a 2NT response to Stayman that says 'I am non-min, have 5 decent ♦'s and a 4 card major'. With his superb fitting hand, East would punt 4 of the major. A pretty good contract. So we have: -

4) 1NT - 2♣ - 2NT = non minimum, 5 decent ♦'s and a 4 card major
5) 1NT - 2♣ - 3♣ = non minimum, 5 decent ♣'s and a 4 card major

Why use 2NT (instead of 3♦) for the ♦ hand? Because we need to have room for responder to ask for the major suit without going above 3 of the major with the reply. Before we have a few examples, let's define the complete bidding structure after these two bids: -

Opener's response shows 5 ♦'s: -   Opener's response shows 5 ♣'s: -

After   1NT - 2♣ - 2NT : -   After   1NT - 2♣ - 3♣ : -

3♣	= transfer to 3♦ (1)		pass	= to play in opener's 5 card ♣ suit	
3♦	= which major?		3♦	= which major?	
3NT	= to play (no 4 card major)		3NT	= to play (no 4 card major)	
			4♣	= RKCB for ♣'s	
4♦	= RKCB for ♦'s (2)				

(1) Unlikely to be weak since there is a major suit fit (if responder is weak then he has both majors). Possibly a very weak 4360, 3460, 3451 or similar hand but it's more likely that responder has a big hand and is angling for a ♦ slam. This may be preferable to launching straight into RKCB (4♦) as opener is then declarer.
(2) Unlikely to be used as responder would normally transfer to ♦'s first.

If responder has a 4 card major, he normally bids 3♦ to establish the possible fit. With a weak hand he passes the 3♥/♠ reply; with a game going or slam hand he bids on.

Example 1

West	East	West	East		
♠ QJ54	♠ K973	1NT	2♣		(1) 5 ♦'s and a 4 card major
♥ K4	♥ Q1052	2NT (1)	3♦ (2)		(2) which major?
♦ AQ953	♦ J842	3♠ (3)	4♠		(3) ♠'s
♣ A8	♣ 6	pass			

A reasonable game that would normally be missed.

————————————

Example 2

West	East	West	East		
♠ Q542	♠ 1093	1NT	2♣		(1) 5 ♦'s and a 4 card major
♥ AJ	♥ Q1052	2NT (1)	3♣ (2)		(2) transfer to ♦'s
♦ AK953	♦ J10764	3♦	pass		
♣ K8	♣ 6				

Under normal methods, this hand would be played in the inferior 2♠ (1NT - 2♣ - 2♠ - pass).

————————————

But responder may be interested in the minor suit slam. It is probably best to agree that 4♦ after the transfer to 3♦ is RKCB for ♦'s. When East has a 4 card major it is normally best to look for the major suit fit, but if slamming it may be best to go for the minor suit slam if the major suit is weak: -

Example 3

West	East	West	East		
♠ AQ84	♠ 10973	1NT	2♣		(1) 5 ♦'s and a 4 card major
♥ A9	♥ K2	2NT (1)	3♣ (2)		(2) transfer to ♦'s
♦ K9863	♦ AQ102	3♦	4♦ (3)		(3) RKCB for ♦'s
♣ K8	♣ A94	4♥ (4)	6♦		(4) 3 key cards
		pass			

6♠ is a reasonable contract but 6♦ is virtually 100%.

If East looks for a major suit fit but none materialises, he can fall back on the minor suit: -

Example 4

West	East	West	East	
♠ AQ	♠ K1093	1NT	2♣	(1) 5 ♦'s and a 4 card major
♥ A1054	♥ J2	2NT (1)	3♦ (2)	(2) which major?
♦ K9863	♦ AQ102	3♥ (3)	?	(3) ♥'s
♣ K8	♣ A94			

East is in a spot now. It was pairs scoring and so he hoped for a ♠ slam. Now he wants to check on key cards with ♦'s as trumps, but a RKCB bid would be for ♥'s as trumps.

The solution? Double RKCB is of no use. (East may well be only interested in one of West's suits) We need to have two RKCB bids, one for the major and one for the minor. You cannot play Kickback for ♦'s as 4♥ would be a sign off. Best is to play 4 of the minor as RKCB for the minor and play Kickback (or 4NT if you prefer) for the major.

West	East	So our bidding sequence continues: -
1NT	2♣	(4) RKCB for ♦'s
2NT	3♦	(5) 3 key cards
3♥	4♦ (4)	
4♥ (5)	6♦	
pass		

Note that under traditional methods East would probably not discover the superb ♦ fit. A likely auction is 1NT - 2♣ - 2♥ - 3NT - pass. East does not have the values to press on over 3NT (unless he knows about the superb ♦ fit).

Example 5

West	East	West	East	
				(1) 5 ♦'s and a 4 card major
				(2) which major?
				(3) ♠'s
♠ AQ54	♠ K1093	1NT	2♣	(4) RKCB for ♠'s
♥ A10	♥ J2	2NT (1)	3♦ (2)	(5) 2 key cards + ♠Q
♦ K9863	♦ AQ102	3♠ (3)	4NT (4)	(6) king ask
♣ K8	♣ A94	5♠ (5)	5NT (6)	(7) ♣K
		6♣ (7)	6♦ (8)	(8) ♦K?
		7♠ (9)	pass	(9) yes

Of course it may not be so easy if you don't play this variation of RKCB.

But even then 6♠ will probably get a good score as most of the field will not know about the ♦ fit and be in 4♠ (1NT - 2♣ - 2♠ - 4♠).

So, there's little doubt that these super-accepts enable thin games to be reached when responder has a very poor hand. And when responder has an invitational or better hand? Super, these bids are very explicit and should enable the correct game/slam to be reached with ease.

Let's just summarize the bids after responder has established opener's two suits via a 3♦ 'which major' enquiry: -

Opener has ♣'s and ♥'s

After   1NT - 2♣ - 3♣ - 3♦ - 3♥: -

3♠   =
3NT = to play
4♣   = RKCB for ♣'s
4♦   =
4♥   = to play
4♠   = RKCB for ♥'s

Opener has ♣'s and ♠'s

After   1NT - 2♣ - 3♣ - 3♦ - 3♠ : -

3NT = to play
4♣   = RKCB for ♣'s
4♦   =
4♥   =
4♠   = to play
4NT = RKCB for ♠'s

Opener has ♦'s and ♥'s

After   1NT - 2♣ - 2NT - 3♦ - 3♥: -

3♠   =
3NT = to play
4♣   =
4♦   = RKCB for ♦'s
4♥   = to play
4♠   = RKCB for ♥'s

Opener has ♦'s and ♠'s

After   1NT - 2♣ - 2NT - 3♦ - 3♠ : -

3NT = to play
4♣   =
4♦   = RKCB for ♦'s
4♥   =
4♠   = to play
4NT = RKCB for ♠'s

And what about these spare bids of the other major and the other minor?

They may be used for whatever you wish, maybe cue bids, but be wary of the auction going past the RKCB bid.

4NT in the ♥ sequences and 4♥ in the ♠ sequences could be used as quantitative NT bids, but there's not much point as opener has already shown a maximum hand.

Summary of Stayman Super-accepts

1NT - 2♣ - 2NT   =   maximum, 5 ♦'s and a 4 card major
1NT - 2♣ - 3♣   =   maximum, 5 ♣'s and a 4 card major
1NT - 2♣ - 3♦   =   maximum, both majors
1NT - 2♣ - 3♥   =   maximum, 5 ♥'s
1NT - 2♣ - 3♠   =   maximum, 5 ♠'s

The Downside

And what are the drawbacks of these super-accepts?

1) we may occasionally get too high (3♥/♠).
2) these 3♥ and 3♠ contracts will sometimes be played from the wrong hand.
3) the defence know opener's shape.

Not really problems, if 3♥/♠ fails then the opponents can surely make something. Anyway, this really is a small price to pay for all the games (and slams) that will otherwise be missed. So the defence know opener's shape, but you will not reach the right contract unless his shape is determined.

Here we consider the sequences: -

1NT - 2♣ - 2♥ - 2NT - 3♥   and   1NT - 2♣ - 2♠ - 2NT - 3♠

What can they possibly mean? Obviously forcing to game. But why not simply bid 3NT? Maybe opener has opened with a 5 card major and is giving responder a choice? Possibly, but if opener elected to open 1NT instead of 1♥/♠ then he presumably has a hand suited to NT and partner's bidding has not changed that.

Hand A

However, some people's style is to open 1NT on hands like this and then a bid that says 'I have values for game and my major is 5 card and I have a weak suit' may come in very handy.

♠ AQJ94
♥ KJ4
♦ 63
♣ AQ6

Example

West	East	West		East	
♠ AQJ94	♠ K86	1NT		2♣	
♥ KJ4	♥ A852	2♠		2NT	
♦ 63	♦ Q75	3♠	(1)	4♠	(2)
♣ AQ6	♣ J75	pass			

(1) West is worried about ♦'s and so emphasises his ♠'s, this bid is forcing to 3NT/4♠.
(2) With good ♠'s, East elects to go for the major suit game.

Now you could elaborate on this principle, with West bidding the suit which he is worried about. But that really would be giving too much information away to the defence, especially if the final contract is 3NT.

The bottom line. Many experienced players will open 1NT on any balanced hand with a 5 card major. If you go along with this philosophy then this is certainly a good convention for you. It is only available when partner has an invitational hand.

Note

If you play Stayman Super-accepts then this convention may not be required. However, some players prefer to reserve the Stayman super-accepts for hands that are absolutely top of the range like this.

♠ AQJ94
♥ KJ9
♦ 103
♣ AQ9

And note also that the Stayman Super-accept is perhaps unwise when playing a weak NT, but this sequence is fine as responder has invitational values.

2.9   Looking For Slam (after Stayman)

We have defined most of responder's 2nd bids after Stayman, but there are a few remaining. Consider: -

After 1NT - 2♣ - 2♥ , what is 3♠, 4♣ or 4♦ ?

After 1NT - 2♣ - 2♠ , what is 3♥, 4♣, 4♦ or 4♥ ?

There certainly is a good case for having splinters, but what is the best way to go about it? What sort of hand do we need for a splinter?

Example 1

West 1	West 2	East	West	East
♠ A984	♠ AKJ4	♠ Q763	1NT	2♣
♥ KJ	♥ KJ	♥ AQ74	2♠	?
♦ A984	♦ A984	♦ 2		
♣ KJ8	♣ 982	♣ AQ73		

Let's suppose that you play 4♦ as a splinter in this situation. East bids 4♦ and West likes his hand. 4NT (RKCB) looks right. 6♠ is reached, making easily with West 2 but failing with West 1. What is the problem? East really needs better trumps to splinter and we need to be able to make a general slam try below the level of game. So one of these bids needs to be reserved as a general slam try (showing either no shortage and/or dodgy trumps).

One method is to use 3 of the other major as the general slam try, with 4♣, 4♦ and 4♥ (if ♠'s are trumps) as splinters. This works reasonably well, but is incomplete (no ♠ splinter if ♥'s are trumps). Also, many players are used to having 4♣ as Gerber (of course I mean RKCB).

Is there a solution? Yes, we retain 4♣ as RKCB. Our general slam try is either an ASID sequence or 4♦. We use 3 of the other major as an ambiguous splinter.

So, after   1NT - 2♣ - 2♥ -   and after   1NT - 2♣ - 2♠ -

3♠ = ambiguous splinter   3♥ = ambiguous splinter
4♣ = RKCB for ♥'s   4♣ = RKCB for ♠'s
4♦ = slam try, no shortage   4♦ = slam try, no shortage

2.9.1 Splinters After Stayman Has Found A Fit

So we have decided upon 3 of the other major as an ambiguous splinter. Ambiguous splinters really do have an advantage over the direct splinter in that they lose nothing and do not give anything away to the defence if opener has an unsuitable hand for investigating slam. Opener can sign off in 4 of the major or ask about the shortage. The next bid up asks: -

So, after   1NT - 2♣ - 2♥ - 3♠,

3NT asks   4♣ = ♣ singleton/void
4♦ = ♦ singleton/void
4♥ = ♠ singleton/void

and after   1NT - 2♣ - 2♠ - 3♥,

3♠ asks   3NT = ambiguous void
4♣ = ♣ singleton
4♦ = ♦ singleton
4♥ = ♥ singleton

In the ♠ sequence, we have a couple of spare bids (3NT and 4♠). We will use 3NT to show an ambiguous void, with 4♣ as a relay to find out where. There is no room in the ♥ sequence for something similar so the shortage may be singleton or void.

After 1NT - 2♣ - 2♠ - 3♥ - 3♠ - 3NT,

4♣ asks   4♦ = ♦ void
4♥ = ♥ void
4♠ = ♣ void

Example 2

West	East	West	East	
♠ A4	♠ K83	1NT	2♣	(1) ambiguous splinter
♥ Q1084	♥ KJ75	2♥	3♠ (1)	(2) where?
♦ KQ54	♦ 7	3NT (2)	4♦ (3)	(3) ♦ shortage
♣ KQ8	♣ AJ1062	4♥ (4)	pass	(4) not interested

Example 3

West	East	West	East	
				(1) ambiguous splinter
				(2) where?
♠ A42	♠ 3	1NT	2♣	(3) ♠ shortage
♥ Q1084	♥ KJ75	2♥	3♠ (1)	(4) RKCB. Even with this flat West hand 6♥
♦ KQ5	♦ A87	3NT (2)	4♥ (3)	is fine as there are no wasted values.
♣ KQ8	♣ AJ1062	4♠ (4)	etc to 6♥	

Example 4

West	East	West	East		(1) ambiguous splinter
♠ KQ2	♠ 3	1NT	2♣		(2) not interested
♥ Q1084	♥ KJ75	2♥	3♠	(1)	
♦ KQ5	♦ A87	4♥	(2) pass		
♣ KQ8	♣ AJ1062				

With examples 2-4 there is an alternative approach available. This is fully described in section 4.2, but you could transfer to the minor and then bid 3 of the major (game forcing). The problem using the transfer to the minor method with these example hands is that when opener agrees your major then you are already at the 4 level and so you really need a better hand to venture forth opposite a possible minimum.

The splinter bids are, by definition, interested in slam.

Example 5

West	East	West	East		(1) ambiguous splinter
♠ AJ82	♠ KQ107	1NT	2♣		(2) where?
♥ J84	♥ -	2♠	3♥	(1)	(3) it's a void
♦ KQ5	♦ A832	3♠	(2) 3NT	(3)	(4) where?
♣ AQ8	♣ KJ762	4♣	(4) 4♥	(5)	(5) void ♥
		4NT	etc to 7♠		

This East hand could have splintered over the 1NT directly (see section 5.4) but chose the Stayman route because of the good quality of the ♠ suit and relatively poor ♦'s. Another approach is that East could transfer into ♣'s and then bid ♠'s, we cover transfers to minors in section 4.

Hands that are definitely slamming.

Hand A	Hand B	
		Now we saw in the previous examples that responder's hand may be slam invitational or definitely slamming. There is, however, a problem
♠ 4	♠ -	with hands that are definitely slamming with ♠ shortage.
♥ KQ107	♥ KQ107	With these hands we would be bidding 4♥ in response to partner's
♦ A832	♦ A832	shortage enquiry and the problem is that he may then pass!
♣ KJ76	♣ KJ762	So with these very strong hands with ♠ shortage we have to take another

route. With Hand A you could either try SARS or else you could choose to splinter directly (direct splinters are covered later in section 5.4). With Hand B you could transfer to ♣'s and then bid ♥'s or you could again choose to splinter directly.

There is also a similar problem with a hand that has a ♣ void as 4♠ shows this, and partner may pass 4♠. So with a ♣ void and a slam forcing hand you also have to choose an alternative approach.

2.9.2   4♦ - The General Slam Try

The bidding has started 1NT - 2♣ - 2♥/♠. If responder is interested in slam in the suit then he has a number of options including key card ask, (ambiguous) splinter or ASID. Without shortage you cannot splinter, ASID may not help when you have found the fit but don't know if slam is there - you want partner to try for slam. Sometimes, with no clear course of action, it may be best to pass the buck. So we define: -

> 1NT - 2♣ - 2♥/♠ - 4♦

as a slam try in the agreed suit but usually without a shortage. It invites opener to look for slam if he has decent trumps and a non-min. If opener is interested, then RKCB (I prefer 4♠ when ♥'s are trumps) is the usual continuation.

Hand A	Hand B	Partner opens a strong NT, you bid Stayman and partner responds 2♠ (A) or 2♥ (B). There really is little point in enquiring about partner's shape (using ASID) and you have no shortage to splinter. You want to invite slam but have nothing special to say. So bid 4♦, this agrees trumps and leaves it up to partner. If he bids RKCB (I prefer 4♠ as the RKCB bid with ♥'s) then he can find out all about your hand.
♠ AJ84	♠ A9	
♥ A92	♥ KQ107	
♦ KJ9	♦ A87	
♣ A87	♣ K862	

Example 1

West	East	West	East		(1) general slam try agreeing ♥'s
					(2) minimum.
♠ KQ	♠ A9	1NT	2♣		
♥ J842	♥ KQ107	2♥	4♦	(1)	
♦ KJ5	♦ A87	4♥	(2) pass		
♣ AJ73	♣ K862				

Example 2

West	East	West	East		(1) general slam try agreeing ♠'s
					(2) RKCB for ♠'s
♠ KQ76	♠ AJ84	1NT	2♣		(3) 3 key cards
♥ KQ5	♥ A92	2♠	4♦	(1)	
♦ A106	♦ KJ9	4NT (2)	5♣	(3)	
♣ K93	♣ A87	6♠	pass		

Note that 6♠ is pretty solid whereas 6NT would be on a guess. Another testament to the good 4-4 fit.

2.9.3   4♣ - Gerber/RKCB After Stayman

Here we consider the sequences: -

1) 1NT - 2♣ - 2♦ - 4♣
2) 1NT - 2♣ - 2♥ - 4♣
3) 1NT - 2♣ - 2♠ - 4♣

(1) is a simple ace ask (Gerber).
(2) and (3) are RKCB.
4NT bids are quantitative.

2.9.3.1   4♣ - Gerber After A 2♦ Response To Stayman

Much the same as the standard Gerber bid after a 1NT opening, except that responder is known to have a 4 card major.

Hand A	Hand B	
		Hand A first looks for a ♠ fit. With no fit, 6NT is still a good bet, but best to check on the aces. You never know!
♠ AQJ10	♠ K8	
♥ KQ6	♥ KQJ6	Hand B was looking for 7♥. You could now check on aces and try 7NT.
♦ QJ4	♦ AJ6	This hand should, however, be looking for a ♣ fit and should bid 3♣
♣ K73	♣ KQ109	(SARS) looking for 7♣.

So, we only really use Gerber after Stayman if we have no other good 4 card suit (we would try SARS). Thus typically 4333 or 3433 shapes.

Example 1

West	East	West	East		
				(1)	With a good 5 card suit West elects to upgrade to 1NT, fine.
♠ K9	♠ AQJ10	1NT (1)	2♣	(2)	Gerber
♥ J109	♥ KQ6	2♦	4♣ (2)	(3)	1 ace
♦ AK5	♦ QJ4	4♥ (3)	4NT (4)	(4)	glad I checked!
♣ QJ1098	♣ K73	pass			

Example 2

West	East	West	East		
				(1)	bid 3♣ (SARS) here and onto 7♣ when the ♣ fit is uncovered.
♠ AJ7	♠ K8	1NT	2♣		All the aces and all the kings does not
♥ A72	♥ KQJ6	2♦	? (1)		mean that 7NT is safe.
♦ K85	♦ AJ6				
♣ AJ72	♣ KQ109				

2.9.3.2   **4♣ - RKCB After A 2♥/♠ Response To Stayman**

When opener acknowledges a major suit, 4♣ is the key card ask. I prefer to call it RKCB and retain the name Gerber when specifically asking for aces.

Hand A	Hand B	
♠ KQJ3	♠ K8	Same hands as before. This time Hand A gets a 2♠ response to Stayman. So 4♣, RKCB, to check on key cards on the way to 6♠.
♥ K76	♥ KQJ6	
♦ A105	♦ AJ6	Hand B discovers the ♥ fit. 7♥ is surely there if all the key cards are present.
♣ KQ10	♣ KQ109	

_____

Example 1

West	East	West		East		(1) RKCB
♠ A874	♠ KQJ3	1NT		2♣		(2) 3 key cards
♥ A82	♥ K76	2♠		4♣	(1)	
♦ KJ7	♦ A105	4♦	(2)	6♠		
♣ A72	♣ KQ10	pass				

Here we see the power of the 4-4 fit yet again. In 6NT we need to find the ♦Q, in 6♠ we are safe provided the trumps split 3-2. (3 rounds of trumps, eliminate ♣'s and throw in on the 3rd round of ♥'s). Another example of why you should still bid Stayman when 4333, and this time both hands are 4333!

_____

Example 2

West	East	West		East		(1) RKCB
♠ AJ5	♠ K8	1NT		2♣		(2) 3 key cards
♥ A852	♥ KQJ6	2♥		4♣	(1)	
♦ K7	♦ AJ6	4♦	(2)	etc to 7♥		
♣ AJ72	♣ KQ109					

_____

Example 3

West	East	West		East		(1) RKCB
♠ AJ5	♠ KQ	1NT		2♣		(2) 3 key cards
♥ A852	♥ KJ106	2♥		4♣	(1)	(3) ♥Q?
♦ J7	♦ AKQ	4♦	(2)	4♠	(3)	(4) no
♣ AJ72	♣ KQ109	4NT	(4)	6♥ or 6NT		

If you don't play RKCB here then it may be difficult to establish that the ♥Q is missing. It's up to you what you play at (4) to deny the trump queen. I assume the next bid although a return to the trump suit is probably a better treatment.

2.9.4   4NT And 4 Of The Other Major After Stayman

4NT is always quantitative. We have the following sequences to consider: -

1) 1NT - 2♣ - 2♦ - 4NT
2) 1NT - 2♣ - 2♥ - 4NT
3) 1NT - 2♣ - 2♠ - 4NT

also, there are three redundant sequences: -

4) 1NT - 2♣ - 2♦ - 4♠
5) 1NT - 2♣ - 2♥ - 4♠
6) 1NT - 2♣ - 2♠ - 4♥

We shall define all of these as quantitative.

2.9.4.1   4NT And 4♠ After Opener Has Denied A 4 Card Major

First, the sequences   1NT - 2♣ - 2♦ - 4♠ and 1NT - 2♣ - 2♦ - 4NT.

We use the 4♦ and 4♥ bids here as Extended Texas Transfers and so 4♠ is free. We shall define both 4♠ and 4NT as quantitative. Responder has one or two 4 card majors (otherwise he would not have gone via Stayman) but opener has none. Now a normal 4NT quantitative bid is 15-17 pts, so let's make it easier for opener by saying how good the quantitative bid is.

1NT - 2♣ - 2♦ - 4♠ =	quantitative, 15-16. One or two 4 card majors
1NT - 2♣ - 2♦ - 4NT =	quantitative, 17. One or two 4 card majors

Opener now has slightly more to go on. He simply uses the normal replies to a quantitative 4NT bid. I.e. sign off in 4NT, look for a minor suit fit or bid 6NT. Note that opener must have a good minor suit to look for a minor suit slam – responder does not have another decent 4 card suit or he would have used SARS.

Example 1

West	East	West	East		
				(1)	15-16
				(2)	I have good ♦'s, forcing
♠ Q94	♠ AJ76	1NT	2♣		
♥ 84	♥ A7	2♦	4♠ (1)		
♦ AKQ9	♦ J532	5♦ (2)	6♦		
♣ AJ84	♣ KQ6	pass			

West liked his hand and the ♦ suit, so he accepted the slam invitation but tried for the ♦ slam. East was pleased to oblige.

Example 2

West	East	West	East		(1) 15-16
♠ J9	♠ AQ76	1NT	2♣		
♥ KJ4	♥ A7	2♦	4♠	(1)	
♦ AK94	♦ J532	4NT	pass		
♣ A984	♣ KQ6				

This time, West does not have enough opposite 15-16 and so he signs off. He would have taken his chances opposite 17: -

---

Example 3

But it's always best to look for a decent fit, here 6♦ is superior to 6NT: -

West	East	West	East		(1) 17
					(2) I have good ♦'s, forcing
♠ J9	♠ AQ76	1NT	2♣		
♥ KJ4	♥ A7	2♦	4NT	(1)	
♦ AK94	♦ Q532	5♦ (2)	6♦		
♣ A984	♣ KQ6	pass			

West knows that East does not have a good 4 card 2nd suit (he did not try SARS). So there is no point in looking for a ♣ slam. The ♦ suit, however, is robust, so try it at (2).

East also knows what's going on, of course. He knows that West will only suggest ♦'s with a good suit and so he accepts ♦'s as trumps.

Example 4

If opener has a reasonable 5 card suit then he bids it at the six level: -

West	East	West	East		(1) 17
					(2) I have a 5 card ♣ suit
♠ J9	♠ AQ76	1NT	2♣		(3) excellent
♥ K42	♥ A7	2♦	4NT	(1)	
♦ AK4	♦ J532	6♣ (2)	pass	(3)	
♣ AJ984	♣ KQ6				

2.9.4.2   4NT And 4♥ After Opener Has Replied 2♠ To Stayman

A similar situation here, there is again no major suit fit. Opener has 4 ♠'s and responder has 4 ♥'s.

1NT - 2♣ - 2♠ - 4♥   =   quantitative, 15-16. Four card ♥ suit.
1NT - 2♣ - 2♠ - 4NT   =   quantitative, 17. Four card ♥ suit.

Much the same as earlier, opener may sign off, look for a minor suit fit or bid 6NT. Again, responder is unlikely to have another decent 4 card suit as he would probably have looked for a fit via SARS.

Example 4

It may just be that opener has a 5 card ♠ suit: -

West	East	West	East		(1) 15-16, quantitative
♠ AQ974	♠ J103	1NT	2♣		
♥ QJ9	♥ AK76	2♠	4♥	(1)	
♦ J6	♦ A72	4♠	(2) pass		
♣ AJ8	♣ 96				

The 4♠ bid at (2) is best defined as a 5 card suit and offering 4♠ or 4NT as a final resting place. With a 5 card ♠ suit and a max hand, opener bids 6♠ (or 5♠ if you prefer), offering the choice of 6♠ or 6NT.

Example 5

Occasionally we may luck out with this use of 4♥ as a quantitive bid if opener has good 3 card support for ♥'s and goes for the Moysian fit: -

West	East	West	East		(1) 15-16, quantitative (and obviously 4 ♥'s
♠ AK94	♠ J53	1NT	2♣		as responder went via Stayman).
♥ QJ9	♥ AK76	2♠	4♥	(1)	
♦ J6	♦ A72	pass			
♣ A984	♣ KJ6				

2.9.4.3   4NT And 4♠ After Opener Has Replied 2♥ To Stayman

So, the two remaining sequences. But things are slightly different this time as opener may have 4 ♠'s in addition to his 4 ♥'s.

1NT - 2♣ - 2♥ - 4♠	=	quantitative, 15-16. Four card ♠ suit.
1NT - 2♣ - 2♥ - 4NT	=	quantitative, 17. Four card ♠ suit.

In addition to the normal options (4NT, 6NT or a minor suit slam), there is also the possibility of a ♠ fit.

Example 6

West	East	West	East		
♠ A1064	♠ KQJ7	1NT	2♣		(1) quantitative, 4♠'s
♥ AK95	♥ 42	2♥	4♠	(1)	
♦ A8	♦ K532	6♠	pass		
♣ J97	♣ AK6				

West has just enough to accept East's invitation with ♠'s as trumps. East did not go via SARS because his ♦ suit is a bit ropey for a ♦ slam.

Example 7

West	East	West	East		
♠ A8	♠ KQJ7	1NT	2♣		(1) quantitative, 4♠'s
♥ AK95	♥ 42	2♥	4♠	(1)	
♦ Q876	♦ K532	4NT	pass		
♣ QJ9	♣ AK6				

West has the same values, but with no good fit there is no slam. As East did not try SARS, West knows that a possible ♦ fit would not be a good suit for slam.

Example 8

West	East	West	East	
♠ A1064	♠ KQJ7	1NT	2♣	(1) quantitative, 4♠'s
♥ AQ95	♥ 42	2♥	4♠ (1)	
♦ A8	♦ K432	pass		
♣ J97	♣ AQ6			

A ♠ fit this time, but West is minimum and so no slam (well, not a particularly good one).

_____

Example 9

West	East	West	East	
♠ A1064	♠ KQJ7	1NT	2♣	(1) max quantitative, 4♠'s
♥ AQ95	♥ 42	2♥	4NT (1)	
♦ A8	♦ KJ32	6♠	pass	
♣ J97	♣ AK6			

West has the same minimum hand, but this time East's quantitative bid shows max (17 points). West accepts because there is a fit.

_____

Example 10

West	East	West	East	
♠ A106	♠ KQJ7	1NT	2♣	(1) quantitative, 4♠'s
♥ AJ95	♥ 42	2♥	4♠ (1)	
♦ AQJ7	♦ K432	5♦	6♦	
♣ J9	♣ AK6	pass		

West is maximum. With good intermediates, an excellent ♦ suit and good ♠ support, the ♦ slam is worth investigating.

_____

Example 11

With no ♦ fit, you are generally heading for 6NT and hope it makes? …

West	East	West	East	
♠ A106	♠ KQJ7	1NT	2♣	(1) quantitative, 4♠'s
♥ AJ95	♥ K82	2♥	4♠ (1)	
♦ AQJ7	♦ 432	5♦ (2)	5♠ (3)	
♣ J9	♣ AK6	6♠	pass	

After West's 5♦ at (2) we are heading for slam. But it does no harm for East to emphasise his good ♠'s at (3). West is only too happy to oblige.

3   Jacoby Transfers

A transfer bid is a bid of one suit that requests partner to bid another (usually the next) suit. There are various transfer bids but here we are concerned with transfers after partner has opened 1NT. Why transfer? There are various reasons and perhaps the most obvious when playing a strong NT is that the strong hand becomes declarer. Is that important? Not always, but very often: -

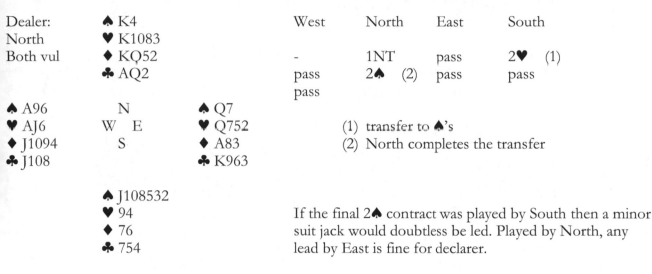

Dealer:	♠ K4			West	North	East	South
North	♥ K1083						
Both vul	♦ KQ52			-	1NT	pass	2♥ (1)
	♣ AQ2			pass	2♠ (2)	pass	pass
				pass			

♠ A96	N	♠ Q7
♥ AJ6	W E	♥ Q752
♦ J1094	S	♦ A83
♣ J108		♣ K963

(1) transfer to ♠'s
(2) North completes the transfer

♠ J108532
♥ 94
♦ 76
♣ 754

If the final 2♠ contract was played by South then a minor suit jack would doubtless be led. Played by North, any lead by East is fine for declarer.

After an opening of 1NT we use 4-way Jacoby Transfers as follows: -

2♦ = transfer to ♥
2♥ = transfer to ♠
2♠ = transfer to ♣
2NT = transfer to ♦

Note. Many players prefer to use 2♠ as minor suit Stayman and 2NT as an (ambiguous) transfer to a minor. However, we can locate minor suit fits using our shape ask after Stayman (SARS) and so we will use these 4 way transfers.

The 2♠ and 2NT bids here must be alerted (but the rules keep changing). There is no required point count for a transfer. Transfers to a major are 0+ pts and a 5+ card suit. Transfers to a minor need a few pts and a 6 card suit (as it is the 3 level) or else a very good (game forcing) hand with a good five card minor.

In this chapter we are concerned with major suit transfers. Transfers to a minor suit are covered in chapter 4.

Major Suit Jacoby Transfers

After partner's opening bid of 1NT, the Jacoby Transfer by responder is a bid of 2♦/♥ which requests opener to bid 2♥/♠. The bid always promises 5+ cards in the suit shown and the point range is unlimited.

So, after a 1NT opening: -   2♦ is a transfer to 2♥
                        and 2♥ is a transfer to 2♠.

One of the advantages of playing transfers is that opener gets to play the hand. It is usually better for the stronger hand to be declarer and if you play a strong NT then this aim is achieved. It is also usually better for the NT bidder to be declarer as, with a balanced hand, he is much more likely to have a tenace that needs protecting: -

Dealer:	♠ QJ102		West	North	East		South
West	♥ 76						
Both vul	♦ A97		1NT	pass	2♦	(1)	pass
	♣ Q832		2♥	pass	3NT	(2)	pass
			4♥	(3)	pass		
♠ A53	N	♠ K7					
♥ Q52	W E	♥ AK983					
♦ K53	S	♦ 862	(1) Transfer				
♣ AK95		♣ J104	(2) game values with 5 ♥'s				
	♠ 9864		(3) ♥'s are fine				
	♥ J104						
	♦ QJ104						
	♣ 76						

So what about this hand? Whether 3NT or 4♥ is the final contract is not so important (both are cold if played by West). The important thing is that West must be declarer, especially in 4♥ when N-S could wrap up the first 3 ♦ tricks and then the contract depends upon the ♣ finesse when East plays it. It is usually best for the more balanced hand to be declarer as he may well have tenace(s) to protect. This, of course, is even more true when a playing strong NT rather than a weak NT.

When Is A Transfer Not A Transfer?

So a 2♦ bid is a transfer to ♥'s and a 2♥ bid is a transfer to ♠'s. Is this always the case? There are some conventions that say 'not necessarily so'. Let's have a very brief look at a couple of them: -

a) Walsh Relays

Now we all play that a 2♦ is a transfer to ♥'s, simple, eh? Apparently not. Some players feel the need to complicate the issue : -

After 1NT - 2♦ - 2♥, 2♠ cancels the transfer to ♥'s and is instead shows one of a number of strong hand types, depending upon responder's next bid. I won't bother to list all of the options, suffice it to say that we cover them all by far simpler means. And are there any problems playing Walsh Relays?

Yes.

1- If the next player bids over the 2♥ 'transfer' then subsequent bidding is very messy.
2- Since the 2♦ bid may or may not be a transfer opener has to be very careful about super-accepting. Only one super-accept bid (2♠) is allowed and the continuations are somewhat convoluted.
3- There is considerable loss of accuracy when only one super-accept is available.
4- Of course, if the next opponent interferes over this super-accept (or normal accept) then responder is in a real pickle; opener cannot know if the transfer was anything but genuine.
5- And, most important of all, we have a very useful meaning for 2♠ in this sequence.

b) Compressed Transfers

If you use 2♠ as a transfer explicitly to ♣'s and 2NT as a natural NT raise (or visa-versa) then you have no bid to explicitly transfer to ♦'s. One solution is to instead use the 2♠ bid (or 2NT) as a transfer to ♦'s. Of course you then have no transfer to ♣'s and so you place a double meaning on the 2♦ 'transfer' bid: -

After   1NT - 2♦ - 2♥, 2♠ cancels the transfer to ♥'s and is instead a transfer to ♣'s.

This, of course, suffers from all of the above problems 1-5 and in addition: -

6- A 2♦ bid allows the opposition to come in cheaply when responder has a weak hand with ♣'s.
7- When responder makes an artificial (transfer) bid there is always the danger that the next player will get in a 'cheap' double, to show values and/or as an opening lead indicator. If responder makes two such bids then it really does make life easy for the defenders.

So, in my opinion, it's all nonsense and a transfer is a transfer is a transfer.

I have no doubt that there are also numerous other conventions that people have dreamed up (or will do) that cancel transfers. As Sidney James once said, let's 'carry on regardless'.

3.1   Responder's 2nd Bid

After responder has bid 2♦/♥, a major suit Jacoby Transfer, and opener completes the transfer then responder has various options after opener's reply and everything is covered in this transfer section.

After opener has simply completed the transfer, responder may continue as follows: -

Pass	= a weak hand (0-7)
Bid a new suit	= 4+ card suit, forcing to game
2NT	= 5 card major, invitational (8-9) to 3NT or 4 of the major
3 of the major	= 6 card major, invitational (8-9) to 4 of the major
3NT	= 5 card major, balanced (10-15)
4 of the major	= 6 card major (10-15) and mildly slam invitational (otherwise use Texas).

These are the basic options; other options (ace/key card ask, splinters and other slam suggesting bids) are also covered in other sections.

Let's start with the simplest, pass: -

Hand A	Hand B	Hand C
♠ QJ963	♠ KJ975	♠ J9876
♥ J64	♥ 98	♥ 983
♦ 63	♦ 72	♦ 2
♣ Q85	♣ Q974	♣ J974

With all of these hands, your partner has opened a strong 1NT, you transferred with a bid of 2♥ and partner completed the transfer with 2♠.

Hand A does not have sufficient values to invite a possible NT or ♠ game, and so passes. Similarly Hand B does not have the values to bid (say 2NT or 3♣) and so must pass. Obviously Hand C passes; 2♠ is sure to be a better spot than 1NT.

Example 1

West	East	West	East	
♠ AK5	♠ J9876	1NT	2♥	(1)
♥ Q742	♥ 983	2♠	(2) pass	(3)
♦ Q87	♦ 2			
♣ KQ2	♣ J974			

(1) transfer
(2) normal accept
(3) a better spot than 1NT.

Hand D

♠ J8652
♥ 103
♦ K103
♣ A52

And how about this hand? Eight points and a five card suit. So invite with 2NT after transferring? No. This hand is from a club tournament and every table except one (mine) invited game. 3♠ and 3NT both went down. This hand has a miserable trump suit. High cards belong in long suits, not three carders. This hand should simply pass the 2♠ transfer completion. A very easy way to earn a top board.

We meet this hand again on page 163 when we cover super-accepts by opener.

3.1.1   Invitational Bids: - 2NT Or 3 Of The Major

When responder has invitational values, about 8-9 pts, then he has two options to invite game after transferring. When the major suit is 6 cards long, 3 of the major invites. With just a 5 card major the invitational bid is 2NT. Note that these are the only two possibilities with invitational hands as any other bid is game forcing.

Hand E	Hand F	Hand G	
♠ QJ1063	♠ KJ975	♠ KQ8762	Partner opened a strong 1NT, you bid 2♥ and partner completed the transfer with 2♠.
♥ J64	♥ 103	♥ K103	Hand E bids 2NT, showing exactly 5 ♠'s and invitational
♦ 63	♦ 92	♦ 92	values. Hand F would like to show his ♣ suit, but 3♣ is
♣ KJ8	♣ KJ74	♣ 74	game forcing, so bid 2NT.
			Hand G has a 6 card suit; so 3♠, invitational.

Example 1

West	East	West	East		
				(1)	transfer
				(2)	normal accept
♠ A95	♠ KQ8762	1NT	2♥	(1)	(3) invitational, 6 card suit
♥ QJ42	♥ K103	2♠	(2)	3♠	(3) (4) I like the 6-3 fit.
♦ A87	♦ 92	4♠	(4)	pass	
♣ KQ2	♣ 74				

Example 2

West	East	West	East		
				(1)	transfer
				(2)	normal accept
♠ A6	♠ KJ975	1NT	2♥	(1)	(3) invitational, 5 card suit
♥ QJ42	♥ 103	2♠	(2)	2NT	(3) (4) I'll be happy if I make 8 tricks
♦ A876	♦ 92	pass	(4)		
♣ A92	♣ KJ74				

After a 2NT invitation by responder; opener will usually pass, sign off in 3 of the major or bid game in either NT or the major.

But there are other options …

3.1.1.1   <u>Finding A 5-3 Fit In The Other Major After 2NT</u>

Hand H   You open this hand 1NT and the bidding has gone   1NT - 2♥ - 2♠ - 2NT - ?

♠ Q5
♥ AQ942
♦ KJ5
♣ A92

You are near maximum, but with poor ♠'s a 4♠ contract is not an option. 3NT could well be right, but 4♥ would be preferable if partner has decent 3 card support. How do we tell partner that we are maximum with a 5 card ♥ suit? Simple, we just bid it (the ♥ suit)!

Example 3

West	East	West	East	
				(1) transfer
				(2) normal accept
♠ Q5	♠ K9876	1NT	2♥ (1)	(3) invitational, 5 ♠ card suit
♥ AQ942	♥ K103	2♠ (2)	2NT (3)	(4) I am max with 5 ♥'s
♦ KJ5	♦ 1072	3♥ (4)	4♥ (5)	(5) excellent
♣ A92	♣ Q4	pass		

Example 4

West	East	West	East	
				(1) transfer
				(2) normal accept
♠ Q5	♠ K9876	1NT	2♥ (1)	(3) invitational, 5 ♠ card suit
♥ AQ942	♥ 103	2♠ (2)	2NT (3)	(4) I am max with 5 ♥'s
♦ KJ5	♦ 1072	3♥ (4)	3NT (5)	(5) max is fine
♣ A92	♣ KQ4	pass		

So the sequence   1NT - 2♦ - 2♥ - 2NT - 3♠ is forcing, showing a maximum with 5 ♠'s
        and   1NT - 2♥ - 2♠ - 2NT - 3♥ is forcing, showing a maximum with 5 ♥'s.

3.1.1.2   Game Tries After 2NT

So we use 3 of the other major when accepting the game invitation but looking for a possible 5-3 fit in the other major; but what are 3♣ and 3♦ in this situation?

Hand J   You open this hand 1NT and the bidding has gone   1NT - 2♥ - 2♠ - 2NT - ?

♠ AJ9   You are only slightly more than minimum but with good ♠'s a retreat into
♥ AQ104   3♠ would be pessimistic if partner had something decent in ♣'s.
♦ 85
♣ KJ72   So we use these otherwise redundant bids of 3♣/♦ as help suit game tries.

Example 5

West	East	West	East		
				(1)	transfer
				(2)	normal accept
♠ AJ9	♠ KQ876	1NT	2♥ (1)	(3)	invitational, 5 ♠ card suit
♥ AQ104	♥ J3	2♠ (2)	2NT (3)	(4)	can you help in ♣'s?
♦ 85	♦ 964	3♣ (4)	4♠ (5)	(5)	yes
♣ KJ72	♣ Q104	pass			

A very reasonable 4♠ contract, the sort that you want to be in at teams. But what if responder does not have decent ♣'s?

Example 6

West	East	West	East		
				(1)	transfer
				(2)	normal accept
♠ AJ9	♠ KQ876	1NT	2♥ (1)	(3)	invitational, 5 ♠ card suit
♥ AQ104	♥ J3	2♠ (2)	2NT (3)	(4)	can you help in ♣'s?
♦ 85	♦ Q104	3♣ (4)	3♠ (5)	(5)	no
♣ KJ72	♣ 964	pass			

East has the same hand but with the minor suits reversed, 4♠ would be a poor contract this time.

Unfortunately there is no bid for a game try in the other major, if you wish to make a game try then you have to choose the most suitable minor suit.

Summary of opener's options when responder transfers and then invites with 2NT

The sequence   1NT - 2♦ - 2♥ - 2NT - pass   is minimum and normally denies 3 ♥'s,

    1NT - 2♦ - 2♥ - 2NT - 3♣   is a ♣ help suit game try,

    1NT - 2♦ - 2♥ - 2NT - 3♦   is a ♦ help suit game try,

    1NT - 2♦ - 2♥ - 2NT - 3♥   is a sign off,

    1NT - 2♦ - 2♥ - 2NT - 3♠   is looking for a 5-3 ♠ fit (else 3NT),

and   1NT - 2♦ - 2♥ - 2NT - 3NT   normally denies 5 ♠'s or 3 ♥'s.

The sequence   1NT - 2♥ - 2♠ - 2NT - pass   is minimum and normally denies 3 ♠'s,

    1NT - 2♥ - 2♠ - 2NT - 3♣   is a ♣ help suit game try,

    1NT - 2♥ - 2♠ - 2NT - 3♦   is a ♦ help suit game try,

    1NT - 2♥ - 2♠ - 2NT - 3♥   is looking for a 5-3 ♥ fit (else 3NT),

    1NT - 2♥ - 2♠ - 2NT - 3♠   is a sign off,

and   1NT - 2♥ - 2♠ - 2NT - 3NT   normally denies 5 ♥'s or 3 ♠'s.

3.1.2   Bidding Game: - 3NT Or 4 Of The Major

When responder has game forcing values, about 9+ pts, then he has a lot more options available. We start by considering the cases where responder simply wants to play in game (either 3NT or 4 of the major).

1) 3NT = Responder rebids 3NT on all 5332 type hands with about 10-15 points. Also with 5422 type hands when the 4 card suit (a minor) is not very sturdy (and the two doubletons are quite reasonable).

2) 4♥/♠ = 4 of the major promises 9-15 points and a 6+ card suit. In fact if playing Texas Transfers (section 6.2) then these Jacoby sequences should be the top of the range and mildly slam invitational.

Hand A	Hand B	Hand C
♠ QJ1063	♠ KJ975	♠ KQJ762
♥ J64	♥ K8	♥ K103
♦ A3	♦ A2	♦ A2
♣ K84	♣ J432	♣ J4

Partner opened a strong 1NT, you bid 2♥ and partner completed the transfer with 2♠.

Hand A bids 3NT, showing exactly 5 ♠'s and game values.

Hand B does not wish to introduce this anaemic ♣ suit, so bids 3NT.

Hand C has a 6 card suit; so 4♠. Partner is invited to bid on if he likes ♠'s.

Example 1

West	East	West	East		
♠ 106	♠ KJ975	1NT	2♥	(1)	(1) transfer
♥ AQ42	♥ K8	2♠	(2)	3NT	(3)
♦ KQ87	♦ A2	pass			
♣ KQ5	♣ J432				

(1) transfer
(2) normal accept
(3) 5 card ♠ suit

With 3 card support it is usually best for opener to opt for the major suit contract rather than NT.

Example 2

West	East	West	East		
♠ A109	♠ KQJ76	1NT	2♥	(1)	
♥ QJ84	♥ K103	2♠	(2)	3NT	(3)
♦ KQJ8	♦ 972	4♠	(4)	pass	
♣ Q8	♣ J4				

(1) transfer
(2) normal accept
(3) 5 card ♠ suit
(4) I prefer the 5-3 fit

As I said, the sequence of transfer and then 4 of the major is mildly slam invitational: -

Example 3

West	East	West	East		(1) transfer
					(2) normal accept
♠ A109	♠ KQJ762	1NT	2♥	(1)	(3) 6 card ♠ suit, mild slam invite
♥ QJ84	♥ K103	2♠ (2)	4♠	(3)	(4) RKCB
♦ KQJ8	♦ A2	4NT (4)	etc to 6♠		
♣ A8	♣ J4				

With excellent trumps and a max, West has no problem in going slamming.

_____

Now this is all quite straightforward, at least I think it's all straightforward, but this hand is from the March 2004 issue of the Dutch magazine 'Bridge'.

Hand D   You were asked what to bid with this East hand after the sequence had started: -

♠ 5	West	East
♥ KQJ654		
♦ Q105	1NT	2♦ (1)
♣ 765	2♥	?

The article said 3♥, invitational. Now an invitational bid here is 8-9 points, so OK? I don't think so. This hand is not 8 points, it's more like 10! There is a fit (partner must have at least 2 ♥'s) and this hand is certainly worth game in my view. So 4♥.

But there is, of course, a catch here. I would not be in this position as I would have bid 4♥ (or preferably 4♦, a Texas Transfer or even better 4♣, South African Texas Transfer) at (1).

| | The article then went on to say that with only a 5 card suit then the invitational bid is |
| Hand E | 2NT; so change the East Hand D slightly: - |

♠ 54	West	East
♥ KQJ65		
♦ Q105	1NT	2♦ (1)
♣ 765	2♥	2NT

I have no problem with that, Hand E is a good 8 count but is worth no more than an invitation. Hand D is much stronger than Hand E, hand evaluation is more than just counting points.

3.1.3   The Jacoby Major-Minor Two Suiter

So we have covered the single-suited hands and the balanced hands, that leaves the two suiters. If you transfer and then bid another suit the sequence shows 4+ cards in the second suit and is game forcing. There is, however, one exception. That is when the second suit is the other major. The 5-4, 4-5, 6-4 etc. major-major hands were dealt with in section 2.6 and hands that are 5-5 in the majors will be dealt with later in section 3.1.4. So here we are just considering a 2nd suit that is a minor.

Hand A	Hand B	Hand C	
♠ QJ1063	♠ AKJ97	♠ QJ762	Partner opened a strong 1NT. All three hands transfer to ♠'s. Hand A should then bid 3♣, not so much because he wants to play in ♣'s, but to imply weakness in the other suits. Hand B also bids 3♣, but this time because he is looking for the best slam. Hand C is better off just bidding 3NT. Both short suits are covered.
♥ J6	♥ Q8	♥ K10	
♦ J3	♦ K2	♦ A2	
♣ KQJ8	♣ KQ82	♣ Q942	

This bidding of a 2nd suit is game forcing and may, or may not, show slam interest. Since the bid shows where at least nine of responder's cards lie, it is very useful to declarer in establishing if there is a weak suit for NT: -

Example 1

West	East	West	East
♠ KQ94	♠ 86	1NT	2♦
♥ KJ	♥ AQ1052	2♥	3♣
♦ 632	♦ 75	3♥ (1)	4♥
♣ AQ96	♣ KJ75	pass	

(1) West knows that it is only a 5-2 ♥ fit, but he also knows that the ♦'s may well be wide open. The ♥ game is not certain, but worth a shot (and better than 3NT). West should not bid 4♥ (fast arrival) at (1) because he does not want to rule out a ♣ slam if partner has a good hand.

With example 1 we saw that East only had ambitions for game and was showing his shape so that opener could decide the best game. But this bidding of a 2nd suit is often a prelude for slam.

Example 2

West	East	West	East	
♠ KQ94	♠ A86	1NT	2♦	(1) I prefer ♥'s to NT, and quite like ♣'s
♥ KJ	♥ AQ1052	2♥	3♣	(2) cue bid
♦ 632	♦ 7	3♥ (1)	3♠ (2)	(3) suggesting a ♣ slam
♣ AQ96	♣ KJ75	4♣ (2)	6♣ (3)	(4) West prefers ♣'s to ♥'s
		pass (4)		

Quite often opener will like responder's 2nd suit and he can cue bid to show encouragement (although not above 3NT, as responder may only have values for 3NT or 4 of his major).

Example 3

West	East	West	East	
				(1) cue bid
				(2) slam interest
♠ A94	♠ K6	1NT	2♦	
♥ K6	♥ Q9852	2♥	3♣	
♦ KQ75	♦ A6	3♠ (1)	4♣ (2)	
♣ KJ96	♣ AQ75	etc to 6♣		

Occasionally West may make a mild slam try (a cue bid) but responder was just showing his shape in case 3NT was not secure: -

Example 4

West	East	West	East	
				(1) cue bid
♠ Q4	♠ J10975	1NT	2♥	
♥ AJ6	♥ K2	2♠	3♣	
♦ KQ752	♦ 86	3♥ (1)	3NT	
♣ KJ6	♣ AQ75	pass		

If West did not have good cover in both of the red suits, he would pull 3NT to 4♠.

If opener prefers responder's major suit to the minor or NT but is not interested in slam, then he should bid 4 of the major directly (fast arrival).

Example 5

West	East	West	East	
				(1) no slam interest
♠ Q2	♠ 75	1NT	2♦	
♥ K76	♥ QJ985	2♥	3♣	
♦ AQJ75	♦ K8	4♥ (1)	pass	
♣ KJ6	♣ AQ75			

Note the difference between this West hand and the West hand of examples 1 & 2 when West chose the slow 3♥ bid. The difference is that in examples 1 & 2 the West hand had excellent 4 card ♣ support and so a ♣ slam was a possibility.

If opener is interested in slam, then he cue bids. If, however, he has no ace to cue then instead of cueing a king he could simply bid 3 of the major (this is encouraging, 4 of the major is not).

Example 6

West	East	West	East		(1) slam interest
♠ KQ2	♠ A5	1NT	2♦		
♥ A106	♥ QJ985	2♥	3♦		
♦ K8	♦ A1075	3♥ (1)	etc to 6♥		
♣ KJ765	♣ A8				

If opener attempts to sign off in 3NT or 4 of the major, then responder may over-rule him: -

Example 7

West	East	West	East		(1) no slam interest
♠ Q102	♠ 5	1NT	2♦		(2) RKCB (Kickback) *
♥ K76	♥ AQJ98	2♥	3♣		
♦ AQ75	♦ K86	4♥ (1)	4♠ (2)		
♣ KJ6	♣ AQ75	etc to 6♥			

* You may well agree to play DRKCB here.

Sometimes opener may like responder's 2nd suit (as he has a weakness somewhere). Supporting the minor at the 4 level may be dangerous (as responder may only have values for 3NT/4 of the major) but it is fine if opener has decent 3 (or good 2) card support for responder's major: -

Example 8

West	East	West	East
♠ Q1052	♠ KJ6	1NT	2♦
♥ AK	♥ Q9854	2♥	3♦
♦ AQ75	♦ KJ86	4♦	etc to 6♦
♣ J76	♣ A		

East knows that West must have reasonable ♥'s and good ♦'s for his 4♦ bid, and so goes for the ♦ slam.

Fast And Slow Arrival After A Jacoby Two Suiter

Now I said that 3 of the major is encouraging and that 4 of the major (or 3NT) is not. Let's start with a hand from the club: -

Example 9

West	East	West	East
♠ 953	♠ AK864	1NT (1)	2♥
♥ AQ4	♥ K7	2♠	3♣
♦ AK1093	♦ Q4	3NT (2)	pass (3)
♣ K8	♣ A974		

West had both red suits well stopped and so bid 3NT. A comfortable 6♠ slam was missed, just unlucky or was anyone to blame?

Now this one is tricky as there is no blatantly obvious culprit. The 1NT opening at (1)? It is 16 points but worth much more. A 5 card suit headed by the AK is an excellent +, as are the 10,9 in the suit. Two aces and no jacks are a definite + also. Whether that all adds up to too strong for a 1NT opening is debatable. So let's say it is top of the range but acceptable.

Then what about East's pass at (3)? 16 points, but again very good ones. A 5 card suit headed by the AK is a good +, and an outside 4-carder headed by the ace is another +. Two aces and no jacks are a definite + also. This hand is worth 17+. So it's 17 + 15-17. 32 is usually only good enough for slam if there is a fit and South did not know that North had 3 ♠'s. Could anyone have done anything else?

Yes! The best bid for West at (2) is 3♠ (or a 3♦ cue bid if you prefer). It would be nice to have a ♠ honour but with this max West must make a move. East then knows that West has 3 card ♠ support and slam interest (slow arrival). That's all East needs and the slam is then easy.

Example 10

Now club players can be excused for getting it wrong, but how about internationals? The following deal is from the 2002 Camrose series. This was the bidding at three tables: -

West	East	West	East
♠ K105	♠ A4	1NT (1)	2♦
♥ K105	♥ J87432	2♥	3♦
♦ 7542	♦ KQJ109	4♥ (2)	? (3)
♣ AKQ	♣ -		

1NT at (1) was strong (I think?). I don't think it's worth a strong NT, of course, with the 4333 type shape, AKQ in a 3 card suit and the only 4 card suit headed by the 7. Two 10's are a + factor, but not enough for me. Anyway, that's not the issue here, what does 4♥ mean at (2) and what should East do at (3)? One East thought that 4♥ was a 'picture jump' showing a good trump holding and bid to 6♥. Another was not sure and bid 5♥, passed. Only one (Tim Reese) got it right. He knew that it was fast arrival and passed at (3). South had a singleton ♦, 5♥ was down and 6♥ went two down.

Before we move on, let's have an example from a Dutch bridge magazine.

East	West	East	
♠ KQ943	1NT	2♥	
♥ 96	2♠	?	(1)
♦ 63			
♣ A1063			

This is from the Jan 2004 issue of the Dutch magazine 'Bridge'. A panel of 16 experts were asked what to bid at (1) when vulnerable at teams scoring. The results were: -

Bid	Score	No of votes	% reader's votes
3NT	100	8	16
3♣	80	5	45
2NT	80	2	36
3♠	60	1	1
4♠	30	0	1

I was absolutely amazed when I read this! There is some consolation in that the correct bid was the most popular choice of readers, although it was less than 50% of them. And 36% choosing a non-forcing 2NT is a poor show. 3♣ is totally obvious to me, but let's see what some of these experts said (*in italics*) - my comments are in normal type: -

Den Broeder: *3NT. Because it's teams and we're vulnerable, I want to be in game with these 9 points. If I bid 3♣ that may seduce partner into bidding a too high 5♣.*

Partner will only bid 5♣ if he has weak red suits and then 3NT is not making!

Smit: *3NT. I will not bid a suit that I do not want partner to support.*

I disagree with this philosophy. 3♣ simply describes the hand perfectly and you will not get a 4♣ support bid if 3NT is going to make.

Niemeijer: *3NT. It is between 2NT and 3NT. I reserve the 3♣ bid for slam interest or where 5♣ is an alternative to 3NT.*

2NT a possibility? See my comment on this bid later. At least he has (sort of) said why he does not bid 3♣. I totally disagree, of course. 3♣ could well be looking for slam (responder will clarify later) but for now it warns opener about the red suit weaknesses.

Cosijn: *3♣. Because of the fact that 4♠ even with a 5-2 fit, could well be the best contract. And occasionally partner has ♣Kxxxx with 3 aces and the trumps split in 6♣.*

I agree with the first point – very relevant. The second point is not really an issue.

Zandvoort: *3♣. I want to be in game and 3♣ initiates the search for the best game. Or more opposite ♣KQxxx and 3 aces. My partnership agreement is that we only bid 3♣/♦ after transferring if you are happy if partner supports with 4 card support. Thus only slam interest or distributional.*

Again a very valid first point. Slam is not an option, ♣KQxxx and 3 aces is unlikely, and many would consider it too good for a 1NT opener. The last point about supporting is fine as long as partner will bid 3NT with the other two suits well stopped . And as for partner supporting with 4♣ here, there are much more sophisticated methods (cue bid or shortage ask) as we will see shortly.

Van Arum: *2NT. Not nice with this hand but 3♣ is game forcing. If partner reverts to 3♠ then I'll bid 4♠.*

'Not nice', I totally agree. If partner passes and we miss game what will you say to your team-mates? This hand is far too strong for 2NT. It has 9 points, and the fact that it has two weak doubletons makes it even stronger! Long suits, and points in the long suits are a big + in any book on hand evaluation. This hand must force to game, no but's about it.

Example 11

Let's have an example West hand to support Cosijn's case that a 5-2 ♠ game may be best:

West	East	West	East
♠ A8	♠ KQ943	1NT	2♥
♥ AK75	♥ 96	2♠	3♣ (1)
♦ J75	♦ 63	4♠	pass
♣ KQ72	♣ A1063		

Not very sophisticated, and we shall cover better bidding methods here next in section 3.1.3.1; but certainly an example of why 3NT at (1) is silly.

Example 12

And as for Van Arum's 2NT bid? Well, really! Game has excellent chances opposite most minimum openers, this East hand is far too good for an invitation: -

West	East	West	East
♠ J8	♠ KQ943	1NT	2♥
♥ AJ83	♥ 96	2♠	2NT ??
♦ KJ75	♦ 63	pass	
♣ KQ7	♣ A1063		

It looks like a pretty decent 3NT contract to me.

Both Niemeijer and Den Broeder state that 5♣ will be too high. I agree, it probably will be, but the point that seems to be missed is that the 3♣ bid warns partner about shortage in the red suits so that he can elect for 4♠ if he too has shortage in one or both. It is not an invitation to bid 5♣! Example 11 is a case in point.

———————————

But I guess that one has to listen when half of an expert panel expresses an opinion, so what about these types of hand after partner's strong 1NT opening?

East 1	East 2	East 3	West	East
♠ K9743	♠ K9743	♠ QJ762	1NT	2♥
♥ Q6	♥ Q6	♥ K10	2♠	?
♦ 63	♦ K3	♦ A2		
♣ A1063	♣ J1063	♣ Q942		

Doubtless these would receive even more votes for 3NT? I accept the point with East 2 and would not argue with 3NT – although 3♣ could still work out best. But with East 1 I would definitely still bid 3♣ – the point is that we do not expect partner to bid above 3NT at his next turn and we then bid 3NT ourselves and partner is warned about our two doubletons. East 3 is Hand C from the start of this section and 3NT is fine with these red suit honours.

———————————

Let's just summarize what we mean by the 3 of a minor bid in this situation: -

- It may be strong and looking for slam, but it may only have game values.
- Opener is not normally expected to support the minor unless he has a very good reason to – he must have good support for both of responder's suits.
- With just game values, responder is inviting game in his major, a 5-2 fit, if opener is weak in an unbid suit.
- If responder has slam ambitions then he will make this clear next turn.

So there you have it, even a majority of experts apparently fail to realise what a 3♣/♦ bid really means and what subsequent bidding should be. In particular, direct support of the minor at the 4 level is a rare bid (cue bid instead). Even better is for opener to enquire about responder's shape and this is all covered next: -

Shortage Ask After A Jacoby (Major-Minor) Two Suiter

Hand A   You hold this hand and open a strong NT. Partner bids 2♦ (transfer to ♥'s) and you
                complete the transfer. Partner's next bid is 3♣. So partner is possibly interested in slam,
♠ 985   but is this hand good enough to investigate 6♣? And how do you set about it?
♥ KQ   You know that partner has at most 4 cards divided between ♦'s and ♠'s. 3NT is
♦ AQ84   probably dicey but 4♥ must be a good bet. But surely 6♣ is there if partner has a
♣ KQ83   singleton ♠. How do we investigate? We come back to this hand in example 2.

But first of all, take a look at this similar example.

Example 1

West	East	West	East		(1)	cue bid
♠ KQ4	♠ AJ975	1NT	2♥			
♥ AQ7	♥ K86	2♠	3♣			
♦ 9653	♦ 2	3♥ (1)	3♠ (1)			
♣ AJ6	♣ KQ75	4♣ (1)	4♦ (2) ?			

Some straightforward cue bidding, but what is 4♦ at (2)? Is it the Ace, the King or a singleton? West
needs to know, as a singleton is sufficient for slam but the ace or king are not.

It is best not use splinters directly after a transfer if you have a 2nd suit. Instead, we prefer to bid our
second suit. Also, we really need a 6 card suit to splinter (unless partner has super-accepted). Anyway,
West liked the transfer to ♠'s but did not have enough for a super-accept (this is covered later in section
3.2). After East has shown a ♣ suit, West's hand has become enormous. All he really needs to know is if
East is short in ♦'s. We come back to this example 1 (with new bidding) soon.

In the situations where responder has transferred to a major and then bid a minor suit, he has at
most 4 cards in the two unbid suits. Also note that it is unlikely that responder has a minimal hand with
decent honours in both of these unbid suits as then he would prefer a 3NT rebid rather than showing a
4 card minor. Expect weakness in at least one of these unbid suits. If opener has adequate cover in both
of these unbid suits then he may bid 3NT, but often he will wish to know more about responder's
shape. This is achieved by bidding the next free bid (not a return to responder's major) which always
asks for responder's shortage:

_____

Warning: This shortage ask is something new and unless you have agreed it, most
              would take it as a cue bid. Be very careful. If you (or your partner) are likely
              to forget this convention (and make a cue bid) then skip this section!

So we are considering the following 4 sequences: -

1NT - 2♦ - 2♥ - 3♣   responder has 5 ♥'s, 4+ ♣'s
1NT - 2♥ - 2♠ - 3♣   responder has 5 ♠'s, 4+ ♣'s
1NT - 2♦ - 2♥ - 3♦   responder has 5 ♥'s, 4+ ♦'s
1NT - 2♥ - 2♠ - 3♦   responder has 5 ♠'s, 4+ ♦'s : -

(responder has 5 ♥'s, 4+ ♣'s)

After 1NT - 2♦ - 2♥ - 3♣, 3♦ asks: -

3♥ = singleton ♦
3♠ = singleton ♠
3NT = 2-2 in ♠'s & ♦'s
4♣ = void ♦
4♦ = void ♠
4♥ = no slam interest

(responder has 5 ♠'s, 4+ ♣'s)

After 1NT - 2♥ - 2♠ - 3♣, 3♦ asks: -

3♥ = singleton ♦
3♠ = singleton ♥
3NT = 2-2 in ♥'s & ♦'s
4♣ = void ♦
4♦ = void ♥
4♥ =
4♠ = no slam interest

(responder has 5 ♥'s, 4+ ♦'s)

After 1NT - 2♦ - 2♥ - 3♦, 3♠ asks: -

3NT = 2-2 in ♠'s & ♣'s
4♣ = singleton or void ♣
4♦ = singleton or void ♠
4♥ = no slam interest

(responder has 5 ♠'s, 4+ ♦'s)

After 1NT - 2♥ - 2♠ - 3♦, 3♥ asks: -

3♠ = singleton ♣
3NT = 2-2 in ♥'s & ♣'s
4♣ = singleton ♥
4♦ = void ♣
4♥ = void ♥
4♠ = no slam interest

Obviously we wish to keep the responses at or below 4 of the major and so there is no room to differentiate between singletons and voids in the ♥/♦ sequence. No problem. You could have additional relays to clarify it, but this can normally be sorted out later.

These responses may be remembered by noting that shortage in the minor is mentioned before shortage in the major. The 'flat' 5422 type hand is always 3NT. 4 of the major is a sign off – but opener may (rarely) choose to play in 5 of the minor.

But be careful with the 3NT bid – it is forcing! The 3NT bid should be considered as forcing because responder is interested in slam – he did not 'sign off' in 4 of the major. Responder will bid 3NT with the appropriate shape even if he is definitely slamming. This is no problem as opener would not be asking for shortage (thus usually investigating slam) if he wanted to play in 3NT.

First of all, let's go back to our Example 1 and change West's third bid: -

Example 1 (continued)

West	East	West		East		
♠ KQ4	♠ AJ975	1NT		2♥		(1) shortage?
♥ AQ7	♥ K86	2♠		3♣		(2) singleton ♦
♦ 9653	♦ 2	3♦	(1)	3♥	(2)	
♣ AJ6	♣ KQ75	etc to 6♠				

And how does our shortage ask work with our Hand A?

Example 2

West	East	West		East		
♠ 985	♠ 6	1NT		2♦		(1) shortage?
♥ KQ	♥ AJ1085	2♥		3♣		(2) singleton ♠
♦ AQ84	♦ K93	3♦	(1)	3♠	(2)	
♣ KQ83	♣ AJ94	etc to 6♣				

West could just bid 6♣, or else try RKCB but then he gets to 6♣ anyway. If you play Kickback here then West can bid 4♦ RKCB. Anyway, 6♣ is easily reached after the singleton ♠ is uncovered. I guess that you could choose 6♥ at pairs scoring.

We have the same West hand here, but this time there's no slam: -

Example 3

West	East	West		East		
♠ 985	♠ J6	1NT		2♦		(1) shortage?
♥ KQ	♥ AJ1085	2♥		3♣		(2) 2-2 in ♠'s & ♦'s
♦ AQ84	♦ K9	3♦	(1)	3NT	(2)	(3) With these great ♥'s, West judged
♣ KQ83	♣ AJ94	4♥	(3)	pass		that 4♥ is just as good as 5♣.

West was hoping for ♠ shortage, in which case there might have been slam. However, opener must pull this 3NT bid – it is forcing. Opener would not be asking for shortage if he had adequate cover in both the short suits, and responder may well have slam aspirations.

Sometimes these methods may lead to greater things: -

Example 4

West	East	West	East		(1) shortage?
					(2) void ♠
♠ 985	♠ -	1NT	2♦		
♥ KQ	♥ AJ1085	2♥	3♣		
♦ AQJ4	♦ K96	3♦ (1)	4♦ (2)		
♣ KQ83	♣ AJ942	etc to 7♣ (or maybe 7♥ at pairs)			

It really would have been silly for West to try to settle for 3NT or 4♥ at his 3rd bid.

───────────────────────

Nothing is lost, of course, if responder's shortage is not what opener hoped for: -

Example 5

West	East	West	East		(1) shortage?
					(2) singleton ♦
♠ 985	♠ 763	1NT	2♦		
♥ KQ	♥ AJ1085	2♥	3♣		
♦ AQJ4	♦ 3	3♦ (1)	3♥ (2)		
♣ KQ83	♣ AJ94	4♥	pass		

───────────────────────

If responder definitely does not like NT, he may sign off in 4 of the major himself: -

Example 6

West	East	West	East		(1) shortage?
					(2) no slam ambitions.
♠ 985	♠ 7	1NT	2♦		
♥ KQ	♥ AJ1085	2♥	3♣		
♦ AQJ4	♦ 932	3♦ (1)	4♥ (2)		
♣ KQ83	♣ AJ94	pass			

Remember, opener's shortage enquiry means that he likes responder's suits, and so responder going past 3NT into 4 of the major is fine.

───────────────────────

3.1.4   <u>5-5 In The Majors</u>

Here we consider the situation where responder has two five card majors. Remember that all 5-4's, 6-4 etc. are shown via Stayman, so we are concerned with the situations where responder is at least 5-5 in the majors.

We have already covered weak hands, we bid 2♣ and then our best 5 card major if partner responds 2♦ (Garbage Stayman). We do not play Crawling Stayman as it is unsatisfactory when 5-4 (and for most other situations).

So here we consider invitational and strong 5-5's. There are a few methods used to show these 5-5 hands.

Some players use the direct jump to 3♥/♠ (3♥ either weak or invitational, 3♠ game forcing). We have a better use for these jumps and they really take up too much room, they are covered in section 5.2.

One rather out-dated method with 5-5's is Extended Stayman (1NT - 2♣ - 2♦ - 3♦). But the problem is that there is no differentiation between invitational and strong hands. Also, of course, we use this sequence as a Quest Transfer.

Another practice in common use by many players is: -

1NT - 2♦ - 2♥ - 2♠	shows 5-5 in the majors and is invitational	**Note**. We don't
1NT - 2♥ - 2♠ - 3♥	shows 5-5 in the majors and is game forcing	use this

The major drawback with using the second sequence is that there is little room for manoeuvring, especially when looking for slam. Actually, since the first sequence is at a very low level we can use it for both invitational and strong 5-5 hands. The 2nd sequence will be re-defined later in section 3.1.5.

Before we start, does the sequence 1NT - 2♦ - 2♥ - 2♠ have another meaning? Some players who use the direct jumps to show the 5-5 hands use this 2♠ bid here as a Walsh Relay (which involves various hand types and negates the transfer). I don't particularly like this – a transfer is a transfer and you may well run into problems after a super-accept or if the opponents intervene. So no Walsh relays and 1NT - 2♦ - 2♥ - 2♠ shows our major suit 5-5's, both invitational and game forcing.

Invitational Major Two Suiters.

Another common use is that 1NT - 2♦ - 2♥ - 2♠ shows 5-5 or 4-5 in the majors and is invitational. This is quite reasonable, but needs to be expanded upon to include invitational 5-4's. In this book I give a complete scenario for all invitational and game forcing 5-4, 4-5 and 5-5's major suited hands (see summary in section 7.3.1) but if, for some strange reason, you don't like Quest Transfers then the following is a respectable scheme for all of the invitational hands. The responses must, of course, be kept below 3♥ as partner may be minimum: -

After 1NT - 2♦ - 2♥ - 2♠, 2NT enquires: -

3♣ = 5 ♥'s & 4 ♠'s

3♦ = 4 ♥'s & 5 ♠'s   **Note.** We don't use this.

3♥ = 5 ♥'s & 5 ♠'s

Now the initial transfer promises 5 ♥'s but the 2♠ bid means that it may be only a 4 card ♥ suit. I have stated earlier that I do not like a bid that transfers and then later gets negated, but this time it's slightly different. If partner super-accepts (section 3.2) there is no problem as you then (hopefully) have a 4-4 ♥ fit with a max partner and so simply bid the ♥ game.

So this scheme is (reasonably) sound and opener should be able to select the best contract. Game forcing 5-4 & 4-5's then go via Stayman and a jump to the 3 level over 2♦. Game forcing 5-5's would then use 1NT - 2♥ - 2♠ - 3♥.

Fine, everything is covered but Quest Transfers really are superior and have numerous other benefits (including the obvious one that opener is usually declarer) and our method of showing both invitational and game forcing 5-5's (coming up next) is at a lower level and so is much more accurate.

———————

OK, but with only one sequence (1NT - 2♦ - 2♥ - 2♠) to show both invitational and game forcing 5-5's, how does opener know if responder has just invitational or game going values?

Simple, he just asks! The next bid up (2NT) asks and, what's more, responder's reply will indicate his shortage and so aid declarer in any borderline game decisions: -

When responder has just invitational values, his response must obviously be kept at or below 3♥. We do not have the full range of bids available as in the game forcing case (where we can go up to 4♥) and so we use just two bids (3♦ and 3♥) to show where our shortage (could be singleton or void) is.

So when responder has an invitational hand we have: -

After 1NT - 2♦ - 2♥ - 2♠, 2NT by opener asks: -

3♦ = ♣ shortage, invitational.
3♥ = ♦ shortage, invitational.

After either of these invitational responses opener may pass (a 3♥ response) or bid 3♥, 3♠, 4♥, 4♠ or (very unlikely) 3NT to play.

And if responder has game going values he has many more options: -

3♣ =	a game forcing hand *	4♣ =	void ♣		
3♦ =	see above	4♦ =	void ♦		
3♥ =	see above	4♥ =	no slam interest	See note after	
3♠ =	singleton ♣			example 14 for a	
3NT =	singleton ♦	5♣ =	EDRKCB	possible use of the	
		5♦ =	EDRKCB	4♠/4NT bids.	

EDRKCB is explained shortly. But what's with this * game forcing hand 3♣ bid? I give some examples of this in a minute, but it is used when responder has a weak doubleton (or triplet) minor in order to warn opener of two possible losers off the top there. This 3♣ bid is a puppet to 3♦ and responder then usually defines his shortage although it may just be because responder wants to use DRKCB (at a low level). Note that we don't use 4NT above (as DRKCB) because the responses may get us uncomfortably high.

After 1NT - 2♦ - 2♥ - 2♠ - 2NT - 3♣, 3♦ by opener asks: -

3♥ = small doubleton ♣
3♠ = small doubleton ♦
3NT = DRKCB
4♣ = small triplet ♣ (thus a ♦ void)
4♦ = small triplet ♦ (thus a ♣ void)
4♥ = The 4♥ response is used to show 5611 and 6511 hands and is defined (together with a slight addition to the meaning of the 4♣ and 4♦ responses) in section 3.1.4.2.

The 3♦/♥ responses are an interesting example of change of captaincy. After a 1NT opening, responder starts off as captain. After an invitational 3♦/♥ response opener knows that responder has about 8 points (probably way less in HCPs because of re-evaluation due to shape) and takes charge, either bidding game or not. The slam interest sequences are more of a dual captaincy situation, opener knows responder's shape pretty well and that responder has slam aspirations, responder knows the combined points total.

Anyway, it's time for a few examples: -

Example 1

West	East	West		East		(1) transfer
						(2) normal accept
♠ AK10	♠ J9752	1NT		2♦	(1)	(3) 5-5 in the majors
♥ 985	♥ KJ1042	2♥	(2)	2♠	(3)	(4) relay
♦ KQ7	♦ 6	2NT	(4)	3♥	(5)	(5) invitational, ♦ shortage
♣ A732	♣ J5	3♠		pass		

West has good trumps, but with wasted values in partner's short suit he signs off.

Example 2

West	East	West		East		(1) transfer
						(2) normal accept
♠ AK10	♠ J9752	1NT		2♦	(1)	(3) 5-5 in the majors
♥ 985	♥ KJ1042	2♥	(2)	2♠	(3)	(4) relay
♦ KQ7	♦ J5	2NT	(4)	3♦	(5)	(5) invitational, ♣ shortage
♣ A732	♣ 6	4♠		pass		

This time game is far more likely to succeed. So the knowledge of partner's shortage is an important factor for opener deciding whether to go to game or not.

And explicit information about responder's shape will guide slam decisions when responder has game forcing values: -

Example 3

West	East	West		East		(1) transfer
						(2) normal accept
♠ AKJ4	♠ Q6752	1NT		2♦	(1)	(3) 5-5 in the majors
♥ AQ5	♥ KJ1042	2♥	(2)	2♠	(3)	(4) relay
♦ Q9	♦ A6	2NT	(4)	3♠	(5)	(5) game force, singleton ♣
♣ 9852	♣ 6	etc to 6♠				

Example 4   But if responder has the wrong singleton then it's easy to stay low.

West	East	West		East		(1) transfer
						(2) normal accept
♠ AKJ4	♠ Q7652	1NT		2♦	(1)	(3) 5-5 in the majors
♥ AQ5	♥ KJ1042	2♥	(2)	2♠	(3)	(4) relay
♦ Q9	♦ 6	2NT	(4)	3NT	(5)	(5) game force, singleton ♦
♣ 9852	♣ A6	4♠		pass		

Example 5

So that's all very fine, but what are these weak doubleton and triplet showing bids?

West	East	West	East	
				(1) transfer
				(2) normal accept
♠ AQ94	♠ KJ752	1NT	2♦ (1)	(3) 5-5 in the majors
♥ AJ8	♥ KQ1094	2♥ (2)	2♠ (3)	(4) relay
♦ Q87	♦ J6	2NT (4)	?	
♣ A82	♣ K			

West now has a problem if East's reply of a singleton ♣ said nothing about his doubleton ♦ holding. Basically, the Jacoby bidder usually has 3 cards in the minors, often split 2-1, and it may be essential for opener to know if there are two losers in a suit. This 'small doubleton or small triplet' is defined as two top losers.

West	East	
		So, in this example 5 we have solved the problem by having the 3♣ response to 2NT as showing game forcing values with a weak doubleton (or triplet).
1NT	2♦	
2♥	2♠	Opener then relays with 3♦ and responder shows his weak suit and minor suit distribution.
2NT	3♣ (5)	(5) game forcing
3♦ (6)	3♠ (7)	(6) relay
4♠	pass	(7) weak doubleton ♦

Note that as a result of us having these weak suit bids, if responder does directly show a singleton or void then his doubleton must be Ax or Kx.

Example 6   But if East's minor suits were reversed, then slam is there: -

West	East	West	East	
				(1) transfer
				(2) normal accept
♠ AQ94	♠ KJ752	1NT	2♦ (1)	(3) 5-5 in the majors
♥ AJ8	♥ KQ1094	2♥ (2)	2♠ (3)	(4) relay
♦ Q87	♦ K	2NT (4)	3♣ (5)	(5) game forcing
♣ A82	♣ J6	3♦ (6)	3♥ (7)	(6) relay
		? (8)		(7) weak doubleton ♣

Now West is definitely interested in slam, and the next logical step is to ask about key cards. East is 5-5 in the majors and has no idea which is the key suit. In fact, both suits are key! The king in any 5 card suit is very important and so in this situation we employ Double (or two-suit) Roman Key Card Blackwood, DRKCB.

This is covered (and our example continued) in the following section: -

140

3.1.4.1   <u>Asking For Aces Or Key Cards When Responder Is 5-5 In The Majors</u>

The trump suit has not yet been established, only opener knows. After the response to the 2NT enquiry (or after the response to the 3♦ weakness enquiry), opener uses the next available bid (not 4 of a major suit – that would be an attempt to sign off) to ask for key cards. Since no trump suit is yet defined we use two suit, or Double RKCB (DRKCB), so there are 6 key cards.

We use the next free bid as our DRKCB ask and so the responses are: -

Next step   =   0 or 3 key cards
Next step + 1 =   1 or 4 key cards
Next step + 2 =   2 or 5 key cards, no ♥Q or ♠Q
Next step + 2 =   2 or 5 key cards + ♥Q or ♠Q or both

Note that only opener knows which suit is trumps and so the 2 key card response cannot be specific about which queen.

So how does our example 6 progress?

West	East	West	East			
♠ AQ94	♠ KJ752	1NT	2♦	(1)	(1)	transfer
♥ AJ8	♥ KQ1094	2♥ (2)	2♠	(3)	(2)	normal accept
♦ Q87	♦ K	2NT (4)	3♣	(5)	(3)	5-5 in the majors
♣ A82	♣ J6	3♦ (6)	3♥	(7)	(4)	relay
		3♠ (8)	4♥	(9)	(5)	game forcing
		6♠ (10)	pass		(6)	relay

(7)   weak doubleton ♣
(8)   DRKCB
(9)   2 key cards + a ♥/♠ queen
(10) one key card missing, so 6♠.

If East had had 3 key cards (so the ♦A here), then it's 7♠.

Wow! We covered a lot in that example. It's probably best to have a couple more to make sure that it all works: -

———————————————

Let's have an all-singing all-dancing example. We are using DRKCB but responder is known to have at most 3 cards in the minors — minor suit kings are unimportant and the next bid after the key card response asks for key queens.

Here we need to know about asking for the major suit queens after the initial response to DRKCB. The next bid (not 4 or 5 of a major if no trump suit has been agreed) asks for the queens, the responses are: -

Next step   =   no queen
Next step + 1   =   ♥Q
Next step + 2   =   ♠Q
Next step + 3   =   both queens

Example 7

West	East	West		East	
♠ A106	♠ KQJ75	1NT		2♦	(1)
♥ AJ87	♥ KQ1094	2♥	(2)	2♠	(3)
♦ K87	♦ A64	2NT	(4)	4♣	(5)
♣ QJ2	♣ -	4♦	(6)	4♥	(7)
		4NT	(8)	5♠	(9)
		7♥		pass	

(1) transfer
(2) normal accept
(3) 5-5 in the majors
(4) relay
(5) game force, void ♣
(6) DRKCB
(7) 3 key cards
(8) queens?
(9) both

If opener attempts to sign off and responder has slam ambitions, then he must take over: -

Example 8

West	East	West		East	
♠ K6	♠ QJ875	1NT		2♦	(1)
♥ AJ8	♥ KQ1094	2♥	(2)	2♠	(3)
♦ Q876	♦ AK4	2NT	(4)	4♣	(5)
♣ KQ52	♣ -	4♥	(6)	4♠	(7)
		5♦	(8)	6♥	
		pass			

(1) transfer
(2) normal accept
(3) 5-5 in the majors
(4) relay
(5) game force, void ♣
(6) sign off
(7) DRKCB
(8) 2 key cards, no ♥/♠ queen

If West had held ♣A, he would not have counted it in his key card response. When partner is known to have a void, holdings in the void suit are not included in responses to Blackwood. Note that 4♠ at (7) is OK as DRKCB here as it cannot be a correction of the final contract, ♥'s are agreed.

This next example is from the April 1994 ACBL Bulletin. The holders got to 4♥ and asked how 6♥ could be reached. Let's see how we do it assuming no super-accept of the initial 2♦ transfer: -

Example 9

West	East	West	East			
					(1)	transfer
					(2)	normal accept
♠ AK6	♠ Q10875	1NT	2♦	(1)	(3)	5-5 in the majors
♥ Q987	♥ AKJ104	2♥ (2)	2♠	(3)	(4)	relay
♦ Q87	♦ A6	2NT (4)	3♠	(5)	(5)	game force, singleton ♣
♣ KQ2	♣ 4	?	(6)			

(6) West has two options here. He has good ♥'s but his values in ♣'s are wasted. If he attempts to sign off then East is worth another effort and should bid DRKCB over 4♥.

So, if West decides to have a go, the bidding proceeds: -

West	East		
3NT (6)	4♣ (7)	(6)	DRKCB
4♦ (8)	4NT (9)	(7)	3 key cards
6♥	pass	(8)	queens?
		(9)	♠Q

And if West signs off, then East takes over and the bidding proceeds: -

West	East		
4♥ (6)	4♠ (7)	(6)	sign off
5♥ (8)	6♥	(7)	DRKCB
pass		(8)	2 key cards + a ♥/♠ queen

In the ACBL article, the question was also asked how to avoid the slam if West had say ♠J9 doubleton? DRKCB sorts that out and you end up in a manageable 5♥. The only type of holding that West could have where 5♥ may fail is this

♠ J9 ♥ Q98 ♦ KQJ7 ♣ KQJ7.

Just possible I suppose if you opened 1NT with these six quacks.

When the response to DRKCB is 2 key cards plus a ♥/♠ queen then asker may need to know which queen is held (or if it's both queens). So the next free bid asks about queens and the responses are: -

Next step   =   ♥Q
Next step + 1 =   ♠Q
Next step + 2 =   both queens

Example 10

West	East	West		East				
♠ A943	♠ KQ752	1NT		2♦	(1)	(1)	transfer	
♥ AJ8	♥ KQ1094	2♥	(2)	2♠	(3)	(2)	normal accept	
♦ A87	♦ 9	2NT	(4)	3♣	(5)	(3)	5-5 in the majors	
♣ A82	♣ 96	3♦	(6)	3♥	(7)	(4)	relay	
		3♠	(8)	4♥	(9)	(5)	game forcing	
		4NT	(10)	5♥	(11)	(6)	relay	
		7♠		pass		(7)	weak doubleton ♣	
						(8)	DRKCB	
						(9)	2 key cards + a ♥/♠ queen	
						(10)	clarify queens	
						(11)	both	

Example 11

West	East	West		East				
♠ A943	♠ KQ752	1NT		2♦	(1)	(1)	transfer	
♥ AJ8	♥ K10974	2♥	(2)	2♠	(3)	(2)	normal accept	
♦ A87	♦ Q	2NT	(4)	3♣	(5)	(3)	5-5 in the majors	
♣ A82	♣ Q6	3♦	(6)	3♥	(7)	(4)	relay	
		3♠	(8)	4♥	(9)	(5)	game forcing	
		4NT	(10)	5♦	(11)	(6)	relay	
		6♠		pass		(7)	weak doubleton ♣	
						(8)	DRKCB	
						(9)	2 key cards + a ♥/♠ queen	
						(10)	clarify queens	
						(11)	♠Q only	

Notice that the major suit queen of example 10 is much better than the minor suit queens of example 11.

3.1.4.2 6-5 Or 5-6 In The Majors

Back in section 3.1.4 I said that after 1NT - 2♦ - 2♥ - 2♠ - 2NT - 3♣ - 3♦ that the responses to the 3♦ enquiry could be extended to show 6-5 and 5-6 in the majors. The complete scheme is:

After 1NT - 2♦ - 2♥ - 2♠ - 2NT - 3♣, 3♦ by opener asks: -

3♥   =   small doubleton ♣ (thus a singleton ♦)
3♠   =   small doubleton ♦ (thus a singleton ♣)
3NT =   DRKCB
4♣   =   small triplet ♣ or 6-5 or 5-6 with a weak doubleton ♣ (thus a ♦ void)
4♦   =   small triplet ♦ or 6-5 or 5-6 with a weak doubleton ♦ (thus a ♣ void)
4♥   =   5-6-1-1 or 6-5-1-1

Example 12   There is an alternative way of bidding this example overleaf.

West	East	West		East		
♠ AQ94	♠ KJ752	1NT		2♦	(1)	(1) transfer
♥ AJ8	♥ KQ10964	2♥	(2)	2♠	(3)	(2) normal accept
♦ Q87	♦ J	2NT	(4)	3♣	(5)	(3) in the majors
♣ A82	♣ K	3♦	(6)	4♥	(7)	(4) relay
		4NT	(8)	5♠	(9)	(5) game forcing
		6♠		pass		(6) relay
						(7) 5-6-1-1 or 6-5-1-1
						(8) DRKCB
						(9) 2 key cards + a ♥/♠ queen

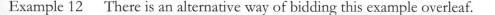

Example 13

There is no mechanism (unless you want to make it really complicated) to show 5-6 or 6-5 and a void with a weak doubleton. The best compromise is to show 5-5 and a weak triplet (thus indicating the important feature – the void). Exclusion DRKCB (see next page) is not recommended with a weak doubleton.

West	East	West		East		
♠ AQ94	♠ KJ752	1NT		2♦	(1)	(1) transfer
♥ AJ8	♥ KQ10963	2♥	(2)	2♠	(3)	(2) normal accept
♦ Q87	♦ -	2NT	(4)	3♣	(5)	(3) 5-5 in the majors
♣ A82	♣ 97	3♦	(6)	4♣	(7)	(4) relay
		4♦	(8)	5♣	(9)	(5) 5-5 game forcing
		7♠		pass		(6) relay
						(7) weak triplet ♣ (so a ♦ void)
						(8) DRKCB
						(9) 2 key cards + a ♥/♠ queen

West knows that 2 ♣'s can be discarded on long ♥'s. The extra ♥ just makes life simpler as only 2 ♦'s now need to be ruffed.

When responder has two singletons, it may simply be better to take charge.

Example 12 (alternative bidding).

West	East	West		East		(1)	transfer
						(2)	normal accept
♠ AQ94	♠ KJ752	1NT		2♦	(1)	(3)	5-5 in the majors
♥ AJ8	♥ KQ10964	2♥	(2)	2♠	(3)	(4)	relay
♦ Q87	♦ J	2NT	(4)	3♣	(5)	(5)	game forcing
♣ A82	♣ K	3♦	(6)	3NT	(7)	(6)	relay
		4♣	(8)	4♦	(9)	(7)	DRKCB
		4NT	(10)	6♥		(8)	3 key cards
		6♠		pass		(9)	queens?
						(10)	♠Q

West knows that responder is at least 5-5 and so corrects to the 5-4 ♠ fit. Opener would also correct if 3-2 in the majors.

This example shows why we need 3NT as the DRKCB bid, you may get too high if DRKCB starts off at 4NT and you need to ask for key queens which partner does not have.

And when responder is 6-5 or 5-6 with a void but a non-weak doubleton, it may also be best to take charge. We have seen that 3NT after the 3♦ relay (at (7) above) is DRKCB. A jump to 5♣ or 5♦ over the 2NT puppet is Exclusion DRKCB (EDRKCB), whereby the answers do not count honours in the exclusion suit: -

Example 14

West	East	West		East		(1)	transfer
						(2)	normal accept
♠ AQ94	♠ KJ752	1NT		2♦	(1)	(3)	5-5 in the majors
♥ AJ8	♥ KQ10964	2♥	(2)	2♠	(3)	(4)	relay
♦ Q87	♦ -	2NT	(4)	5♦	(5)	(5)	EDRKCB
♣ A82	♣ K6	5♥	(6)	5NT	(7)	(6)	3 key cards outside ♦'s
		6♥	(8)	7♥		(7)	queens?
		7♠	(9)	pass		(8)	♠Q
						(9)	West again corrects the final contract.

Note   Note that we do get rather high here and can sometimes have problems if West has just the ♠Q and East does not have the ♥Q. So you may prefer to use the otherwise idle bids of 4♠ and 4NT as EDRKCB for ♣'s and ♦'s respectively

3.1.5   <u>Bidding The Other Major</u>

As we have mentioned before, modern practice by many players is: -

1NT - 2♦ - 2♥ - 2♠   shows 5-5 in the majors and is invitational
1NT - 2♥ - 2♠ - 3♥   shows 5-5 in the majors and is game forcing.

     This was fully covered in the previous section. The major drawback with using the second sequence is that there is little room for manoeuvring, especially when looking for slam. Thus we use the first sequence to show both the invitational and game forcing 5-5's.

So that leaves the sequence	(a)	1NT - 2♥ - 2♠ - 3♥	undefined,
as is the similar sequence	(b)	1NT - 2♦ - 2♥ - 3♠.	
Also, what is	(c)	1NT - 2♥ - 2♠ - 4♥	
and	(d)	1NT - 2♦ - 2♥ - 4♠.	

<u>Splinters?</u>

Let's start with   1NT - 2♥ - 2♠ - 3♥   and   1NT - 2♦ - 2♥ - 3♠.

Hand A	Hand B	Hand C	
			We start by looking at these 3 hands, partner has opened 1NT. Hand A is mildly interested in slam and so a Jacoby Transfer followed by 4♥ is best.
♠ Q3	♠ 3	♠ 3	Hand B has good shape and a singleton, but not really
♥ KQ9642	♥ KQ9642	♥ KQ9642	slam values, so a Texas 4♦ is best.
♦ A4	♦ AJ4	♦ AJ4	Hand C is different; it definitely wants to investigate slam,
♣ K98	♣ J98	♣ K98	especially if partner has few wasted values in ♠'s. With no other 4+ card suit to mention, we clearly want to splinter with Hand C.

     Now   1NT - 2♦ - 2♥ - 3♠/4♣/4♦   and   1NT - 2♥ - 2♠ - 4♣/4♦/4♥   are all played as splinters by some players. But this is a bit wasteful (using three bids) and, as we will see shortly, we need the 4♣ bid as ace/key card ask and we use the 4♦ bid as a general slam try. But there is absolutely no reason why we cannot use 3♥ and 3♠ here as ambiguous splinters, exactly the same as they were with Stayman.

3.1.5.1   <u>Bidding 3 Of The Other Major – Ambiguous Splinters</u>

So we simply adopt the same philosophy as we did after Stayman – ambiguous splinters. After a simple completion of the transfer, 3 of the other major is an ambiguous splinter. It's just the same as the Stayman sequences: -

So, after 1NT - 2♦ - 2♥ - 3♠,

3NT asks   4♣ = ♣ singleton/void
               4♦ = ♦ singleton/void
               4♥ = ♠ singleton/void

and after 1NT - 2♥ - 2♠ - 3♥,

3♠ asks   3NT = ambiguous void
             4♣ = ♣ singleton
             4♦ = ♦ singleton
             4♥ = ♥ singleton

After 1NT - 2♥ - 2♠ - 3♥ - 3♠ - 3NT,

4♣ asks   4♦ = ♦ void
             4♥ = ♥ void
             4♠ = ♣ void

Example 1

West	East	West	East	
				(1) transfer
				(2) normal accept
♠ KJ4	♠ 3	1NT	2♦ (1)	(3) ambiguous splinter
♥ J8	♥ KQ9642	2♥ (2)	3♠ (3)	(4) where?
♦ KQ87	♦ AJ4	3NT (4)	4♥ (5)	(5) ♠ singleton/void
♣ AQ76	♣ K98	pass		

With wasted values in ♠'s, West settles for 4♥.

Example 2

West	East	West	East	
				(1) transfer
				(2) normal accept
♠ Q42	♠ 3	1NT	2♦ (1)	(3) ambiguous splinter
♥ A108	♥ KQ9642	2♥ (2)	3♠ (3)	(4) where?
♦ KQ7	♦ AJ4	3NT (4)	4♥ (5)	(5) ♠ singleton/void
♣ AQ76	♣ K98	4♠ (6)	etc to 6♥	(6) RKCB

This time there's little wastage in ♠'s.

Hand D

    This hand is very powerful and wants to investigate slam even if partner signs off.
    However, there is a slight problem with this particular holding (♠ shortage) when
♠ 3   playing ambiguous splinters in that it goes 1NT - 2♦ - 2♥ - 3♠ - 3NT - 4♥ and partner
♥ KQJ642   may pass! So with this hand type with definite slam interest you cannot splinter and have
♦ AJ4   to simply ask for keycards (with 4♣ after transferring – as we shall see shortly).
♣ AQ8

3.1.5.2   Bidding 4 Of The Other Major

Here we consider the two remaining, perhaps strange, sequences (c) and (d): -

(c) 1NT - 2♥ - 2♠ - 4♥   (see note at the bottom of the next page)
(d) 1NT - 2♦ - 2♥ - 4♠

On the surface, pretty silly. You have transferred but then leapt to 4 of the other major. Before we write off these sequences as meaningless, consider the sequences: -

1NT - 2♦ - 2♥ - 4NT   and   1NT - 2♥ - 2♠ - 4NT.

These are fully covered in section 3.1.8. They are quantitative, showing 5 of the major and suggesting a slam either in the major or in NT. Also possibly in a minor.

But what if responder has a similar slam invitational hand but with 3 cards in the other major? A quantitative 4NT would make a 5-3 slam in the other major very difficult to find. So why not use these otherwise redundant bids of 4 of the other major to show a similar hand to 4NT quantitative but showing 3 (decent) cards in the unbid major? Of course, this also helps to clarify our 4NT quantitative bid (it usually denies 3 cards in the other major). So, we have: -

1NT - 2♦ - 2♥ - 4♠   quantitative, 3532 or 3523 shape
1NT - 2♥ - 2♠ - 4♥   quantitative, 5332 or 5323 shape

Example 3

Opener should then be in a position to have a good shot at the best contract, game or slam.

West	East	West	East	
♠ A5	♠ KQ976	1NT	2♥	(1) quantitative, 3 ♥'s
♥ KJ932	♥ AQ5	2♠	4♥ (1)	(2) with good ♥'s but a minimum, West
♦ Q64	♦ 82	pass (2)		settles for the 5-3 fit at the game level.
♣ KQ8	♣ A106			

Example 4

West	East	West	East	
♠ 85	♠ KQ976	1NT	2♥	(1) quantitative, 3 ♥'s
♥ KJ932	♥ AQ5	2♠	4♥ (1)	
♦ AK6	♦ 82	6♥ (2)	pass	
♣ KQ8	♣ A106			

(2) 4NT is not available as Blackwood here (it is a sign off). 4♠ is also to play of course. So with excellent ♥'s West simply accepts the slam invitation. You could play 5♦ as a cue bid here but it's best played as looking for a ♦ slam (see example 5).

It looks like 11 tricks in NT if the ♠A is offside, but West knows of the 5-3 ♥ fit and also that East has a doubleton minor. The 12th trick should come from a minor suit ruff.

After responder's 4-of-a-major bid it is still best to reserve bids of 5♣/♦ and 6♣/♦ as looking for a minor suit slam as in the traditional case where responder bids 4NT; responder is known to have a 3 card minor: -

Example 5

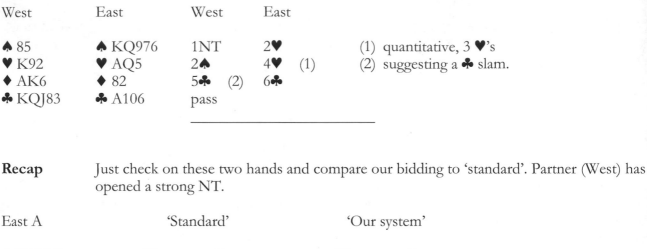

West	East	West	East			
♠ 85	♠ KQ976	1NT	2♥		(1)	quantitative, 3 ♥'s
♥ K92	♥ AQ5	2♠	4♥	(1)	(2)	suggesting a ♣ slam.
♦ AK6	♦ 82	5♣ (2)	6♣			
♣ KQJ83	♣ A106	pass				

Recap   Just check on these two hands and compare our bidding to 'standard'. Partner (West) has opened a strong NT.

East A

♠ K10843
♥ AJ9
♦ 52
♣ Q102

	'Standard'			'Our system'	
	West	East		West	East
	1NT	2♥		1NT	2♥
	2♠	3NT		2♠	3♥… etc.

East B

♠ KQJ83
♥ AJ9
♦ Q2
♣ K108

	'Standard'			'Our system'	
	West	East		West	East
	1NT	2♥		1NT	2♥
	2♠	4NT		2♠	4♥… etc.

Clearly our system is superior as it allows a possible 5-3 ♥ fit to be located at or below game. And, as previously stated, it clarifies the situation when we do rebid 3/4NT (no decent 3 card major).

Note

Some players use sequence (c) 1NT - 2♥ - 2♠ - 4♥ to show a 5-5 hand with slam interest. Clearly quite reasonable, but we use our sequence 1NT - 2♦ - 2♥ - 2♠ - 2NT - ?   to define 5-5's with slam interest. Obviously far better as the level is lower and the ? bid informs opener of shortage etc.

150

3.1.6   <u>4♣ - RKCB After A Jacoby Transfer</u>

We have said that 4NT is quantitative after a Jacoby Transfer (more of this next section). 4♣ is used to ask for aces/key cards. Now you could use simple Gerber here, but a key card ask really is superior. Rather than calling it Key Card Gerber, I prefer to say that 4♣ is Roman Key Card Blackwood.

Hand A	Opposite partner's strong 1NT opening you start off with a transfer. When
	partner simply accepts you really only need to know about key cards for
♠ AQJ964	the ♠ slam. So 4♣, RKCB. If partner had super-accepted (we come on to
♥ 4	this in section 3.2) then 4NT (Kickback) would be RKCB.
♦ KQ2	

		West	East	
♣ KJ10	So: -	1NT	2♥	
		2♠	4♣	4♣ is RKCB for ♠'s.

Example 1

West	East	West	East	
♠ K2	♠ AQ7964	1NT	2♥	(1) RKCB
♥ AJ73	♥ 4	2♠	4♣ (1)	(2) 0 or 3 key cards
♦ AJ64	♦ KQ2	4♦ (2) … etc to 6♠		
♣ Q94	♣ KJ10			

Example 2

West	East	West	East	
♠ 52	♠ AQ7964	1NT	2♥	(1) RKCB
♥ AKQ3	♥ 4	2♠	4♣ (1)	(2) 2 key cards without the queen
♦ AJ64	♦ KQ2	4♠ (2)	pass	
♣ Q94	♣ KJ10			

So we have	1NT - 2♦ - 2♥ - 4♣	is RKCB for ♥'s.
and	1NT - 2♥ - 2♠ - 4♣	is RKCB for ♠'s.

3.1.5   4♦ - The Serious Slam Try

Hand A	Hand B	Hand C	Partner has opened a strong 1NT.
			How do you proceed with these 3 hands?

Hand A	Hand B	Hand C
♠ AQ10964	♠ AQ10964	♠ AQ10964
♥ 64	♥ 64	♥ Q4
♦ Q63	♦ A63	♦ A63
♣ 85	♣ K5	♣ K5

We will be covering Texas Transfers later in section 6.2 and Hand A should use a Texas Transfer rather than a Jacoby Transfer followed by a 4♠ bid. The difference is that Texas is non-encouraging but the Jacoby sequence is mildly slam encouraging.

So Hand B goes via the more encouraging Jacoby route (1NT - 2♥ - 2♠ - 4♠).

Now then. What about Hand C? Not really strong enough to push to slam, but certainly worth an effort. The Jacoby sequence mentioned above probably is a bit too feeble for this nice hand. Taking the plunge (say with 4♣ RKCB after transferring) really is a bit too ambitious. We need an invitational bid below game level. The answer? Transfer and then use the otherwise idle bid of 4♦. This says 'I have a good 6 card suit, no other 4 card suit and have slam ambitions'.

Example 1

West	East	West	East			
♠ K85	♠ AQ10964	1NT	2♥		(1)	looking for slam
♥ AJ8	♥ Q4	2♠	4♦	(1)	(2)	RKCB
♦ QJ94	♦ A63	4NT (2)	…etc. to 6♠ (or 6NT)			
♣ AQ8	♣ K5					

Example 2

West	East	West	East		
♠ J8	♠ AQ10964	1NT	2♥		(1) looking for slam
♥ J105	♥ Q4	2♠	4♦	(1)	
♦ KQJ94	♦ A63	4♠	pass		
♣ AQJ	♣ K5				

This example shows why the invitation should be kept below 4 of the major. Anything more and the contract could be in danger.

The 4NT bid is quantitative, looking for slam. If you open 1NT and partner transfers then he has a five card suit. If he has game going or better values and another 4 card suit, he will usually bid it. Thus this 4NT bid denies another decent 4 card suit. Suppose you have opened a strong 1NT with these hands and partner has transferred to ♠'s followed by a quantitative 4NT. What is your bid?

Hand A	Hand B	Hand C
♠ Q103	♠ Q103	♠ 97
♥ J4	♥ Q4	♥ K93
♦ AQ63	♦ AQ63	♦ AQ63
♣ AQ52	♣ AK52	♣ AQ52

Hand A is minimum and you could pass, but 5♠ is probably safer; this is a sign off.

Hand B is considerably better and the correct bid is 6♠.

Hand C simply passes 4NT.

But what if you have a slam accepting hand with little tolerance for ♠'s. Is there possibly a better strain than NT? Remember, responder has generally denied another 4 card suit.

Hand D	Hand E	Hand F
♠ Q4	♠ Q3	♠ Q7
♥ K94	♥ K93	♥ A43
♦ AQ93	♦ AQ6	♦ J93
♣ AQ92	♣ AQ952	♣ AKQ92

Hand D is worth slam. Traditionally over a quantitative 4NT a hand like this would bid 5♣ in search of a minor suit fit. Under these circumstances there is no point. Simply bid 6NT.

Hand E is different. If a 5-3 ♣ fit exists, then 6♣ may be a better slam than 6NT. Thus a 5♣ or 5♦ bid shows a reasonable 5 card suit and suggests the suit slam if responder has decent 3 card support. Hand F is similar, but here you really want to emphasise that you have a good ♣ suit. So bid 6♣.

Example 1

West	East	West	East
♠ Q4	♠ K8763	1NT	2♥
♥ J74	♥ AK	2♠	4NT (1)
♦ AKQ92	♦ J64	6♦ (2)	pass (3)
♣ A82	♣ KQ6		

(1) quantitative
(2) a very good suit
(3) Three ♦'s with an honour is sufficient to accept the suit as trumps in this situation.

Hand G
♠ K3
♥ K94
♦ AQ
♣ KJ9763

There is, of course, also this type of hand. If you opened this hand with 1NT then 6♣ is probably the best bid now, although you might consider 6NT at pairs scoring.

One small point. A few experts recommend that if you wish to accept the 4NT slam invitation, then you should respond as to Blackwood. I don't like this. As we have seen, we really need these 5 level bids to find our decent 5-3 fits or to sign off in a major.

Finally, let's just look at one possible responder's hand.

Hand H	Now I have emphasised here that a sequence such as 1NT - 2♥ - 2♠ - 4NT denies another 4 card suit. This hand has the values to invite slam with nice top cards –
♠ AKJ73	but not in ♣'s. It would be silly to suggest a ♣ slam with this hand. So rebid 4NT,
♥ QJ	quantitative, after transferring.
♦ KJ	If there is a ♣ slam then opener needs a max with a good ♣ suit and he will bid
♣ 7643	5♣ or 6♣.

Example 2

West (D)	East (H)	West	East		
				(1)	quantitative
				(2)	a good hand but no good suit
♠ Q4	♠ AKJ73	1NT	2♥		
♥ K94	♥ QJ	2♠	4NT (1)		
♦ AQ93	♦ KJ	6NT (2)	pass		
♣ AQ92	♣ 7643				

(2) East has denied a good 2nd suit, and so West's ♣'s and ♦'s are not good enough to suggest that suit for slam in this situation. 6NT is a good contract, 6♣ is not.

3.2   Super-acceptance Of A Transfer.

The law of total tricks (The LAW) implies that it is usually safe to super-accept with 4 trumps. Thus we super-accept with 4 trumps and a min or max hand. Super-accepting with just 3 trumps is a bone of contention, many players will super-accept with 3 good trumps and a non-min hand with good shape.

Now onto an interesting point. The LAW states that it is safe to go to the 3 level (combined number of trumps is 9) if the distribution of points between the two sides is approximately even, or if you have more. This is clearly the case with an opening strong NT, but not so with a weak NT. It is dangerous to super-accept with a weak NT opening, but if partner is bust, then why have the opponents not said anything yet? If you play a weak NT, it's up to you. I play super-accepts with a strong NT only.

Before we continue, it is only fair to say that my view of super-accepting is not universally accepted. I will super-accept with 4 trumps or with just 3 very good trumps, suitable shape and a max. Some players suggest super-accepting with any max, either 3 or 4 'trumps'. Others insist that the only requirement for a super-accept is 4 trumps (The Law says that's OK even if minimum).

With these four hands you opened with 1NT and partner bid 2♦, what now? : -

Hand A	Hand B	Hand C	Hand D
♠ 64	♠ J4	♠ Q4	♠ 64
♥ KQ84	♥ K984	♥ AJ9	♥ AK9
♦ AK82	♦ AK82	♦ AK82	♦ AK82
♣ AJ3	♣ A73	♣ K1082	♣ K1083

Hand A: An obvious super-accept.

Hand B: With 4 trumps I think that a super-accept is in order, but some players will not as they also require a maximum.

Hand C: This one's a maximum but has only 3 trumps. Much more to think about here and it's really up to your (partnership) style.

Hand D: Similar, but with good trumps and the points concentrated in the longer suits I like the hand. I would prefer to super-accept.

I cover super-accepting with just 3 trumps in more detail in section 3.2.1.

There are also umpteen variations on what you should bid when you break the transfer (super-accept). Some players insist that a response of the suit below trumps cannot be made as responder needs that for a re-transfer. Others feel that it is more important to be specific about shape. One popular scheme is to show a 2nd suit. Some players prefer only to show doubletons. Yet others will show doubletons only if they are 'worthless' – Qx (maybe Jx) or worse. Another alternative is to pinpoint a weak suit (either 2 or 3 card) that contains no top (A or K) honour. I give one workable scheme here: -

Super-accepts, showing 4 (possibly 5) cards in the major, can work as follows, where min is (15-16) and max is (16½ -17). In this scheme, the doubleton is weak: -

After 1NT - 2♦ (transfer to ♥) -			After 1NT - 2♥ (transfer to ♠) -		
2♠	doubleton ♠, max pts		2NT	no weak doubleton, max pts	
2NT	no weak doubleton, max pts		3♣	doubleton ♣, max pts	
3♣	doubleton ♣, max pts		3♦	doubleton ♦, max pts	
3♦	doubleton ♦, max pts	*	3♥	doubleton ♥, max pts	*
3♥	4 ♥'s, any shape, min pts	*	3♠	4 ♠'s, any shape, min pts	*

After these bids, responder often continues with a re-transfer if necessary, which opener must accept. We always use the cheapest re-transfer bid available: -

3♦	transfer to 3♥		3♥	transfer to 3♠

* and if the three level bid is unavailable (I call these expensive super-accepts) then: -

4♦	transfer to 4♥		4♥	transfer to 4♠

Responder is then able to pass or to investigate slam. A subsequent 4NT bid is RKCB when ♠'s are trumps and 4♠ is RKCB when ♥'s are trumps.

Example 1

West	East	West		East	
♠ KQ84	♠ AJ1073	1NT		2♥	
♥ 64	♥ AJ	3♥	(1)	4♥	(2)
♦ AK82	♦ Q63	4♠		4NT	(3)
♣ A73	♣ KJ10	5♣	(4)	5♦	(5)
		6♦	(6)	6♠	(7)

(1) West is middle range, but with good trumps and shape he makes the max point super-accept, showing a doubleton ♥.
(2) re-transfer
(3) RKCB for ♠.
(4) 0 or 3
(5) Do you have ♠Q ?
(6) Yes, plus ♦K
(7) East has now located every one of West's high cards, and settles for the small slam.

Example 2

West	East	West		East	
♠ KQ84	♠ AJ1073	1NT		2♥	
♥ KQ6	♥ AJ	3♦	(1)	3♥	(2)
♦ J2	♦ Q63	3♠		4♠	
♣ AQ73	♣ KJ10	pass			

(1) super-accept, weak doubleton ♦
(2) re-transfer

Example 3

West	East	West		East	
♠ KQ84	♠ A10732	1NT		2♥	
♥ K64	♥ J9	3♠	(1)	pass	(2)
♦ K2	♦ Q63				
♣ A932	♣ J76				

(1) super-accept, 4 trumps, min pts
(2) opposite a minimum, even with 4 trumps, game does not look good.

Now that's all very simple, but the next thing that has to be decided is; what does the next bid by responder mean if it's not a re-transfer? It would be nice to use the same bids/meanings as when opener made a simple accept, but we cannot.

To start with, there is always less room. Also we use Kickback as opposed to 4♣ as RKCB. And we don't need 4♦ as a general slam try as any bid other than a sign off in game or part-score is a slam try. Let's try to sort things out: -

Let's start with a new suit. Is it a game try (if below 3 of the major), a cue bid or a 2nd suit? It's up to you, but I prefer that a new minor is natural and looking for slam - either in the agreed major, or in the minor if there is a fit there. Clearly responder does not bother to show a 2nd suit if that's the suit that opener has shown shortage in.

Example 4

West	East	West		East	
♠ K984	♠ AQJ32	1NT		2♥	
♥ AJ4	♥ 75	3♠	(1)	4♦	(2)
♦ K984	♦ AQJ3	4♥	(3)	5♦	(4)
♣ A9	♣ 75	6♦		pass	

(1) super-accept, 4 trumps, min pts
(2) 2nd suit, looking for slam
(3) DRKCB
(4) 2 key cards + ♦Q

4♦ at (2) is looking for slam and invites opener to bid RKCB. If opener bid 4NT then that would be RKCB with ♠'s as trumps. 4♥ is Kickback bid for ♦'s, but since there is a known double fit it is DRKCB with ♦'s assumed as trumps.

6♦ is an excellent contract, a good 4-4 fit often plays better than a 5-4 fit.

So that's OK, but what if the new suit is the re-transfer suit? This situation may arise when ♥'s are trumps.

Now we have seen that 1NT - 2♥ - 3♦ - 3♥ is a re-transfer, which is fine as responder cannot have a ♥ suit as hands that are 5-4 in the majors go via Stayman but we have a problem with the sequences

$$1NT - 2♦ - 2♠ - 3♦.$$
$$1NT - 2♦ - 2NT - 3♦.$$
and $$1NT - 2♦ - 3♣ - 3♦.$$

Is 3♦ a re-transfer or a ♦ suit? You could choose either but I believe that showing a 2nd suit and maybe finding a superior 4-4 fit for slam is more important than the NT opener being declarer. But actually you can have both! We use 3♦ as a re-transfer, thus 3♥ is not needed as a natural sign off and so a 3♥ bid shows ♦'s as a 2nd suit. But of course you have to be very wary here, standard is that 3♥ would be a weak sign off and you don't want partner passing! And a couple more points about showing the 2nd suit. It can only be a minor (Responder would have bid Stayman rather than transferring if he had both majors) and we do not show a second suit if opener has shown a weak doubleton there.

There is one minor 'error' in the above paragraphs. Responder may indeed have a 2nd suit that is a major; but that is only when he is 5-5 in the majors and in that case the 5-4 ♥ fit is preferable to any possible 5-3 ♠ fit.

Example 5

West	East	West	East		
					(1) super-accept, no weak doubleton
					(2) ♦ 2nd suit, looking for slam
♠ AQ4	♠ 75	1NT	2♦		
♥ K984	♥ AQJ32	2NT (1)	3♥ (2)		
♦ K984	♦ AQJ3	? (3)			
♣ A9	♣ 75				

But now we have another problem with these touching (♦/♥) suits. What would 4♥ at (3) mean? Is it a sign off or (D)RKCB for ♦'s? Clearly it needs to be a sign off and so we shall use 4♦ as the (D)RKCB bid. There is a double fit and so we use DRKCB with ♦'s as trumps. If opener just wanted to use RKCB for ♥'s it would be 4♠ Kickback.

Example 5 cont.

West	East		
4♦ (3)	5♣ (4)	(3) DRKCB
6♦	pass	(4) 2 key cards + ♦Q

6♦ is an excellent contract, the good 4-4 fit again playing better than the 5-4 fit.

Let's have a summary to check how far we've got so far: -

Partial summary of responder's 2nd bid after a super-accept of the transfer to ♥'s,

so after 1NT - 2♦ - …

Super Accept ↓	Responder's 2nd Bid								
	2NT	3♣	3♦	3♥	3♠	3NT	4♣	4♦	4♥
2♠		♣'s 2nd suit	re-transfer	♦'s 2nd suit					
2NT		♣'s 2nd suit	re-transfer	♦'s 2nd suit					
3♣			re-transfer	♦'s 2nd suit					
3♦				sign off			♣'s 2nd suit	re-transfer	
3♥							♣'s 2nd suit	♦'s 2nd suit	

Partial summary of responder's 2nd bid after a super-accept of the transfer to ♠'s,

so after 1NT - 2♥ - …

Super Accept ↓	Responder's 2nd Bid								
	3♣	3♦	3♥	3♠	3NT	4♣	4♦	4♥	4♠
2NT	♣'s 2nd suit	♦'s 2nd suit	re-transfer						
3♣		♦'s 2nd suit	re-transfer						
3♦			re-transfer	♣'s 2nd suit					
3♥				sign off		♣'s 2nd suit	♦'s 2nd suit	re-transfer	
3♠						♣'s 2nd suit	♦'s 2nd suit		

So that's fine and we have lots of unallocated bids so far. But we also need to define splinters, cue bids, general slam try etc.

Let's start with cue bids. It's best to re-transfer first if this is at a low level and this is what we do for the cheapest 3 sequences. So re-transfer and then cue bid after the forced reply.

Example 6

West	East	West		East		
♠ AQ4	♠ K52	1NT		2♦		(1) super-accept, no weak doubleton
♥ K984	♥ AQJ32	2NT	(1)	3♦	(2)	(2) re-transfer
♦ A9	♦ 75	3♥		4♣	(3)	(3) cue bid
♣ K984	♣ AJ3	4♦	(3)	4♠	(4)	(4) RKCB (Kickback)
		4NT	(5)	6♥		(5) 3 key cards
		pass				

In the last two 'expensive' super-accept sequences, the re-transfer is up at the four level and so we use 3NT to initiate cue bidding.

Example 7

West	East	West		East		
♠ AJ4	♠ K52	1NT		2♦		(1) super-accept, 4 trumps, min pts
♥ K984	♥ AQJ32	3♥	(1)	3NT	(2)	(2) general slam try
♦ A9	♦ 75	4♦	(3)	4♠	(4)	(3) cue bid
♣ K984	♣ AQ3	4NT	(5)	6♥		(4) RKCB (Kickback)
		pass				(5) 3 key cards

But responder may not be interested in slam and the re-transfer ensures that opener becomes declarer.

Example 8

West	East	West		East		
♠ AK4	♠ Q5	1NT		2♦		(1) super-accept, no weak doubleton
♥ K984	♥ AQ632	2NT	(1)	3♦	(2)	(2) re-transfer
♦ A964	♦ 8732	3♥		4♥		
♣ K9	♣ 65	pass				

And now onto splinters. With the normal accept we needed a 6 card suit to splinter. It's different when opener has super-accepted as he has agreed the trump suit.

Hand E	Hand F	With both of these hands you have slam interest after partner has super-accepted your transfer to ♥'s. Hand E has a 2nd suit but Q532 is not really a slam quality suit and so I would splinter.
♠ Q532	♠ 7	
♥ AQ632	♥ AJ963	With Hand F you could splinter but I would prefer to show the ♦ suit.
♦ 2	♦ K1052	A 3♦ bid would be a re-transfer and we see how to bid this hand later
♣ KQ7	♣ A93	in Example 11.

When Stayman had found a fit we used three of the other major as an ambiguous splinter and that worked fine, so can we do something similar here? 3♠ is available with ♥'s as trumps but with ♠'s as trumps 3♥ is not available. So we'll use 3♠ as an ambiguous splinter when ♥'s are trumps but use direct splinters when ♠'s are trumps. In the ♥ sequences the ambiguous splinter means that all possibilities are covered. With the higher super-accepts in the ♠ sequence there is no room for splinters.

You could develop things further and use spare bids in the cheaper sequences to show voids but I'll leave that up to you. And if you're not totally happy with ambiguous splinters in the ♥ sequences and not with ♠'s then you could choose to use direct splinters in both.

And a word about splintering with a shortage in opener's weak doubleton. Normally one should not splinter with a singleton ace (partner will devalue honours in the suit) but when partner has shown a weak doubleton it is acceptable to splinter with the singleton ace.

So, after   1NT - 2♦ - 2♠/2NT/3♣/3♦/3♥, 3♠ is the ambiguous splinter and

3NT asks   4♣ = ♣ singleton/void
                 4♦ = ♦ singleton/void
                 4♥ = ♠ singleton/void

Example 9

West	East (E)	West	East	(1) super-accept, no weak doubleton
				(2) ambiguous splinter
♠ AK4	♠ Q532	1NT	2♦	(3) where?
♥ K984	♥ AQ632	2NT (1)	3♠ (2)	(4) ♦'s
♦ Q964	♦ 2	3NT (3)	4♦ (4)	(5) RKCB
♣ A9	♣ KQ7	4♠ (5) etc to 6♥		

In the ♠ sequences we splinter directly.

Example 10

West	East	West	East	(1) super-accept, no weak doubleton
				(2) splinter
♠ K984	♠ AQJ632	1NT	2♥	(3) RKCB
♥ AK4	♥ Q53	2NT (1)	4♦ (2)	
♦ Q964	♦ 2	4NT (3) etc to 6♠		
♣ A9	♣ KQ7			

Complete summary of responder's 2nd bid after a super-accept of the transfer to ♥'s, so after 1NT - 2♦ - …

Super Accept ↓	Responder's 2nd Bid								
	2NT	3♣	3♦	3♥	3♠	3NT	4♣	4♦	4♥
2♠		♣'s 2nd suit	re-transfer	♦'s 2nd suit	ambig. splinter				
2NT		♣'s 2nd suit	re-transfer	♦'s 2nd suit	ambig. splinter				
3♣			re-transfer	♦'s 2nd suit	ambig. splinter				
3♦				sign off	ambig. splinter	general slam try	♣'s 2nd suit	re-transfer	
3♥					ambig. splinter	general slam try	♣'s 2nd suit	♦'s 2nd suit	to play

Complete summary of responder's 2nd bid after a super-accept of the transfer to ♠'s, so after 1NT - 2♥ - …

Super Accept ↓	Responder's 2nd Bid								
	3♣	3♦	3♥	3♠	3NT	4♣	4♦	4♥	4♠
2NT	♣'s 2nd suit	♦'s 2nd suit	re-transfer			splinter	splinter	splinter	
3♣		♦'s 2nd suit	re-transfer			splinter	splinter	splinter	
3♦			re-transfer	♣'s 2nd suit		splinter	splinter	splinter	
3♥				sign off	general slam try	♣'s 2nd suit	♦'s 2nd suit	re-transfer	
3♠					general slam try	♣'s 2nd suit	♦'s 2nd suit		to play

When responder has a 2nd suit and also a shortage, should he splinter or show the 2nd suit after a super-accept? It probably depends upon the quality of the suits but as I said earlier I would usually prefer to show the 2nd suit if it's a good one.

Example 11

West	East	West	East		
				(1)	transfer
				(2)	super-accept, 2 ♣'s
♠ AJ3	♠ 7	1NT	2♦ (1)	(3)	♦'s 2nd suit
♥ KQ102	♥ AJ963	3♣ (2)	3♥ (3)	(4)	DRKCB
♦ AQ96	♦ K1052	4♦ (4)	etc to 6♦		
♣ 85	♣ A93				

Note that West bid Blackwood (DRKCB) at (4) despite holding a worthless doubleton. This is fine in this situation as he has already shown this weak doubleton and partner is looking for slam – and hence has the suit covered.

So that's covers super-accepts with 4 card support. I have not gone into it in as much detail as I have for other aspects (because you may choose to adopt a different super-accept philosophy). And there are many improvements/additions that you may wish to make. And there are even a few murky areas – such as what are the (D)RKCB bids in all the situations where responder has shown a 2nd suit. I could write another 20 pages but I don't really want to in an area where you may choose to play something completely different. I'll leave there.

Playing super-accepts clearly has its advantages. And it also has beneficial repercussions elsewhere: -

♠ J8652 You hold this hand and partner opens a strong NT. Obviously you transfer and partner
♥ 103   partner bids 2♠.What now? 8 points so 2NT? No! This is a poor 8 count with a
♦ K103   miserable ♠ suit. Since partner has not super-accepted then game is remote. If you bid
♣ A52   on, you will go down (in either a part-score or game) much more often than you will find
         a makeable game.

This hand was from a club tournament. Nearly everybody was in 2NT or 3♠, with both contracts failing by one trick.

So with this hand it's 1NT - 2♥ - 2♠ - pass. If opener super-accepted then it may depend upon the type of super-accept as to whether you proceed further or not but you normally would bid game.

3.2.1   <u>**Super-accept With 3 Card Support?**</u>

This is really up to the particular partnership. It may well work with 3 good trumps and a bit of shape: -

Example 1

West	East	West	East		
♠ AQ3	♠ J5	1NT	2♦ (1)		(1) transfer
♥ KJ10	♥ AQ963	3♣ (2)	4♦ (3)		(2) super-accept, 2 ♣'s
♦ AQ963	♦ 108	4♥	pass		(3) re-transfer
♣ 85	♣ 9742				

So, a good game contract that will probably be missed if West had simply accepted the transfer.

Super-accepting with only 3 trumps (and a max) is by no means that popular. You may run into difficulties when responder has minimal values – you are at the three level with only 8 trumps.

Example 2

West	East	West	East		
♠ AQ3	♠ 75	1NT	2♦ (1)		(1) transfer
♥ KJ10	♥ 98632	3♣ (2)	3♦ (3)		(2) super-accept, 2 ♣'s
♦ AQ963	♦ 74	3♥	pass		(3) re-transfer
♣ 85	♣ Q742				

Example 3   But then you may reach a good slam: -

West	East	West	East		
♠ AQ3	♠ 75	1NT	2♦ (1)		(1) transfer
♥ KQ10	♥ AJ963	3♣ (2)	3♦ (3)		(2) super-accept, 2 ♣'s
♦ AQ963	♦ K102	3♥	4♣ (4)		(3) re-transfer
♣ 85	♣ A97	4♦ (4)	4♠ (5)		(4) cue bid
		etc to 6♥			(5) RKCB

Note that it is fairly safe for East to bid Blackwood at (5) as West has already shown a weak doubleton ♣ and would normally have a top ♠ honour. If West had simply accepted the transfer, then East probably would not consider investigating slam.

When playing 3-card super-accepts it really is important to have our ability to show a 2nd suit. A good 4-4 fit elsewhere will virtually always be better for slam.

Example 4

West	East	West	East	
♠ AJ32	♠ 76	1NT	2♦	(1)
♥ AK10	♥ QJ963	3♣ (2)	3♥	(3)
♦ A1096	♦ KQ52	etc to 6♦		
♣ 85	♣ A9			

(1) transfer
(2) super-accept, 2 ♣'s
(3) ♦'s 2nd suit

Now example 4 looks fine but there is a problem with super-accepting a transfer to ♥'s with just 3 card support when you also have 4 ♠'s: -

East

♠ KQ954
♥ QJ963
♦ 532
♣ -

East may be 5-5 in the majors! If West were to super-accept with the hand above opposite this East then it would be very difficult to find the ♠ fit, let alone the ♠ slam.

So my advice is do not super-accept a transfer to ♥'s with just three card support when holding 4 ♠'s.

When responder has a 2nd suit and also a shortage, should he splinter or show the 2nd suit after a super-accept? If you allow 3-card super-accepts it is surely best to show the 2nd suit.

Example 5

West	East	West	East	
♠ AJ32	♠ 7	1NT	2♦	(1)
♥ KQ10	♥ AJ963	3♣ (2)	3♥	(3)
♦ AQ96	♦ K1052	4♠ (4)	etc to 6♦	
♣ 85	♣ A93			

(1) transfer
(2) super-accept, 2 ♣'s
(3) ♦'s 2nd suit
(4) DRKCB

It really is a matter of personal preference if you decide to super-accept with just 3 trumps. Sometimes it works, sometimes it does not. With a superb fit like the above example, it certainly seems to make sense. And it may make finding slam in another strain easier. But on the other hand responder may feel more secure if he knows that opener always has 4 cards in the major.

Transfers to a major after a 1NT opening are very common, but transfers to a minor are different. First of all, you will be at the 3 level, and so you really need a six card suit if you don't have a strong (game going) hand. Secondly, there is only one 'obviously' free bid available (2♠). One quite popular method when holding a weak hand and a long minor is simply to bid 2♠, requiring opener to bid 3♣ which is then either passed or corrected to 3♦. There is, however, a far more accurate method of minor suit transfers available, which involves the use of both 2♠ and 2NT as transfer bids.

Now I have said that the 2♠ bid is redundant when we play transfers and also that 2NT is free as we can show an invitational raise via 2♣. But it may be timely to check on some common uses of these 2♠ and 2NT bids in order to ensure that we cover all of these options by other bids and that they really are free: -

1) 2♠ (8 pts) and 2NT (9 pts) are both balanced and invitational to 3NT
2) 2♠ is natural and weak
3) 2♠ shows a weak hand with a long minor suit
4) 2♠ is Baron, seeking a 4-4 fit
5) 2♠ and 2NT (and 3♣) are as defined in Truppet Stayman
6) 2NT is a puppet to 3♣, either weak ♣'s or a 3 suiter looking for slam
7) 2♠ is Minor Suit Stayman
8) 2♠ is either a limit 2NT type bid or a balanced slam try

1)   <u>2♠ (8 pts) and 2NT (9 pts) are both balanced and invitational to 3NT.</u>

This scheme is use by some less experienced players in the UK (they play a weak NT so it's actually 11 pts and 12 pts). I guess that this distinction may aid declarer in a borderline case but it really is squandering two bids for just one meaning and we need all the bids we can get.

2)   <u>2♠ is natural and weak</u>

Hand A	Hand B	
		Before the days of transfers both of these hands would simply respond with their major suit, fine. Nowadays we transfer; nothing is lost with Hand A but with Hand B if we transfer with 2♥ then there is a risk that LHO will double to show ♥'s and the opponents will find a ♥ fit that may otherwise have been lost. A valid point, but not so important as to squander this otherwise very useful bid.
♠ 7	♠ Q10972	
♥ Q10972	♥ 7	
♦ Q76	♦ J76	
♣ J652	♣ J652	

3)   <u>2♠ shows a weak hand with a long minor suit</u>

This is a simple variation used by many less experienced players. 2♠ is simply a puppet to 3♣ and responder either passes or bids 3♦ which opener passes. 2NT directly over the opening 1NT is played as invitational.

4)   <u>2♠ is Baron, asking the range and seeking a 4-4 fit</u>

A Baron bid shows no 5 card suit and is generally looking for a 4-4 fit (usually a minor) for slam purposes. It is common in the UK to play 3♣ over an opening 2NT as Baron and this use of 2♠ over 1NT is gaining in popularity. Over 2♠ opener replies: -

2NT   minimum, may have any shape. Responder will normally start bidding 4 card suits up the line until a fit is found. However, the 2♠ bid may also be used as a quantitative raise and responder will then pass.

3♣ →3♠   with a maximum, 4 card suits are bid up the line.

The 2NT bid is not needed as a natural invitation (the response to 2♠ tells responder if opener is maximum or not) and so may be used for what you wish, usually a puppet to 3♣.

Now this all works, but it is nowhere near as efficient as our SARS sequences. Let's have a look at some other options: -

5)   <u>2♠ and 2NT (and 3♣) are as defined in Truppet Stayman</u>

Truppet Stayman is a convention involving Transfers and Puppets. 2♠ is game forcing and is a puppet to 2NT. After the forced 2NT responder then bids 3♣/♦ with a single suited hand or any other bid to show both minors. The direct 2NT over opener's 1NT is a transfer to ♣'s and 3♣ is a transfer to ♦'s. An invitational 2NT is bid via 2♣.

I guess that this all works OK but we can do everything with simpler methods. We transfer into the minor with our single minor suited hand (weak, invitational or strong). With both minors and a game forcing or slam seeking hand SARS works fine. And, as we shall see in section 4.1, it is very convenient to have an in-between bid available when transferring to the minors. Another disadvantage of Truppet Stayman is that the direct 3♣ bid over 1NT is utilised. We have another use for this and so no Truppets for us.

6)   <u>2NT is a puppet to 3♣, either weak ♣'s or a 3 suiter looking for slam</u>

You respond 2NT with either type of hand. With a ♣ bust you pass opener's 3♣ bid; with a three suiter you bid your singleton/void (or the suit below if you prefer that). This works fine but we can also do both of these; we transfer with the weak ♣ hand and we also have splinters which will be defined in section 5.4. With this scheme there is no obvious mechanism for showing the weak ♦ hand.

7)   <u>2♠ is Minor Suit Stayman</u>

This is quite popular for those who do not use 4-way transfers, and there are different variations within Minor Suit Stayman. I'll cover two common variants: -

7a)   <u>'Garbage' Minor Suit Stayman</u>

With this variation, popular in the States, the 2♠ bid does not promise anything in the way of values and so opener cannot bid above 3♦. The responses to 2♠ are: -

2NT	no 4 card minor
3♣	4 (or 5) ♣'s
3♦	4 (or 5) ♦'s

With two 4 card minors, opener bids the better one.
What can I say? 'Primitive' is apt, but this is popular, even with some experts.
Responder will bid 2♠ with any of three hand types: -

1- A weak hand with a long ♦ suit.
2- A weak hand with both minor suits.
3- A hand interested in slam, usually containing both minors.

Now this works (otherwise it would not be played by so many people) but it really is rather limited. Let's consider the three hand types: -

1- OK with ♦'s, but there is no provision for a weak hand with ♣'s.
2- How often do you come across a weak hand that can play in either minor at the 3 level but not in 1NT? And since opener may have no 4 card minor, it may well have to play at the 3 level opposite 3 card support.
3- This is fine, but our SARS sequences are far superior as you can find out opener's exact minor suit holding rather than just establishing that he has a 4 card minor. And, with this scheme, when opener shows a 4 card minor responder does not know if it is a 4 or 5 carder or if opener also has 4 cards in the other minor.

So, not really very satisfactory. Let's look at another variant of Minor Suit Stayman: -

7b)   Game Forcing Minor Suit Stayman

With this variant responder must have at least game going values and is usually looking for a minor suit slam. Responder may have just one or both minors. The responses to 2♠ are:

2NT   no 4 card minor but slam interest
3♣   4 (or 5) ♣'s
3♦   4 (or 5) ♦'s
3♥   two 4 card minors with a ♥ control
3♠   two 4 card minors with a ♠ control
3NT   no 4 card minor and no slam interest

I guess that this variation works but there are a few drawbacks: -

1- We have no bid to show our weak hand with a long minor suit.
2- The responses do not tell us if opener has a 4 or 5 card minor.
3- What does responder do with a hand two 4 card minors but no ♥/♠ control?

And, of course, we can get all of this information and more with our SARS sequences.

Whichever variation of Minor Suit Stayman you use, 2NT is free for the conventional limit raise.

8)   2♠ is either a limit 2NT type bid or a balanced slam try

This system is popular in the UK, they use 2♠ to ask opener's strength and the direct 2NT is generally used to sign off with a weak hand and a long minor suit (a puppet to 3♣ which responder either passes or corrects to 3♦).

The responses to 2♠ are: -

2NT   minimum
3♣   maximum.

There are then various different subsequent bids to show all sorts of hand types.

Now this is all fine, but I am a simple soul and do not like to complicate things unnecessarily. SARS is extremely efficient if looking for 4-4 minor suit fits and transfers to the minors are excellent and are pretty well established worldwide.

───────────────

There are also umpteen other variations for these 2♠/NT bids but I don't really like any of them and we'll stick with transfers to the minors because: -

- It is simple.
- It is what a large number of people worldwide play.
- It complements the rest of our structure perfectly.
- It is, as Tina Turner states, 'Simply The Best'.

Transfers To The Minors

So, that's settled. We are going to use 2♠ and 2NT as transfers to the minors. They are also used in conjunction with transfers to the majors and the whole set-up is often referred to as 4-way transfers. After a 1NT opening we now have : -

2♠ transfer to ♣'s   and   2NT transfer to ♦'s

If responder has a poor hand and simply wants to play in 3 of a minor, he passes opener's normal acceptance of the transfer: -

1NT - 2♠ - 3♣ - pass   or   1NT - 2NT - 3♦ - pass

Example 1

West	East	West		East	
♠ AJ4	♠ 983	1NT		2NT (1)	(1) transfer to ♦'s
♥ AQ6	♥ J5	3♦	(2)	pass (3)	(2) I have poor ♦'s
♦ 753	♦ KJ9862				(3) then 3♦ is best.
♣ AJ108	♣ 97				

_____

Example 2

West	East	West		East	
♠ A104	♠ J983	1NT		2NT (1)	(1) transfer to ♦'s
♥ AQJ	♥ 5	3♦	(2)	pass (3)	(2) I have poor ♦'s
♦ 753	♦ KJ9862				(3) then 3♦ is best.
♣ AJ108	♣ 97				

Note that in example 2 there may be a 4-4 ♠ fit. Unfortunately with this weak hand type responder cannot do everything and it's best not to look for the major suit fit.

_____

4.1　Super-acceptance Of Minor Suit Transfers

If opener has a good holding in the transfer suit then he should try for 3NT by making the 'in-between' bid; so 2NT in the case of a transfer to ♣'s and 3♣ when the transfer was to ♦'s. If he has a bad holding, he should simply complete the transfer. In the case of an in-between reply, responder will bid 3NT with a good hand/suit or simply complete the transfer with a bad hand.

And the requirements for the in-between bid? There are differing opinions, but best is that 3 cards to a top honour (A,K or Q) or any 4 will do. The over-riding consideration for a super-accept is this support for partner's long minor; the overall strength is less important.

When opener super-accepts he promises good support for responder's minor and responder should bid 3NT with a decent suit even if the hand does not quite contain invitational values.

Example 3

West	East	West	East	
♠ AJ4	♠ Q93	1NT	2NT (1)	(1) transfer to ♦'s
♥ AQ6	♥ 95	3♣ (2)	3NT (3)	(2) Let's try 3NT if you have anything remotely decent (a super-accept).
♦ Q53	♦ KJ9862	pass		(3) I'm not ashamed of my hand, Barcus is willing.
♣ QJ108	♣ 97			

A good 3NT contract has been reached on minimal values. Note that the important factor in opener deciding to super-accept or not is not whether he is min or max, but whether he has good cards in responder's suit.

And what happens if responder has a miserable hand and opener super-accepts?
Then responder simply signs off himself: -

1NT - 2♠ - 2NT - 3♣ - pass　　　or　　　1NT - 2NT - 3♣ - 3♦ - pass

Example 4

West	East	West	East	
♠ AJ4	♠ 853	1NT	2NT (1)	(1) transfer to ♦'s
♥ AQ6	♥ 85	3♣ (2)	3♦ (3)	(2) super-accept
♦ Q53	♦ J98762	pass		(3) I'll be happy if I go just one down in 3♦
♣ QJ108	♣ 97			

Responder, of course, may have his sights set on greater things than just 3NT. He is not just limited to 3 of the minor or 3NT, the initial transfer may be any strength and, as we shall see, there are numerous hand types.

Further Development Of The Auction Using 4-way Transfers

Up to now we have only used these transfers to a minor with weak hands. As with major suit transfers, they can be used with stronger hands. Since we are necessarily at the three level there is no room for invitational bids, so any bid by responder after making a minor suit transfer is game forcing. A new suit at a minimal level is natural, and since the hand is necessarily strong the original minor may be just 5 card.

4.2	**The Minor-Major Two Suiter**

Hand A	How do you bid Hand A after partner has opened a strong NT? Some players bid Stayman, and after a 2♦/♥ response a 3♣ bid shows a strong hand and a ♣ suit.
♠ AJ103	But does it also show ♠'s? Enough. There is a much better way to be specific about this
♥ 93	hand type and we need this sequence for our SARS shape ask.
♦ Q9	So we transfer into the minor and subsequently bid 3♠,
♣ AKJ97	I.e. 1NT - 2♠ - 2NT/3♣ - 3♠, showing 5+ ♣'s, 4 ♠'s and game forcing.

Now this is an excellent method and is what I shall be using in the examples but there is one possible improvement that you might like to consider if you are a firm believer that the NT opener should always be declarer. Instead of bidding your 4 card major after the minor suit transfer, you bid the other major (à la Smolen). This has the obvious advantage that opener is declarer but you do lose an awful lot of bidding space when ♥'s are the suit (a transfer to the next suit up is fine, a transfer to the suit below uses a complete bidding level! – that's why I don't like Smolen.). I'll assume the natural approach, thus: -

1NT - 2♠ - 2NT - 3♥/♠	is game forcing and shows 5 ♣'s and 4 ♥/♠'s
1NT - 2♠ - 3♣ - 3♥/♠	is game forcing and shows 5 ♣'s and 4 ♥/♠'s
1NT - 2NT - 3♣ - 3♥/♠	is game forcing and shows 5 ♦'s and 4 ♥/♠'s
1NT - 2NT - 3♦ - 3♥/♠	is game forcing and shows 5 ♦'s and 4 ♥/♠'s

Quite often opener will have no ambitions other than a simple 3NT: -

Example 1

West	East	West	East		West	East
♠ 863	♠ KQ97	1NT	2NT (1)		(1)	transfer to ♦'s
♥ AKQ63	♥ 52	3♦ (2)	3♠ (3)		(2)	normal accept
♦ J3	♦ AK872	3NT	pass		(3)	natural
♣ AJ6	♣ K7					

With poor holdings in both of East's suits, West signs off. But responder may choose to bid on with a stronger hand.

If opener likes responder's 2nd suit then he can make a move towards slam. It's best to play that a cue bid agrees the major suit and if opener is interested in a minor suit slam he should bid 4 of the minor to set trumps. Even if opener has super-accepted the minor suit transfer, it would still be preferable to play in a major suit 4-4 fit.

But one very important decision to make is which bid to use as the RKCB bid. Clearly we will use Kickback for the major, but what about the minor? Which is best, four of the minor or Kickback?

The answer is that it is usually best for responder to be the Blackwood bidder - he knows if slam is in the air and with the more shapely hand it's best for him to ask. So after responder has made his 2nd bid of indicating his major suit then if opener bids the minor then that simply sets trumps (and responder will often bid the next suit up, Kickback). And if opener makes a cue bid (thus agreeing the major) then responder will again use Kickback. If opener bids a major suit it is never RKCB.

Let's try to summarize this: -

Opener's 3rd Bid After Responder Shows A Minor-Major Two Suiter.

After 1NT - 2♠ - 2NT/3♣ - 3♥: -

3♠ = cue bid agreeing ♥'s
3NT = natural
4♣ = agrees ♣'s as trumps
4♦ = cue bid agreeing ♥'s
4♥ = agrees ♥'s as trumps *1

*1 may have the ♣A.

After 1NT - 2♠ - 2NT/3♣ - 3♠: -

3NT = natural
4♣ = agrees ♣'s as trumps
4♦ = cue bid agreeing ♠'s
4♥ = cue bid agreeing ♠'s
4♠ = agrees ♠'s as trumps *1

After 1NT - 2NT - 3♣/♦ - 3♥: -

3♠ = cue bid agreeing ♥'s
3NT = natural
4♣ = cue bid agreeing ♥'s
4♦ = agrees ♦'s as trumps
4♥ = agrees ♥'s as trumps *2

*2 may have the ♦A.

After 1NT - 2NT - 3♣/♦ - 3♠: -

3NT = natural
4♣ = cue bid agreeing ♠'s
4♦ = agrees ♦'s as trumps
4♥ = cue bid agreeing ♠'s
4♠ = agrees ♠'s as trumps *2

A subsequent Kickback bid by responder is RKCB for the suit agreed.

But there is a slight ambiguity if opener bids 3NT at his 3rd turn. Consider the auction 1NT - 2NT - 3♣/♦ - 3♥ - 3NT - 4♥. What is the 4♥ bid? Is it Kickback for ♦'s or setting ♥'s as trumps?

Since responder has only 4 ♥'s and opener may have only two, this is Kickback.

So that's it. The Kickback suit is always RKCB when bid by responder but is natural (or a cue bid) if bid by opener. This is an example of what I mean: -

1NT - 2NT - 3♣/♦ - 3♥ - 3NT - 4♥   is RKCB for ♦'s
1NT - 2NT - 3♣/♦ - 3♥ - 4♣ - 4♥   is to play
1NT - 2NT - 3♣/♦ - 3♥ - 4♣ - 4♠   is RKCB for ♥'s

Example 2

West	East	West	East		
♠ AJ103	♠ KQ97	1NT	2NT (1)	(1)	transfer to ♦'s
♥ AJ9	♥ 52	3♣ (2)	3♠ (3)	(2)	super-accept
♦ Q93	♦ AK872	4♥ (4)	4NT etc to 6♠	(3)	natural
♣ QJ9	♣ K7			(4)	cue bid agreeing ♠'s

The sequence is also game forcing if opener does not super-accept: -

Example 3

West	East	West	East		
♠ AJ103	♠ KQ97	1NT	2NT (1)	(1)	transfer to ♦'s
♥ AJ9	♥ 52	3♦ (2)	3♠ (3)	(2)	simple accept
♦ 953	♦ AK872	4♣ (4)	4♠	(3)	natural
♣ AJ10	♣ K7	pass		(4)	cue bid agreeing ♠'s

Example 4

And responder may push on if opener backs off: -

West	East	West	East		
				(1)	transfer to ♦'s
♠ AJ103	♠ KQ97	1NT	2NT (1)	(2)	simple accept
♥ AJ9	♥ 5	3♦ (2)	3♠ (3)	(3)	natural
♦ 953	♦ AK8762	4♣ (4)	4NT (5)	(4)	cue bid agreeing ♠'s
♣ AJ10	♣ K7	5♣ (6)	6♠	(5)	RKCB
		pass		(6)	3 key cards

Example 5

Or opener may be interested in a minor suit slam: -

West	East	West	East		
♠ J63	♠ KQ97	1NT	2NT (1)	(1)	transfer to ♦'s
♥ AJ9	♥ 5	3♣ (2)	3♠ (3)	(2)	super-accept
♦ QJ93	♦ AK8762	4♦ (3)	4♥ (4)	(3)	natural
♣ AQJ	♣ K7	5♦ (5)	6♦	(4)	RKCB (Kickback)
		pass		(5)	2 key cards + ♦Q

With only an invitational hand it's probably best for responder to transfer to the minor and pass if there is no super-accept.

Example 6

West	East	West	East		
♠ K93	♠ J742	1NT	2♠ (1)	(1)	transfer to ♣'s
♥ AK92	♥ 5	3♣ (2)	pass	(2)	normal accept
♦ AJ92	♦ 103				
♣ J6	♣ AQ9872				

But if opener super-accepts the minor suit transfer then responder should go for game.

Example 7

West	East	West	East		
♠ Q953	♠ J742	1NT	2♠ (1)	(1)	transfer to ♣'s
♥ AQ9	♥ 5	2NT (2)	3NT (3)	(2)	super-accept
♦ AJ9	♦ 103	pass			
♣ K65	♣ AQ9872				

(3) Responder could well bid 3♠ here, but with a long running (after opener has super-accepted) minor suit it may be easier to make 9 tricks in NT as the ♠ suit is rather poor.

It's all very straightforward, I know, but for completeness I'll have to give examples 1-4 (so 8-11 here) from section 2.3 (3) which were so problematic when we did not transfer into the minor: -

Example 8 (1)

West	East 1	East 2	West	East 1	West	East 2
♠ A4	♠ 75	♠ Q1087	1NT	2♠	1NT	2♠
♥ KJ9	♥ Q1087	♥ 75	2NT	3♥	2NT	3♠
♦ A962	♦ K7	♦ K7	4♥	pass	3NT	pass
♣ KJ76	♣ AQ543	♣ AQ543				

When we met these hands earlier West did not know which major East had and so could not play in the Moysian ♥ fit with East 1.

Example 9 (2)

West	East 3	East 4	West	East 3	West	East 4
♠ A4	♠ K5	♠ Q1087	1NT	2♠	1NT	2♠
♥ KJ9	♥ Q1087	♥ 7	2NT	3♥	2NT	3♠
♦ A962	♦ 7	♦ K5	4♣ (1)	etc to 6♣	3NT (2)	pass
♣ KJ76	♣ AQ10543	♣ AQ10543				

(1) West likes East's 2nd suit and so agrees to investigate the ♣ slam.
(2) West does not like East's 2nd suit and so leaves it up to partner to make any further move.

When we met this example before, West had no idea which major East had and so could not investigate slam on the basis of the good ♥'s.

Example 10 (3)

West	East	West	East	
♠ Q743	♠ K8	1NT	2♠	(1) cue bid agreeing ♥'s
♥ AQ74	♥ K963	2NT	3♥	(2) RKCB for ♥'s
♦ A3	♦ 84	4♦ (1)	4♠ (2)	
♣ KJ8	♣ AQ764	etc to 6♥		

When we met this example before the ♥ fit was found immediately but East has no idea about the superb ♣ fit and so quite reasonably simply bid game.

Example 11 (4)

West	East	West	East	
♠ AQ74	♠ K963	1NT	2♠	(1) cue bid agreeing ♠'s
♥ Q743	♥ K8	2NT	3♠	(2) RKCB for ♠'s
♦ A3	♦ 84	4♦ (1)	4NT (2)	
♣ KJ8	♣ AQ764	etc to 6♠		

And much the same here. When we met it before West could do no better that support ♠'s at his 3rd turn and the slam was missed.

4.3   The Minor-Minor Two Suiter

Here we are covering the four sequences: -

Sequence A/B: 1NT - 2♠ - 2NT/3♣ - 3♦   and
Sequence C/D: 1NT - 2NT - 3♣/♦ - 4♣

So what type of hand do we need for a transfer to one minor and then bidding the other? It needs to be pretty strong, of course, as the auction is game forcing. Let's consider a few candidates: -

Hand 1	Hand 2	Hand 3	Hand 4	Hand 5
♠ KQ7	♠ Q8	♠ 87	♠ A	♠ 10
♥ 7	♥ J7	♥ 2	♥ A2	♥ 7
♦ AQ976	♦ KQJ42	♦ Q8752	♦ KJ872	♦ 10986543
♣ KQ98	♣ AQ42	♣ K8752	♣ AQJ76	♣ AKJ4

Hand 1   is strong enough to look for slam but the hand is playable in 3 suits. We come on to this later and a splinter is best with this hand type. We see this hand again in sections 5.2 and 5.4

Hand 2   We saw this hand earlier - example 7 in the SARS section 2.5.2. With just 9 cards in the minors it is usually best to use SARS because: -
   1.   Opener will know that when you do use sequence A or B then you have at least 10 cards in the minors.
   2.   It is easy to locate either a 4-4 ♣ fit or 5-3 ♦ fit (or better) using SARS.
   3.   NT may be the best strain.

Hand 3   We see this hand later (section 5.2) when we come on to discuss the meaning of a direct jump to 3♣. This hand is weak and a convention that I don't like uses the 3♣ bid to show a weak hand 5-5 in the minors. I cover this later, but I would simply pass 1NT. This hand is not strong enough for Sequence A/B which is game forcing.

Hand 4   is typical for sequence A/B. It is looking for slam and we meet this hand soon.

Hand 5   just wants to play in the best minor suit game. So transfer to ♦'s and then bid 4♣. You should then end up in the correct game.

When partner opens 1NT and we only have minor suits then NT is very often the best strain. However, there are exceptions. Typical such exceptions are: -

1) We have a poor hand with no real entries outside a ruff, or possibly too many quick losers in NT.
2) We are looking for slam!

1)   **Let's look at the poor hands first (partner opens a strong NT): -**

Hand A	Hand B	Partner opens 1NT. Hand A is very weak, with no game possibilities.

Partner opens 1NT. Hand A is very weak, with no game possibilities. Best is to simply transfer into ♦'s and play in 3♦, there is no room to subsequently mention the ♣ suit.

Hand B is different. There is good chance of game (5♦ or 5♣) if partner has a suitable hand. So transfer in to ♦'s and then bid 4♣, forcing.

Hand A
♠ 4
♥ 9
♦ J98632
♣ J9842

Hand B
♠ 4
♥ 9
♦ K108632
♣ KJ974

Example 1

West	East (B)	West	East	(1) transfer to ♦'s

♠ J96
♥ AK87
♦ Q4
♣ AQ65

East (B)
♠ 4
♥ 9
♦ K108632
♣ KJ974

West   East
1NT   2NT (1)
3♦ (2)   4♣   (3)
?   (4)

(1) transfer to ♦'s
(2) normal accept
(3) 2nd suit, forcing

Exactly what West should bid at (4) and how the auction stops in 5♣ is covered when we complete this example in section 4.3.3. If partner super-accepts the transfer to ♦'s then responder should still bid 4♣ at (3) as there may be a superior ♣ fit.

2)   **We are looking for slam!**

Hand C   Hand D

Partner again opens a strong NT. This time we have a great two suiter. Partner must have at least 3 card support for one of our minors (he opened 1NT). So we transfer into our longest minor and then bid the other.

Hand C
♠ 4
♥ 9
♦ AK842
♣ KQ9754

Hand D
♠ 4
♥ 9
♦ KQ9754
♣ AK842

Thus we have: -

With Hand C:	1NT - 2♠ - 2NT - 3♦ etc.	Sequence A	(super-accept)
or :	1NT - 2♠ - 3♣ - 3♦ etc.	Sequence B	(normal accept)
With Hand D:	1NT - 2NT - 3♣ - 4♣ etc.	Sequence C	(super-accept)
or :	1NT - 2NT - 3♦ - 4♣ etc.	Sequence D	(normal accept)

We only transfer into a minor and then bid the other when holding 10+ cards in the minors; with 5-4 or 4-5 we would use SARS.

Now we have an idea about suitable hands for sequences A - D, but what are the continuations?

4.3.1   Asking For Aces Or Key Cards When Responder Has A Minor-Minor Two Suiter

After sequence A/B opener or responder may eventually ask for key cards. After sequence C/D it is only responder who may ask – we come onto that shortly. Since responder has at least ten cards in the minors in all of the sequences we need to use DRKCB (or EDRKCB). The actual bid for this ask depends upon the particular sequence, but the replies are as expected: -

After a keycard ask the responses are: -

Next step   =   0 or 3 key cards
Next step + 1 =   1 or 4 key cards
Next step + 2 =   2 or 5 key cards, no ♣Q or ♦Q
Next step + 3 =   2 or 5 key cards + ♣Q or ♦Q or both

After a 0/3 or 1/4 response the next free bid asks for queens. The responses are: -

Next step   =   no queen
Next step + 1 =   ♣Q
Next step + 2 =   ♦Q
Next step + 3 =   both queens

And after a 2/5 response showing a queen, the next free bid asks for clarification: -

Next step   =   ♣Q
Next step + 1 =   ♦Q
Next step + 2 =   both queens

Further Extensions To DRKCB (and EDRKCB)

Now we have seen when looking at the similar 5-5 major suited hands, that the key queens are very important cards, usually more important than a non-key king. But very occasionally asker may need to know about outside kings, the way to ask is that the free bid above a queen ask or queen clarification asks about non-key kings. If the response to DRKCB was 2/5 denying a queen then it's the next free bid that asks for kings. And after a queen ask or clarification and response then the next free bid asks for kings.

The responses to a king ask are: -

Next step   =   no king
Next step + 1 =   ♥K
Next step + 2 =   ♠K
Next step + 3 =   both kings

This king ask is normally only employed when all the key cards and key queens are present and a grand slam is in the offing.

So here we are specifically considering the sequences: -

Sequence A: 1NT - 2♠ - 2NT - 3♦ ... (super-accept)
Sequence B: 1NT - 2♠ - 3♣   - 3♦ ... (normal accept)

It does not matter if opener has super-accepted or not as the continuations are identical.

With Sequence A or B (as opposed to Sequence C or D) we are at a nice low level and either party can describe their hand/get in the appropriate Blackwood bid or whatever in relative ease. Responder's 3♦ bid is forcing to game and typically shows 5-5 or 4-6 or 5-6 in the minors (usually more ♣'s than ♦'s or equal length). Opener has two possible bids below 3NT (3♥ and 3♠) and these will be defined shortly

Opener's options are thus 3♥/♠ (to be defined) 3NT (natural) or 4♣/♦. The 4♣/♦ bids state that 3NT is questionable and that a ♣ or ♦ contract would be preferable.

We will be covering everything in detail shortly, but let's first set the groundwork. Clearly opener will bid 3NT with cover in both majors, but what should opener do if he cannot bid 3NT? Presumably he cannot bid 3NT because he has one or two doubtful majors. In that case he has good cards in one or both minors and slam could well be there if responder has a decent hand. But how should opener continue? What would a 3♥ or 3♠ bid mean?

Without discussion these would probably be cue bids, but with a weak major it is surely best for opener to find out about responder's major suits, in particular shortage.

Here we are specifically concerned with sequence A/B. 3NT is natural. 4♣ and 4♦ are best used to set trumps when opener has no desperate need to establish responder's shortage. These bids generally deny a major suit ace. We shall use 3♥ as the shortage ask and we use 3♠ as a general waiting bid when opener has no 4 card minor (so can't bid 4♣/♦), is not really interested in shortage and cannot bid 3NT. All of this is covered shortly.

So after 1NT - 2♠ - 2NT/3♣ - 3♦   we have: -

3♥   =   shortage ask
3♠   =   a waiting bid
3NT =   natural, both majors covered
4♣   =   ♣'s are trumps
4♦   =   ♦'s are trumps

Here we have 4 distinct bids (4♣ & 4♦ are similar) that opener may make and we will be covering them all in detail in this order: -

4.3.2.1   3NT   - natural, both majors covered.
4.3.2.2   3♥   - shortage ask.
4.3.2.3   4♣/♦   - natural, setting the trump suit
4.3.2.4   3♠   - a waiting bid.

4.3.2.1   <u>3NT - Natural, After Sequence A/B</u>

With cover in both majors, opener tries 3NT: -

Example 1

West	East	West	East		
				(1)	transfer to ♣'s
				(2)	normal accept
♠ AQ64	♠ 9	1NT	2♠ (1)	(3)	2nd suit, forcing
♥ AQ64	♥ 103	3♣ (2)	3♦ (3)	(4)	both majors covered
♦ Q64	♦ A9872	3NT (4)	pass (5)		
♣ K5	♣ AJ874				

(5) East has shown his shape and is more than happy if West has both majors covered and suggests 3NT.

But opener does not really need such robust majors. He should assume that responder has a decent hand and so all he really needs is stops in both majors.

Example 2

West	East	West	East		
				(1)	transfer to ♣'s
				(2)	normal accept
♠ QJ64	♠ 9	1NT	2♠ (1)	(3)	2nd suit, forcing
♥ KJ64	♥ 103	3♣ (2)	3♦ (3)	(4)	both majors covered
♦ KQ4	♦ A9872	3NT (4)	pass		
♣ K5	♣ AJ874				

Very occasionally responder will wish to pull this 3NT to 5 of a minor.

Example 3

West	East	West	East		
				(1)	transfer to ♣'s
				(2)	normal accept
♠ K87	♠ 10	1NT	2♠ (1)	(3)	2nd suit, forcing
♥ AJ10	♥ 7	3♣ (2)	3♦ (3)	(4)	both majors covered
♦ Q753	♦ AKJ4	3NT (4)	5♣ (5)	(5)	pass or correct
♣ AJ2	♣ 10986543	5♦	pass		

But if responder has a strong slam seeking hand he will make a noise over 3NT.

Example 4

West	East	West	East			
					(1)	transfer to ♣'s
					(2)	normal accept
♠ QJ64	♠ 9	1NT	2♠	(1)	(3)	2nd suit, forcing
♥ KJ64	♥ A	3♣ (2)	3♦	(3)	(4)	both majors covered
♦ KQ4	♦ A9872	3NT (4)	?	(5)		
♣ K5	♣ AQ8764					

Now the continuations after 3NT when responder wishes to look for slam have to be defined: -

After 1NT - 2♠ - 2NT/3♣ - 3♦ - 3NT we have: -

4♣ = DRKCB
4♦ =
4♥ = EDRKCB
4♠ = EDRKCB
4NT = quantitative
5♣ = pass or correct

Example 4 cont.

	West	East			
	3NT (4)	4♣	(5)	(5)	DRKCB
	4NT (6)	6♣		(6)	2 key cards + a queen
	6♦	pass			

Example 5

West	East	West	East			
					(1)	transfer to ♣'s
					(2)	super-accept
♠ QJ64	♠ -	1NT	2♠	(1)	(3)	2nd suit, forcing
♥ KQ6	♥ A	2NT (2)	3♦	(3)	(4)	both majors covered
♦ KQ4	♦ A98762	3NT (4)	4♠	(5)	(5)	EDRKCB
♣ K52	♣ AJ8764	5♥ (6)	5♠	(7)	(6)	2 key cards + a queen
		6♣ (8)	6♦	(9)	(7)	clarify queens
		pass			(8)	♦Q only

East is not certain about the grand at (9) — he was hoping for a two queen reply. He knows that West has the ♦KQx(x) and that the ♣Q is missing. There is no real way to establish if the ♣K is doubleton or not and so stopping in 6♦ is very sensible.

Now very occasionally (when both key queens are present) responder may wish to ask for major suit kings.

Example 6

West	East	West		East		(1) transfer to ♣'s
						(2) normal accept
♠ QJ64	♠ A	1NT		2♠	(1)	(3) 2nd suit, forcing
♥ QJ64	♥ A2	3♣	(2)	3♦	(3)	(4) both majors covered
♦ AQ4	♦ KJ872	3NT	(4)	4♣	(5)	(5) DRKCB
♣ K5	♣ AQJ76	4NT	(6)	5♠	(7)	(6) 2 key cards + a queen
		5NT	(8)	6NT		(7) non-key kings?
		pass				(8) neither

If East had bid 5♥ at (7) then that would ask for clarification of queens. So the next free bid asks for kings (confirming that all key cards and key queens are present). Either major suit king would have been enough for the grand.

Sometimes responder will have to ask for queens before a king ask.

Example 7

West	East	West		East		(1) transfer to ♣'s
						(2) normal accept
♠ K964	♠ A	1NT		2♠	(1)	(3) 2nd suit, forcing
♥ Q864	♥ A2	3♣	(2)	3♦	(3)	(4) both majors covered
♦ AK4	♦ Q10872	3NT	(4)	4♣	(5)	(5) DRKCB
♣ KQ	♣ AJ976	4♦	(6)	4♥	(7)	(6) 3 key cards
		4NT	(8)	5♥	(9)	(7) queens?
		6♣	(10)	7NT		(8) ♣Q only
		pass				(9) non-key kings?
						(10) ♠K

Note the importance of playing DRKCB as opposed to RKCB. East needed to establish both the ♦K,Q and the ♣Q before investigating the grand.

3♥ - The Shortage Ask After Sequence A/B.

Let's see how the shortage ask works. Responder has at least 10 cards in the minors (with 5-4 or 4-5 he uses SARS) and so has at most 3 cards in the majors.

after 1NT - 2♠ - 2NT/3♣ - 3♦,   3♥ enquires about responder's shortage: -

3♠	=	singleton ♥
3NT	=	singleton ♠
4♣	=	void ♥
4♦	=	void ♠
4♥	=	EDRKCB
4♠	=	EDRKCB
4NT	=	DRKCB
5♣	=	no slam interest – pass or correct.

Responder uses the 4♥/♠/NT bids when he has a hand that is too strong to allow opener to take charge (a possible grand slam).

> **Warning:** This shortage ask and the 3♠ waiting bid are something new and unless you have agreed it, most players would take them as a cue bids. Be very careful. If you (or your partner) are likely to forget this convention (and make a cue bid) then skip this section!

If opener bids 4♥ after ascertaining the shortage this is DRKCB.

Example 1

West	East	West	East			
					(1)	transfer to ♣'s
					(2)	super-accept
♠ J72	♠ 9	1NT	2♠	(1)	(3)	2nd suit, forcing
♥ AJ7	♥ 63	2NT	(2) 3♦	(3)	(4)	shortage?
♦ KQ64	♦ A8732	3♥	(4) 3NT	(5)	(5)	singleton ♠
♣ AQ5	♣ KJ874	4♥	(6) 5♣	(7)	(6)	DRKCB
		6♦	pass		(7)	2 key cards, no queen

That clearly works fine. But after a response to the shortage ask that defines the singleton/void opener may wish to show no further slam interest. This is easy when the response is at a low level (4♣/♦ = no slam interest and 4♥ = DRKCB) but if 4♣/♦ are not available then we have to define the no slam interest bids. Simple, we use 5♣/♦ when the 4 level is unavailable. Thus we have: -

After 1NT - 2♠ - 2NT/3♣ - 3♦ - 3♥: -

Responder replies: -			Opener's next bid: -				
3♠	=	singleton ♥	→	4♥	=	DRKCB,	4♣/4♦	=	no slam interest
3NT	=	singleton ♠	→	4♥	=	DRKCB,	4♣/4♦	=	no slam interest
4♣	=	void ♥	→	4♥	=	DRKCB,	5♣/4♦	=	no slam interest
4♦	=	void ♠	→	4♥	=	DRKCB,	5♣/5♦	=	no slam interest

After any of the 'no slam interest' bids by opener, 4♥ by responder is always DRKCB. Now there would appear to be a problem when opener has bid 5♣ or 5♦. But actually there is not; if responder has a void and is still interested in slam after opener has signed off opposite the void, then responder has a hand strong enough that he should have 'broken' the shortage ask by bidding EDRKCB over opener's 3♥ bid.

Example 2

West	East	West		East		
♠ J72	♠ 63	1NT		2♠	(1)	(1) transfer to ♣'s
♥ AJ7	♥ 9	2NT	(2)	3♦	(3)	(2) super-accept
♦ KQ64	♦ A8732	3♥	(4)	3♠	(5)	(3) 2nd suit, forcing
♣ AQ5	♣ KJ874	4♦	(6)	5♦		(4) shortage?
		pass				(5) singleton ♥
						(6) wrong shortage

Example 3

West	East	West		East		
♠ J72	♠ A3	1NT		2♠	(1)	(1) transfer to ♣'s
♥ AJ7	♥ 9	2NT	(2)	3♦	(3)	(2) super-accept
♦ KQ64	♦ A8732	3♥	(4)	3♠	(5)	(3) 2nd suit, forcing
♣ AQ5	♣ KJ874	4♦	(6)	4♥	(7)	(4) shortage?
		4♠	(8)	4NT	(9)	(5) singleton ♥
		5♠	(10)	6♦ or 6NT	(11)	(6) wrong shortage
		pass				(7) DRKCB
						(8) 3 key cards
						(9) queens?
						(10) both

(11) East knows that 7♦ may well make, but not if West is 4243.

185

With a rock crusher responder cannot let opener take control and so he has to 'break the shortage ask' by bidding DRKCB or EDRKCB over the 3♥ shortage ask. Remember, responder knows that opener is interested in at least one of the minor suits (not necessarily ♣'s even after a super-accept) and has a major suit ace when making a shortage ask.

Example 4

West	East	West	East		
				(1)	transfer to ♣'s
				(2)	super-accept
♠ J72	♠ AK	1NT	2♠ (1)	(3)	2nd suit, forcing
♥ AJ7	♥ 9	2NT (2)	3♦ (3)	(4)	shortage?
♦ KQ64	♦ A8732	3♥ (4)	4NT (5)	(5)	DRKCB
♣ AQ5	♣ KJ874	5♣ (6)	5♥ (7)	(6)	3 key cards
		6♦ (8)	7♣ (9)	(7)	queens?
		7♦	pass	(8)	both
				(9)	pass or correct

And when responder has a void and wants to take control, it's EDRKCB.

Example 5

West	East	West	East		
				(1)	transfer to ♣'s
				(2)	super-accept
♠ J72	♠ -	1NT	2♠ (1)	(3)	2nd suit, forcing
♥ AJ7	♥ KQ	2NT (2)	3♦ (3)	(4)	shortage?
♦ KQ64	♦ A8732	3♥ (4)	4♠ (5)	(5)	EDRKCB
♣ AQ5	♣ KJ8764	4NT (6)	5♥ (7)	(6)	3 key cards
		6♦ (8)	7♣	(7)	queens?
		7♦	pass	(8)	both

When responder wants to settle in 5 of a minor he should bid 5♣ and offer opener the choice of minor suit.

Example 6

West	East	West	East		
				(1)	transfer to ♣'s
				(2)	normal accept
♠ Q87	♠ 6	1NT	2♠ (1)	(3)	2nd suit, forcing
♥ AJ10	♥ 7	3♣ (2)	3♦ (3)	(4)	shortage?
♦ K7532	♦ AQ84	3♥ (4)	5♣ (5)	(5)	pass or correct
♣ AJ	♣ 10986543	5♦	pass		

(5) East cannot be sure which suit West likes. It's probably ♦'s but it could just be ♣'s. East wants to play in game in the best one and so bids 5♣ which West will correct.

4♣/♦ - Setting The Trump Suit After Sequence A/B.

When West has reasonable holdings in both majors there is little point in asking for shortage (and he should have a ♥/♠ ace for the shortage ask). If the majors are not good enough for 3NT then he has to find another bid. With definite preference for one minor (a 4 card suit) then he bids 4 of the minor to set trumps: -

Example 1

West	East	West		East		
						(1) transfer to ♣'s
						(2) super-accept
♠ QJ2	♠ 63	1NT		2♠	(1)	(3) 2nd suit, forcing
♥ Q84	♥ 9	2NT	(2)	3♦	(3)	(4) I prefer ♦'s
♦ KQ65	♦ A8732	4♦	(4)	5♦		
♣ AQ5	♣ KJ874	pass				

Note that it is unlikely that West has a major suit ace when he bids 4♣/♦ as he would normally then ask for shortage.

When opener bids 4♣/♦ over 3♦ it sets the trump suit (although we still use DRKCB of course). It's easiest on the memory if we use 4♥/♠ as the EDRKCB bids.

After 1NT - 2♠ - 2NT/3♣ - 3♦ - 4♣

4♦	=	DRKCB
4♥	=	EDRKCB
4♠	=	EDRKCB

After 1NT - 2♠ - 2NT/3♣ - 3♦ - 4♦

4♥	=	EDRKCB
4♠	=	EDRKCB
4NT	=	DRKCB

Example 2

West	East	West		East		
						(1) transfer to ♣'s
						(2) super-accept
♠ QJ6	♠ A3	1NT		2♠	(1)	(3) 2nd suit, forcing
♥ QJ5	♥ 2	2NT	(2)	3♦	(3)	(4) I prefer ♦'s
♦ AJ96	♦ KQ732	4♦	(4)	4NT	(5)	(5) DRKCB
♣ AJ5	♣ KQ987	5♥	(6)	6♦		(6) 2 key cards, no queen
		pass				

3♠ - A Waiting Bid After Sequence A/B.

When opener makes the 'waiting' 3♠ bid then the onus is back on responder. The 3♠ bid generally denies a major suit ace (otherwise opener would ask for shortage) and also denies good enough majors to bid 3NT. Responder will often sign off in five of a minor. But with a good hand (either a major suit ace or a void) he may press on. The responses to the 'waiting' 3♠ are: -

after 1NT - 2♠ - 2NT/3♣ - 3♦ - 3♠ we have: -

3NT	=	DRKCB
4♣	=	EDRKCB (♥'s)
4♦	=	EDRKCB (♠'s)
4♥	=	
4♠	=	
4NT	=	please bid 5♣ or 5♦

Example 1

Here West has a holding not good enough for 3NT and so with no definite preference for either minor he passes the buck with a 'waiting' 3♠ bid: -

West	East	West	East			
					(1)	transfer to ♣'s
					(2)	super-accept
♠ Q92	♠ 63	1NT	2♠	(1)	(3)	2nd suit, forcing
♥ QJ64	♥ -	2NT	(2) 3♦	(3)	(4)	waiting
♦ KQ6	♦ A8753	3♠	(4) 4NT	(5)	(5)	please bid 5♣ or 5♦
♣ AQ5	♣ KJ8742	5♣	pass			

The 3♠ waiting bid is generally not interested in slam, just the best minor suit game. But East may have a more powerful hand: -

Example 2

West	East	West	East			
					(1)	transfer to ♣'s
					(2)	super-accept
♠ Q92	♠ A	1NT	2♠	(1)	(3)	2nd suit, forcing
♥ QJ42	♥ 3	2NT	(2) 3♦	(3)	(4)	waiting
♦ KQ6	♦ A8753	3♠	(4) 3NT	(5)	(5)	DRKCB
♣ AQ5	♣ K98742	4♠	(6) 4NT	(7)	(6)	2 key cards + a queen
		5♥	(8) 6♣	(9)	(7)	clarify queens
		pass			(8)	both
					(9)	pass or correct

The Continuations After Sequence C/D,   1NT - 2NT - 3♣/♦ - 4♣

So here we are considering the sequences: -

Sequence C: 1NT - 2NT - 3♣   - 4♣ ...   (super-accept)
Sequence D: 1NT - 2NT - 3♦   - 4♣ ...   (normal accept)

With big hands and equal length minors (5-5) it is best to transfer into ♣'s as there is then more bidding space to investigate slam.

So here responder has more ♦'s than ♣'s, usually 6 ♦'s and 4 or 5 ♣'s. But note that with a good hand with 6 ♦'s and 5 ♣'s it may well be best to use sequence A/B as there is so much more room for investigating slam.

After   1NT - 2NT - 3♣/♦ - 4♣, opener does not know if responder is weak or not. What's more there is precious little room and opener cannot bid much higher because responder needs room for a possible Blackwood bid. If opener were to bid 4NT then 5♣ or 5♦ by responder would be a sign off and so there is no room for Blackwood. Responder could elect to use Sequence A or B of course when everything is simple. But if responder has longer ♦'s than ♣'s and slam interest he may choose the more space consuming route in order to emphasise his ♦'s.

Hand E	Take Hand E for example. Partner has opened 1NT and this hand wants to be in slam. 6 or 7♣ will be fine with a 4 card ♣ fit, but with no ♣ fit a 6-3♦ fit will do nicely.
♠ -	So this hand really has to use Sequence C/D. Now it is also possible to bid SARS or a
♥ A73	splinter with this type of hand and I would not argue (but the ♥'s are a bit too weak for
♦ KJ9754	a splinter), but most people would prefer the more natural approach to emphasise their
♣ AK84	good suits, so transfer into the long suit and then bid the other.

As it certainly is possible that responder has slam in mind and needs bidding space opener cannot bid too high. Thus we restrict opener's next bid to 4♦; this is a simple waiting bid. This then leaves responder maximum room to investigate slam.

After the 4♦ waiting bid responder's options are: -

4♥   =   EDRKCB
4♠   =   EDRKCB
4NT =   DRKCB
5♣   =   pass or correct

Example 1   An example from a club teams event. 3NT was reached at one table and 5♦ at the other (neither were successful). The bidding given shows how the best contract can be reached if you play 4-way transfers.

West	East	West	East
♠ K87	♠ 10	1NT	2NT (1)
♥ AJ10	♥ 7	3♦ (2)	4♣ (3)
♦ AJ	♦ 10986543	4♦ (4)	5♣ (5)
♣ Q7532	♣ AKJ4	pass	

(1) transfer to ♦'s
(2) not quite good enough to super-accept
(3) ♦-♣ two suiter, game forcing
(4) forced (waiting)
(5) East signs off. He bids 5♣ which West will normally correct to 5♦ unless he has 4+ ♣'s.

Note that in this sequence East may be weak(ish) and West cannot take control (with DRKCB or whatever). The 4♦ bid at (4) is mandatory.

If opener has a very suitable hand he may occasionally over-rule responder's decision to sign off in 5 of a minor. Opener knows that responder probably has a singleton in each major.

Example 2

West	East	West	East
♠ J7	♠ 10	1NT	2NT (1)
♥ AJ10	♥ 7	3♣ (2)	4♣ (3)
♦ AK2	♦ 10986543	4♦ (4)	5♣ (5)
♣ Q7532	♣ AKJ4	6♣ (6)	pass

(1) transfer to ♦'s
(2) super-accept
(3) ♦-♣ two suiter, game forcing
(4) forced (waiting)
(5) East signs off.
(6) With excellent minors and a major suit ace, 6♣ is a good bet.

Example 3 But it will very often be responder who is looking for slam: -

West	East	West	East		(1) transfer to ♦'s
					(2) normal accept
♠ K875	♠ 4	1NT	2NT	(1)	(3) 2nd suit, forcing
♥ AJ10	♥ 9	3♦ (2)	4♣	(3)	(4) waiting
♦ AJ	♦ KQ9754	4♦ (4)	4NT	(5)	(5) DRKCB
♣ Q753	♣ AK842	5♥ (6)	6♣	(7)	(6) 2 key cards + a queen
		pass			(7) pass or correct

Example 4 With a void, responder uses EDRKCB: -

West	East	West	East		(1) transfer to ♦'s
					(2) normal accept
♠ K875	♠ -	1NT	2NT	(1)	(3) 2nd suit, forcing
♥ KJ10	♥ A73	3♦ (2)	4♣	(3)	(4) waiting
♦ AQ	♦ KJ9754	4♦ (4)	4♠	(5)	(5) EDRKCB
♣ Q753	♣ AK84	5♣ (6)	5♥	(7)	(6) 1 key card
		6♦ (8)	7♣	(9)	(7) queens?
		pass			(8) both
					(9) pass or correct

Finally, remember this example 1 from the start of section 4.3 (page 178)? We now know how East signs off in 5 of a minor: -

Example 1(4.3) cont.

West	East (B)	West	East		(1) transfer to ♦'s
					(2) normal accept
♠ J96	♠ 4	1NT	2NT	(1)	(3) 2nd suit, forcing
♥ AK87	♥ 9	3♦ (2)	4♣	(3)	(4) waiting
♦ Q4	♦ K108632	4♦ (4)	5♣	(5)	(5) pass or correct
♣ AQ65	♣ KJ974	pass			

But make the West hand slightly more suitable and he could go on to slam: -

West	East (B)	West	East		(1) transfer to ♦'s
					(2) normal accept
♠ A96	♠ 4	1NT	2NT	(1)	(3) 2nd suit, forcing
♥ A876	♥ 9	3♦ (2)	4♣	(3)	(4) waiting
♦ QJ	♦ K108632	4♦ (4)	5♣	(5)	(5) pass or correct
♣ AQ65	♣ KJ974	6♣	pass		

The Single Minor Suited Hand

Partner opens 1NT, we have a long minor suit and immediately have options. We have already met a few of these: -

1 - pass 1NT
2 - transfer into our minor and then pass
3 - invite 3NT by bidding 2NT (via Stayman as we play 4-way transfers)
4 - transfer into our minor and then bid 3NT only over a super-accept
5 - bid 3NT directly
6 - transfer into our minor and then bid 3NT
7 - transfer into our minor and then bid 5 of the minor
8 - bid a quantitative 4NT directly
9 - transfer into our minor and then bid a quantitative 4NT
10 - transfer into our minor and then splinter
11 - transfer into our minor and then ask about key cards
12 - ask about aces directly (Gerber)

Let's have a quick example of each. Partner opens a strong NT: -

Hand 1	Hand 2	Hand 3	
♠ J63	♠ K7	♠ J76	Hand 1 has no ambitions and 1NT is probably better than 3♦, so pass.
♥ 64	♥ 93	♥ 93	Hand 2 will play better in ♦'s. So transfer and pass 3♦ (convert a super-accept 3♣ into 3♦).
♦ K8563	♦ J109765	♦ KJ975	Hand 3 invites, so 2NT (via 2♣).
♣ Q52	♣ 742	♣ K42	

Hand 4	Hand 5	Hand 6	
♠ Q93	♠ Q93	♠ J3	Hand 4 transfers and then bids 3NT only if partner super-accepts.
♥ 95	♥ Q5	♥ K6	Hand 5 simply bids 3NT without transferring.
♦ KJ9862	♦ KQ6532	♦ KQJ876	Hand 6 is stronger. Slam is possible so transfer and then bid 3NT over a normal accept.
♣ 97	♣ 97	♣ K64	

Hand 7	Hand 8	Hand 9	
♠ -	♠ A6	♠ A6	Hand 7. Anything could be right, but 5♦ is probably a good bet. So transfer and bid it, or maybe bid 5♦ directly.
♥ J5	♥ KJ3	♥ J85	Hand 8 does not want to emphasise this ♦ suit.
♦ QJ1086432	♦ K9864	♦ AQJ96	He could (should) have tried SARS. I guess a quantitative 4NT is not unreasonable?
♣ J73	♣ KJ2	♣ K42	Hand 9 is similar but has a decent ♦ suit, so transfer and then bid a quantitative 4NT.

Hand 10	Hand 11	Hand 12	
			Hand 10 is also slam invitational, but with a singleton we indicate this by splintering.
♠ K85	♠ A	♠ A	
♥ 4	♥ KQ	♥ A	Hand 11 transfers and then bids RKCB (4♦).
♦ AQ9765	♦ QJ98752	♦ KQJ9862	Hand 12 only needs to know about aces, so 4♣ Gerber directly.
♣ J95	♣ KQJ	♣ KQJ10	

Minor Suit Transfer Followed By 3NT

Suppose partner opens a strong NT and we have an excellent hand containing a good long minor suit. One traditional method is to bid 3 of our minor, game forcing and looking for slam. However we now have 4-way transfers and can show these hand types by transferring first. This has a number of advantages: -

1) The NT bidder gets to play the hand more often, whether game or slam.
2) Responder knows immediately if opener has good support for the minor (he will super-accept).
3) It frees the direct jumps for another purpose (see 5.2).

Hand A	Hand B	Hand C	
♠ J3	♠ A6	♠ K7	All of these hands are worthy of an attempt at slam and directly bidding the suit at the three level is a way to handle these strong hands. However, they can all be satisfactorily dealt with using transfers and we have another use for the direct 3 level bids - see 5.2.
♥ K6	♥ 93	♥ A93	
♦ K64	♦ AQJ654	♦ AKJ762	
♣ KQJ876	♣ K64	♣ 64	

So, with these big hands with a minor suit, we transfer. If partner super-accepts then we either bid 3NT or we can investigate slam. 4NT is quantitative (see next section). You have to decide which bids are RKCB; we will continue to use Kickback.

Unlike previous sections, there is a difference when opener has super-accepted. If opener has super-accepted then a 3NT bid by responder means that he needed the additional help from opener. If there was no super-accept then why didn't responder bid 3NT directly over 1NT? The answer is that his hand is too good and the sequence is mildly slam invitational.

So let's start with the super-accept as that's simplest,

1NT - 2♠ - 2NT - 3NT   and   1NT - 2NT - 3♣ - 3NT.

This really is the main point of having the super-accept. If opener has three to an honour in the transfer suit he should super-accept and responder will bid 3NT with a decent suit/hand: -

Example 1

West	East	West	East		
				(1) transfer to ♣'s	
				(2) super-accept	
♠ KJ7	♠ 86	1NT	2♠	(1)	
♥ AJ105	♥ 96	2NT (2)	3NT		
♦ AJ105	♦ 642	pass			
♣ K95	♣ AQ8762				

East can be sure of 6 ♣ tricks and so it only remains for West to find 3 tricks elsewhere.

Now let's move on to when opener has made a normal accept,

1NT - 2♠ - 3♣ - 3NT   and   1NT - 2NT - 3♦ - 3NT

Opener may pass. If he wishes to investigate slam then he can bid Kickback. If he has a hand unsuitable for Blackwood (a weak suit) then he can bid 4 of the minor which invites responder to bid Kickback with a suitable hand or else cue bid.

Example 2

West	East	West	East		
				(1)	transfer to ♣'s
				(2)	normal accept
♠ KQ74	♠ J3	1NT	2♠ (1)	(3)	looking for slam
♥ AJ105	♥ K6	3♣ (2)	3NT (3)	(4)	I'm minimum
♦ AJ	♦ K64	pass (4)			
♣ 952	♣ KQJ876				

This East hand is a bit light to look for slam, but it is worth it if opener has the right cards, a good long suit is a big plus: -

Example 3

West	East	West	East		
				(1)	transfer to ♣'s
				(2)	normal accept
♠ A1074	♠ J3	1NT	2♠ (1)	(3)	looking for slam
♥ AQ9	♥ K6	3♣ (2)	3NT (3)	(4)	RKCB
♦ AQJ	♦ K64	4♦ (4)	etc to 6♣		
♣ 952	♣ KQJ876				

Example 4

West	East	West	East		
				(1)	transfer to ♣'s
				(2)	normal accept
♠ J74	♠ A	1NT	2♠ (1)	(3)	looking for slam
♥ AKQ9	♥ 864	3♣ (2)	3NT (3)	(4)	slam interest
♦ AQ3	♦ K64	4♣ (4)	4♦ (5)	(5)	RKCB
♣ 952	♣ KQJ876	etc to 6♣			

West did not want to bid RKCB at (4) because of potential ♠ losers off the top.

4.4.2   Minor Suit Transfer Followed By 4NT

This is clearly quantitative, but there is a distinction between hands where opener has super-accepted and those where he has not. The difference is that after a normal accept then 3NT is already slam invitational (because responder would have simply bid 3NT over 1NT if he had no slam ambitions). But after a super-accept 3NT simply means that responder needs help in the minor for 3NT.

Note that we do not generally bid 4NT with a singleton, but prefer a slam invitational splinter (see 4.4.4).

Let's start with the situation after a super-accept. Responder simply has a slam invitational hand.

So   1NT - 2♠ - 2NT - 4NT   and   1NT - 2NT - 3♣ - 4NT.

Example 1

West	East	West	East	
				(1) transfer to ♣'s
				(2) super-accept
♠ KJ74	♠ 65	1NT	2♠ (1)	(3) quantitative
♥ A9	♥ K6	2NT (2)	4NT (3)	
♦ AQ32	♦ K64	6♣	pass	
♣ K52	♣ AQJ876			

With a max and good top cards, opener has no problem in accepting the slam invitation.

Example 2

West	East	West	East	
				(1) transfer to ♣'s
				(2) super-accept
♠ KJ74	♠ 65	1NT	2♠ (1)	(3) quantitative
♥ AJ	♥ K6	2NT (2)	4NT (3)	
♦ QJ32	♦ K64	pass (4)		
♣ K52	♣ AQJ876			

But this West hand is minimum and so declines the invitation. A pass of 4NT is probably better than bidding 5♣ (to play).

195

That's pretty straightforward, so let's look at the situation after a normal accept, this time responder has a very good hand as 3NT is already slam invitational.

So   1NT - 2♠ - 3♣ - 4NT   and   1NT - 2NT - 3♦ - 4NT.
_____

Example 3

West	East	West	East		(1) transfer to ♣'s
					(2) normal accept
♠ KJ74	♠ 65	1NT	2♠	(1)	(3) quantitative
♥ AQ9	♥ KJ	3♣	(2)	4NT (3)	
♦ AQ32	♦ K64	pass			
♣ 52	♣ AKJ1076				

With no more than a bare minimum and very poor ♣'s, West cannot accept the slam invitation.
_____

Example 4

West	East	West	East		(1) transfer to ♣'s
					(2) normal accept
♠ K974	♠ 65	1NT	2♠	(1)	(3) quantitative
♥ A92	♥ KJ	3♣	(2)	4NT (3)	
♦ AQ32	♦ K64	6NT	pass		
♣ Q2	♣ AKJ1076				

Here West is absolutely minimum, but 4NT is extremely encouraging and this time the ♣Q is a golden card; that's what makes the difference.

4.4.3   Minor Suit Transfer Followed By 4 Of The Minor

Hand A	Hand B	Hand C	These hands are too good to simply rebid 3NT after transferring. The answer is to transfer and then bid the minor at the 4 level. This shows an excellent hand, looking for slam. Since we have gone past 3NT responder must have very strong slam ambitions.
♠ 6	♠ A6	♠ 64	
♥ K6	♥ 9	♥ K93	
♦ AK4	♦ AKQJ654	♦ AKQJ76	
♣ KQJ8762	♣ K64	♣ K6	

Now here we have a slight problem. We have a very big single suited hand, seriously looking for slam (whether opener has super-accepted or not). But we are rather high and we do not wish our RKCB bid to be above the Kickback level. You could choose to use Kickback, but we really need the Kickback suit as a splinter (next section).

The answer is that 4 of the minor is also RKCB.

So here we are concerned with the sequences: -

1NT - 2♠ - 2NT/3♣ - 4♣   and   1NT - 2NT - 3♣/♦ - 4♦

Example 1

West	East	West	East		
				(1)	transfer to ♦'s
				(2)	normal accept
♠ KQJ4	♠ A6	1NT	2NT (1)	(3)	long ♦'s, RKCB
♥ QJ7	♥ 9	3♦ (2)	4♦ (3)		
♦ 973	♦ AKQJ654	etc to 6♦			
♣ AQJ	♣ K64				

Example 2

West	East	West	East		
				(1)	transfer to ♦'s
				(2)	normal accept
♠ KJ53	♠ Q4	1NT	2NT (1)	(3)	long ♦'s, RKCB
♥ AQ74	♥ K93	3♦ (2)	4♦ (3)		
♦ 953	♦ AKQJ76	etc to 6♦ or 6NT			
♣ AJ	♣ K6				

Note that some experts state that 4 of the minor in the sequences 1NT - 2♠ - 2NT/3♣ - 4♣ and 1NT - 2NT - 3♣/♦ - 4♦ is invitational. This, in my view, is nonsense. There are not many hands where you would want to invite 5♣/♦ and possibly play in 4♣/♦ instead of 3NT.

When one asks for key cards and there are two missing, it is usually preferable to stop in 4NT rather than 5 of the minor, especially at matchpoint scoring.

Example 3

West	East	West		East		(1) transfer to ♦'s
						(2) normal accept
♠ QJ105	♠ K4	1NT		2NT	(1)	(3) long ♦'s, RKCB
♥ AKJ	♥ Q103	3♦	(2)	4♦	(3)	(4) 1 key card
♦ J53	♦ KQ10976	4♠	(4)	4NT	(5)	(5) sign off
♣ KJ3	♣ AQ	pass				

Using 4-of-the-minor as RKCB means that it is virtually always possible to sign off in 4NT. The only possible exception is with ♦'s as trumps and when opener has two key cards plus the ♦Q: -

Example 4

West	East	West		East		(1) transfer to ♦'s
						(2) super-accept
♠ KJ52	♠ Q4	1NT		2NT	(1)	(3) long ♦'s, RKCB
♥ AJ10	♥ KQ3	3♣	(2)	4♦	(3)	(4) 2 key cards + ♦Q
♦ Q53	♦ KJ10976	5♣	(4)	5♦	(5)	(5) sign off
♣ AJ3	♣ KQ	pass				

4.4.4   **Splinters After A Minor Suit Transfer**

Hand A

♠ K85
♥ 4
♦ J95
♣ AQ9765

This hand comes from a club competition, how do you bid it after partner opens 1NT? Obviously you start with a 2♠ transfer to ♣'s and suppose that partner super-accepts with 2NT. What now? You have a slam invitational hand and probably the deciding factor is the ♥ singleton. Partner needs to know this.

So, after a minor suit transfer we need splinters whether opener has super- accepted or not. It's best to play these splinters as slam invitational, i.e. not as strong as the hands in section 4.4.3 where we launched into RKCB.

Thus we have: -

After 1NT - 2♠ - 2NT/3♣ ,

4♦	=	♦ shortage
4♥	=	♥ shortage
4♠	=	♠ shortage

After 1NT - 2NT - 3♣/♦ ,

4♥	=	♥ shortage
4♠	=	♠ shortage
5♣	=	♣ shortage

Example 1   This is the actual hand from the club. If opener likes the shortage he can check for keycards (next free bid – if there is one below 4NT) or simply bid slam.

West	East	West	East		
♠ A97	♠ K85	1NT	2♠	(1)	(1) transfer to ♣'s
♥ 762	♥ 4	2NT (2)	4♥	(3)	(2) super-accept
♦ AKQ7	♦ J95	4♠ (4)	5♣	(5)	(3) ♥ shortage
♣ K108	♣ AQ9765	6♣	pass		(4) RKCB
					(5) 1 key card

Example 2   But with wasted values he signs off.

West	East	West	East	
♠ A74	♠ K85	1NT	2NT (1)	(1) transfer to ♦'s
♥ K62	♥ 4	3♣ (2)	4♥ (3)	(2) super-accept
♦ K108	♦ AQ9765	5♦	pass	(3) ♥ shortage
♣ KQ72	♣ J95			

Example 3   And sometimes 4NT may be better than 5 of the minor.

West	East	West	East	
♠ AJ7	♠ K85	1NT	2♠ (1)	(1) transfer to ♣'s
♥ AQ72	♥ 4	3♣ (2)	4♥ (3)	(2) normal accept
♦ K1072	♦ J95	4NT	pass	(3) ♥ shortage
♣ K10	♣ AQ9765			

Minor Suit Transfer Followed By 5 Of The Minor

If you transfer and then bid 5 of the minor then you have bypassed 3NT and used up valuable bidding space. I guess that the only excuse can be that 5 of the minor is probably the only viable game contract and slam is remote?

So here we are concerned with the sequences: -

1NT - 2♠ - 2NT/3♣ - 5♣   and   1NT - 2NT - 3♣/♦ - 5♦

Example 1

West	East	West	East		
				(1)	transfer to ♦'s
				(2)	normal accept
♠ Q953	♠ -	1NT	2NT (1)	(3)	to play
♥ AQ74	♥ J5	3♦ (2)	5♦ (3)		
♦ 95	♦ QJ1086432				
♣ AKQ	♣ J73				

There are no guarantees, of course. Sometimes game will fail and very occasionally a slam will be missed. But 5 of the minor is generally a good bet on hands like this, especially if played by West. Remember, opener has denied Axx or Kxx by not super-accepting.

A perhaps preferable alternative is to simply bid 5♦ at (1).

****

Any Disadvantages With 4-way Transfers?

Now every convention gives up something (the use of the bid as natural). Here we have used 2NT as a transfer but have overcome any obstacles. So any drawbacks? There are a couple. Since you cannot bid a direct invitational 2NT but have to go via Stayman then the opponents will learn about opener's (and so probably declarer's) shape. Also, the 2♣ bid may be doubled for a lead or whatever. A small price to pay for such a powerful convention.

Alternatives

Some players prefer to have the super-accept and normal accept of minor suit transfers the other way round. This has the advantage that opener is declarer in many high level contracts (but not all). But it has the disadvantage that opener will not be declarer in so many part-scores! Swings and roundabouts. Let's keep it simple and play the 'standard' way.

5 **3 Level Responses**

So, at last, that's Stayman and Jacoby Transfers completely finished with. Let's next consider all direct jumps to the 3 level after partner's 1NT opening. We start with the easy one, 3NT.

5.1 The Direct 3NT

Values for game but insufficient for a slam try. Since Stayman was not used, then obviously no 4 card major? We have been all through this before; I have strong views about when denying a 4 card major is allowed.

Hand A	Hand B	Hand C	Partner opens a strong NT, what do you do?
♠ KQ3	♠ J963	♠ A107	Hand A is a simple 3NT – game values, no 4 card major.
♥ KJ4	♥ AQ3	♥ A1053	Hand B is a classic example of the rare occasion when a 4 card major should be by-passed. Plenty of points, with all outside suits well protected.
♦ Q64	♦ KJ7	♦ J42	
♣ J1094	♣ K102	♣ 1094	Hand C is from section 2.1. It should look for the 4-4 ♥ fit and bid Stayman. If opener responds 2♦/♠ then bid 3NT.

We have seen that with a long minor suit you can transfer into the minor. But if there really is no other possible game than 3NT, then bid it directly. This gives less information away to the defence.

Example 1

West	East	West	East
♠ QJ75	♠ K93	1NT	3NT
♥ AQ5	♥ 97	pass	
♦ K9	♦ AQJ853		
♣ KJ32	♣ 64		

This sequence shows a weaker hand than the sequence 1NT - 2NT - 3♦ - 3NT which is slam invitational.

Summary of these 3NT bids: -

1NT - 3NT	Responder simply has values to play in 3NT
1NT - 2♠ - 2NT - 3NT	Responder needed help in the ♣ suit for 3NT
1NT - 2♠ - 3♣ - 3NT	Is a mild slam try
1NT - 2NT - 3♣ - 3NT	Responder needed help in the ♦ suit for 3NT
1NT - 2NT - 3♦ - 3NT	Is a mild slam try

The 3♣/♦/♥/♠ Bids

There are numerous uses for these direct jumps over partner's 1NT opening, let's look at a few: -

1) 3♣ is Puppet Stayman, asking for 4 and 5 card majors.
2) 3♣/♦/♥/♠ are good 6 card suits and slam tries.
3) 3♣/♦/♥/♠ define various game forcing two suiters.
4) 3♣/♦/♥/♠ show 5-5 minor suit and 5-5 major suit hands.
5) 3♣/♦/♥/♠ are all used as a substitute for Minor Suit Stayman.
6) 3♣/♦ are 6 card suits, game (3NT) invitational.
7) 3♥/♠ show a broken suit (6 or 7 cards) with slam interest.
8) 3♣/♦/♥/♠ are game forcing splinters, showing a singleton/void.

All of the above are in common use, so let's have a look at them all and choose one(?): -

1) __3♣ is Puppet Stayman__

We will sometimes open 1NT with a hand containing a 5 card major. And sometimes partner will need to know this, especially if he has a game going hand containing a small doubleton and 3 card major support. Puppet Stayman is a useful convention over an opening 2NT, a 3♣ bid over the 2NT opening locates both 4 card and 5 card major suits in the 2NT opener's hand. This same 3♣ bid can be used over a 1NT opening; but our SARS system works fine (better) and so we can allocate another meaning to this 3♣ bid.

2) __3♣/♦/♥/♠ are 6 card suits and slam tries.__

Clearly a very sound concept, and perhaps the most obvious and widely used use of these bids.

Hand A	Hand B	Hand C	
			All of these hands are worth an attempt at slam and bidding the suit at the three level is a way to handle these strong hands.
♠ KQJ876	♠ 876	♠ K7	However, they can all be satisfactorily dealt with using
♥ K64	♥ AKQJ93	♥ A93	transfers with the advantage that the NT opener will
♦ K64	♦ 2	♦ AKQJ76	usually be declarer.
♣ 5	♣ K64	♣ 64	So we can find another use for the direct 3 level bids.

3) __3♣/♦/♥/♠ define various game forcing two suiters.__

There are numerous variations here, but we can cover all the permutations with our transfer and Quest Transfer sequences etc. So we'll use these 3 level jumps for another purpose.

4) 3♣/♦/♥/♠ show 5-5 minor suit and 5-5 major suit hands.

The scheme here is –

3♣ = 5-5 in the minors, weak.
3♦ = 5-5 in the minors, strong.
3♥ = 5-5 in the majors, weak.   * note, some play this 3♥ bid as 5-5 invitational, see bottom.
3♠ = 5-5 in the majors, strong.

Now this scheme is gaining in popularity, so it's about time that somebody put an end to the virus! Despite the fact that it is very popular, I think that it's all nonsense. Let's go through all four of the bids one at a time and compare them with our system: -

a. 3♣ = 5-5 in the minors, weak.

Hand F   Now 3♣ is a weak bid which opener is expected to either pass or correct.
                But opener may have no more than a 3 card minor and you are up at the 3 level, why
♠ 87   not simply pass 1NT?
♥ 2   3 of a minor may work out best, but it is squandering an otherwise useful bid.
♦ Q8752   Also, in these days of aggressive bidding, this hand would probably not get a chance to
♣ K8752   say anything as the opponents will have bid.

b. 3♦ = 5-5 in the minors, strong.

Hand G   We met this hand back in section 4.3.1 (page 183) when the bidding started
                1NT - 2♠ - 2NT - 3♦. Now we are at the same level here but things are not the same.
♠ A   With our transfer sequence opener had the opportunity to super- accept or not and so
♥ A2   in our sequence responder knew that opener held 3♣'s to an honour.
♦ KJ872   Also, our transfer sequences cater for 6-5 and 5-6 in the minors and this scheme
♣ AQJ76   cannot do that adequately. And, of course, what about 6-4 and 4-6's?

c. 3♥ = 5-5 in the majors, weak.

Hand H   We met this hand when we had that little detour to discuss Crawling Stayman.
                Our approach is to bid Stayman and if partner bids 2♦ then take a guess.
♠ Q8642   We are at the two level but it may be a 5-2 fit.
♥ Q8642   With this direct 3♥ method you will usually locate a 5-3 fit but you are one level higher.
♦ 76   I prefer our simple method because: -
♣ 3   1- If there is a 5-4 fit opener plays it and we are one level lower.
                2- ½ the time we will locate the 5-3 fit and be at a lower level.
                3- so less than ½ the time this method locates a 5-3 fit which we miss, but they are one
                    level higher.
                4- does your partner ever open 1NT with 2245 or 2254 shape?

* note   playing 3♥ as 5-5 invitational is another established approach, but our sequence
                1NT - 2♦ - 2♥ - 2♠ - 2NT - 3♦/♥ is obviously superior as opener has more information
                about responder's shape (the 3♦/♥ bids show an invitational 5-5 with ♣/♦ shortage).

d. **3♠ = 5-5 in the majors, strong.**

Hand J	We met Hand J back in section 3.1.4 (page 142) and the sequence started 1NT - 2♦ - 2♥ - 2♠ - 2NT - ? . At the ? stage responder has shown a 5-5 major suited
♠ KQJ75	hand and his next bid gives further definition (strength, shape etc.).
♥ KQ1094	Our scheme really is light years ahead of this uncouth 3♠ jump. We are a whole bidding
♦ A64	level lower and also accommodate invitational as well as game forcing hands.
♣ -	

They may be fairly popular, but using these jumps to show a few 5-5 shapes really sucks.

5) **3♣/♦/♥/♠ are all used as a substitute for Minor Suit Stayman.**

Players who play minor suit transfers and have not yet heard of SARS need a method to find minor suit fits after partner's 1NT opening. One such method is: -

3♣ = 5 ♣'s, 4 ♦'s
3♦ = 4 ♣'s, 5 ♦'s
3♥ = 5-5, singleton or void ♥
3♠ = 5-5, singleton or void ♠

All fairly sensible but somewhat limited. Utilising four bids for the infrequent situations where responder has 9 or 10 cards in the minors and game going values is a bit extravagant. Also, there seems to be no mention of responding hands that are 4-4 in the minors. Anyway, we have SARS for 4-4, 5-4 and 4-5's and we transfer (1NT - 2♠ - 2NT/3♣ - 3♦) with 5-5's. These are clearly superior as we are at a lower level and have already exchanged useful information.

6) **3♣/♦ are 6 card suits, game (3NT) invitational.**

Hand D	Hand E	
		With this option, the jump to 3♣/♦ shows a good suit and nothing much outside. The suit should be six or seven card and headed by two
♠ 76	♠ 76	top honours (but AK is too good). Opener should then bid 3NT with a
♥ 64	♥ 64	doubleton A or K or with three small with all outside suits covered.
♦ 653	♦ KQJ7653	Obviously a sound concept. However, you can show many of these hand
♣ AQJ876	♣ 95	types by transferring to the minor and opener is usually declarer.

But consider these two example hands. If opener has ♣Kx opposite Hand D or ♦Ax opposite Hand E then 3NT will make and transferring will miss the game. So a useful treatment and definitely worth considering.

Using this treatment the 3♥/♠ bids are still spare and an excellent scheme for these is: -

7)   3♥/♠ show a broken suit (6 or 7 cards) with slam interest.

Hand H	Hand J	
		You could bid both of these hands by starting with a transfer.
♠ AJ8742	♠ 4	However, being able to indicate that you have a very good hand but with
♥ A2	♥ KJ87642	a broken suit may well be beneficial. Opener will be warned off slamming
♦ KJ10	♦ K87	if he does not have an honour in the suit.
♣ 95	♣ A7	This is clearly a very sensible option for 3♥ and 3♠, so let's describe it in
		a little more detail: -

First of all, what are opener's options? With a minimal hand or with a good hand but lacking a trump honour, opener should simply sign off in 4 of the major. With a small doubleton in the suit then opener may elect to bid 3NT - responder will convert to 4 of the major with a 7 card suit (and maybe with a 6-carder). With slam potential and a high trump, opener should cue bid.

Example 7.1

West	East	West	East	
				(1) broken suit
♠ 963	♠ AJ8742	1NT	3♠ (1)	
♥ KQJ8	♥ A2	4♠	pass	
♦ AQ65	♦ KJ10			
♣ KJ	♣ 95			

Example 7.1 demonstrates the main advantage of this method. West has the knowledge of East's broken suit and so does not even have to investigate slam. If East had transferred then they may well have got too high (5♠ is not secure) in search of slam.

But one more important point is that the wrong hand is declarer! Wouldn't it be nice to be able to stop in 4♠ with West as declarer? We come back to this example in section 5.3.

Example 7.2

West	East	West	East	
				(1) broken suit
♠ 96	♠ AJ8742	1NT	3♠ (1)	
♥ KQJ8	♥ A2	3NT	pass	
♦ AQ65	♦ KJ10			
♣ KJ6	♣ 95			

In example 7.2 West has no fit and so 3NT will be reached however you bid it. However, East may well elect to pull it to 4♠, not really a problem except that the wrong hand is declarer.

Example 7.3

West	East	West	East		
					(1) broken suit
♠ KQ5	♠ AJ8742	1NT	3♠	(1)	(2) cue bid
♥ K763	♥ A2	4♣	(2)	etc to 6♠	
♦ Q965	♦ KJ10				
♣ AQ	♣ 95				

A decent slam, but wouldn't it be a much better one if played by West?

So, quite a useful treatment for these two jumps. The knowledge of the broken suit often enables us to stay lower when we might otherwise get too high, but it's the wrong hand that ends up as declarer. We'll come back to this (and see the examples 7.1 – 7.3 again) in section 5.3.

Let's look at another very sensible option for these 3♣/♦/♥/♠ bids: -

8) 3♣/♦/♥/♠ are game forcing splinters, showing a singleton/void

How do you bid a 4441 (any order) type hand with game going values after partner has opened 1NT? You could try Stayman but if there is no major suit fit, then 5 or 6 of a minor might be on. But indicating your shortage to opener will often avoid silly 3NT contracts.

Having direct splinters to the 3 level is also a very good option, so let's look into it a little deeper: -

Hand A	Hand B	
		Partner opens a strong NT. Using normal methods with Hand A you try Stayman and if there is no fit then there really is no option but to punt
♠ AQ98	♠ KJ3	3NT. It's a shame if you lose the first 5♥ tricks. You could try SARS but
♥ 2	♥ 10874	how do you establish if opener has sufficient ♥ stops so that 3NT is
♦ K853	♦ AQJ85	better than 5 of a minor?
♣ Q1063	♣ 4	And how about Hand B? You could transfer into ♦'s and then bid 3♥, but that leaves ♠'s out of the equation and 4♠ may just be the only makeable game. So let's see how splinters can work.

What does opener do after partner has splintered? The bid is game forcing, so the cheapest bid in a suit sets trumps. 3NT shows that the shortage is well stopped.

And what bid is used by responder to show this splinter suit? Traditionally one simply bids the short suit, and that is a perfectly workable method. But bidding the suit below the shortage (3♠ with short ♣'s) has its advantages: -

1- The next player will not be able to double the splinter bid to show a strong holding in that suit.
2- It frees the bid of the short suit by opener for further exploration.

But there are disadvantages with using the suit below: -

1- Partner may forget?
2- Responder is more likely to become declarer.
3- You do not actually save on bidding space. With the shortage in ♦'s, ♥'s or ♠'s you have one extra step, but with a ♣ shortage you have to bid 3♠ and so lose 3 steps. This really is quite important, as with a ♣ shortage it's quite likely that a major suit will be trumps and it is not so easy now for opener to make a distinction between slam interest or not when he likes ♥'s or ♠'s.

If you prefer to use the 'suit below' then fine, and you will need to define what a bid in the short suit by opener means. Now I am not going to say which scheme is best – because we will be using neither! But we will be using these direct splinters (in a slightly more devious form) and so I'll just give a few examples to demonstrate how useful they can be. We cover the same examples later in section 5.4 using our refined methods.

Example 8.1

West	East	West	East		
♠ AQ105	♠ KJ3	1NT	3♣	(1)	(1) ♣ shortage
♥ AJ5	♥ 10874	4♠	(2) pass		(2) ♠'s but min
♦ K974	♦ AQJ85				
♣ Q3	♣ 4				

3NT is silly and 5♦ may lose 3 tricks. 4♠ is an excellent contract that is unlikely to be reached by other methods.

_____

Example 8.2   Often you can avoid silly 3NT contracts by playing in a minor: -

West	East	West	East		
♠ KQ5	♠ A642	1NT	3♥	(1)	(1) ♥ shortage
♥ Q76	♥ 2	4♦	5♦		
♦ AQ106	♦ K853	pass			
♣ KJ2	♣ Q1063				

_____

Example 8.3   Wouldn't it be great to get to 6♠ on these cards: -

West	East	West	East		
					(1) ♥ shortage
					(2) sets trumps
					(3) cue bid
♠ AJ108	♠ KQ7	1NT	3♥	(1)	
♥ Q976	♥ 2	3♠	(2) 4♦	(3)	
♦ KJ	♦ AQ976	etc to 6♠			
♣ AJ4	♣ KQ98				

Example 8.4   Sometimes East may have a void: -

West	East	West	East		
				(1) short ♥'s
♠ KQ6	♠ AJ98	1NT	3♥	(1)	(2) ♦'s are trumps
♥ J62	♥ -	4♦	?	(2)	(3)
♦ AQ106	♦ KJ853	etc to 6♦		
♣ KJ2	♣ Q876			

You have to decide which bid is RKCB in these situations. In example 8.4, 4♥ at (3) would be the RKCB bid for ♦'s, but maybe we should allow responder to be able to cue bid the shortage suit to show a void? We'll solve this problem when we move onto our version of direct splinters in section 5.4.

So everything is not that straightforward and there is the odd grey area. Another problem is that the 3♠ splinter is rather high. Suppose that East has ♠ shortage and West wants to investigate a ♥ slam: -

Example 8.5

West	East	West	East		
				(1) ♠ shortage
♠ Q976	♠ 2	1NT	3♠	(1)	
♥ AJ108	♥ KQ7	?		(2)	
♦ KJ	♦ AQ976			
♣ AJ4	♣ KQ98			

West wants to try for 6♥, but how does he continue at (2)? 3NT is to play; 4♣/♦ set the trump suit; 4♥ is to play; and 4NT is, well, above 4♥ if responder is not interested in a ♥ slam!

So we cannot really use 3♠ for ♠ shortage, I will leave this to section 5.4 where we cover our method of playing these splinters.

****

So that's it and we have covered all of the options for these 3♣/♦/♥/♠ jumps that are in common use. It's time to pick one.

As far as I'm concerned it's between option 6 combined with option 7 or option 8. Even in this book we can't have everything and since we have to choose one …

Rewind, rewind.

What am I saying? Perhaps we can't have everything, but we can at least try to have the broken suit jumps and also splinters. And while we are at it, can't we arrange for these broken suit jumps to be played by declarer? And perhaps sort out the problems with looking for a major suit slam and also the void problem with the splinters?

Of course we can …

5.3　　　**Broken Suit Transfers (BST)**

Now I believe that this showing of the broken ♥/♠ suit with slam interest is a good idea, the problem was that the wrong hand will always end up being declarer. Now you could adopt the Smolen philosophy but I guess you know what I think of that! No, the answer is that 1NT - 3♦/♥ have to be transfers indicating the broken suit. Excellent. But that then leaves just 3♣ and 3♠ for the splinters, but we will solve that minor irritation in the next section. So we have: -

1NT - 3♦　　=　　transfer to ♥'s, indicating a broken ♥ suit and slam interest.
1NT - 3♥　　=　　transfer to ♠'s, indicating a broken ♠ suit and slam interest.

Next we have to define the subsequent bids. West has two options. If he prefers 3NT then he bids it but responder will often pull this – especially with a 7 card suit. Note that if responder does pull it he bids 4♦/♥ – a re-transfer.

If opener prefers the major suit (either game or slam) it really is best if he always completes the transfer (that's the main point, isn't it?) or else bids game with no slam interest. After a transfer completion responder will cue bid if possible (else 3NT) and opener will then proceed in investigating slam (cue bid or RKCB).

To start with, let's see how it works with the examples from section 5.2, pages 205 – 206.

Example 1 (7.1)

West	East	West	East		
♠ 963	♠ AJ8742	1NT	3♥　(1)		(1) broken suit transfer (BST)
♥ KQJ8	♥ A2	4♠　(2)	pass		(2) no slam interest
♦ AQ65	♦ KJ10				
♣ KJ	♣ 95				

So this time it's the same contract but played by the correct hand.

Example 2 (7.2)

West	East	West	East	
♠ 96	♠ AJ8742	1NT	3♥　(1)	(1) BST
♥ KQJ8	♥ A2	3NT	pass　(2)	
♦ AQ65	♦ KJ10			
♣ KJ6	♣ 95			

Same contract as before. But it's quite likely that East will choose to pull it to 4♠ at (2) (via a 4♥ re-transfer) and BST is then far superior as West is declarer.

Example 3 (7.3)

West	East	West	East		
				(1)	BST
♠ KQ5	♠ AJ8742	1NT	3♥ (1)	(2)	cue bid
♥ K763	♥ A2	3♠	4♥ (2)	(3)	cue bid
♦ Q965	♦ KJ10	5♣ (3)	5♦ (4)	(4)	cue bid
♣ AQ	♣ 95	6♠	pass		

West has weak ♦'s and does not want to bid RKCB at (3) – very wise, swap East's minors and there is no slam. East's cue bid at (4) is 2nd round control.

The same contract as before, but this time it's virtually 100% as West is declarer.

———————————

Example 4   If East has no ace to cue then he bids 3NT: -

West	East	West	East		
				(1)	BST
♠ Q65	♠ KJ8742	1NT	3♥ (1)	(2)	no ace to cue
♥ AJ6	♥ KQ	3♠	3NT (2)		
♦ A962	♦ KQJ	4♠ (3)	pass		
♣ KQ7	♣ 52				

West is max with good trumps, but with no ♣A and a probable ♠ loser (because East has shown a broken suit), discretion is the better part of valour at (3).

———————————

Example 5   But if East shows the ♣A then it's worth a shot: -

West	East	West	East		
				(1)	BST
♠ Q95	♠ KJ8742	1NT	3♥ (1)	(2)	cue bid
♥ AJ6	♥ KQ	3♠	4♣ (2)	(3)	RKCB
♦ A962	♦ Q53	4♦ (2)	4NT (3)		
♣ KQ7	♣ A2	etc to 6♠			

A very respectable slam, even if the ♦K is wrong and you get a ♦ lead.

———————————

Now two examples to emphasise the main points of playing BST — establishing the broken suit and ensuring that opener is declarer: -

Example 6

West	East	West	East		
♠ 653	♠ AJ8742	1NT	3♥ (1)		(1) BST
♥ KQ98	♥ A2	4♠	pass		
♦ AQ62	♦ KJ10				
♣ AJ	♣ Q2				

With probably two trump losers, West does not even try for slam. Note that 4♠ by West is a better contract than 4♠ by East.

Example 7

West	East	West	East		
♠ Q53	♠ AJ8742	1NT	3♥ (1)		(1) BST
♥ K983	♥ A2	3♠	4♥ (2)		(2) cue bid
♦ AQ62	♦ KJ10	4NT (3)	etc to 6♠		(3) RKCB
♣ AJ	♣ Q2				

West has the same strength hand, but this time the ♠Q is so much better than the ♥Q. 6♠ is a good contract, especially when played by West.

And as I mentioned earlier, East should re-transfer over 3NT if he wants (partner) to play in the suit contract: -

Example 8

West	East	West	East		
♠ 96	♠ AJ87542	1NT	3♥ (1)		(1) BST
♥ KJ83	♥ A2	3NT	4♥ (2)		(2) re-transfer
♦ AQ62	♦ KJ10	4♠	pass		(3) RKCB
♣ AQ3	♣ 2				

There's no doubt about it, BST is far superior to a natural jump to 3♥/♠, n'est pas?
But then there are just 3♣ and 3♠ left for the direct splinters. Can we cope?
What a silly question …

5.4   __Direct Ambiguous Splinters__

Hand A	Hand B	So with this type of hand, playable in 3 suits, we want to splinter. The bid is game forcing but not necessarily slam seeking. We allow a (good) 3 card major but minor suits would normally be at least 4 cards long.
♠ A642	♠ AQ3	
♥ 2	♥ 10874	
♦ K853	♦ AJ985	
♣ Q1063	♣ 4	

We have decided to use 1NT - 3♦/♥ as transfers indicating the broken suit. Excellent. But that then leaves just 3♣ and 3♠ for the splinters. No problem: -

1NT - 3♣	=	either ♠, ♣ or ♦ shortage, 3♦ by opener asks and	3♥	=	♠ shortage
			3♠	=	♣ shortage
			3NT	=	♦ shortage

1NT - 3♠   =   ♥ shortage

I indicated earlier that we cannot use 3♠ as ♠ shortage; so with our limited options we have to use 3♥ (after the 3♣/3♦ sequence) as this is the only sequence with enough bids for the ♠ shortage. You could then actually choose whichever sequences you like to show the other three shortages (they all have the same number of free bids), this scheme is as good as any. But there is not that much space and we have to be careful, especially where we need to distinguish between slam seeking and just game going hands. Anyway, it is all covered shortly.

Now these splinter bids are rather high and so we have to set a few ground rules. First, let's consider the situation where opener selects a minor suit as trumps. So he bids 4 of the minor, but what does responder then do? If the 4♣/♦ did not indicate whether opener had slam interest or not then responder is in a spot as it's now decision time (the next bid is the Kickback suit).

There is not enough bidding space for everybody to investigate everything and so it is best for responder to restrict the use of splinters to just game going hands or slam interest hands. Slam forcing hands will have to find another route unless they can cope with opener 'signing off' in 5 of a minor. So when opener wants to play in a minor, 4♣/♦ expresses slam interest but 5♣/♦ are sign offs. After opener bids 4♣ or 4♦ (expressing slam interest) then responder will sign off in 5♣/♦ with no slam ambitions. Otherwise the next free bid is the Kickback suit and so responder usually uses this as RKCB.

So with a minor suit as trumps there is always enough bidding space, but with a major suit it's different. Opener cannot simply bid 4♥/♠ to set trumps as responder does not know if opener has slam interest or not. So 4♥/♠ need to be sign off and with slam interest in a major suit opener has to find another bid. (Fortunately) there is just enough room to do this in every scenario and it is different depending upon what the shortage suit is.

So now we'll cover all of the shortages in detail, the example numbers in brackets are where we met them before in section 5.2, pages 207 – 208.

1- Short ♥'s (1NT - 3♠)

After 1NT - 3♠, showing ♥ shortage, opener's responses are: -

3NT	=	to play
4♣	=	♣'s are trumps, slam interest
4♦	=	♦'s are trumps, slam interest
4♥	=	♠'s are trumps, slam interest
4♠	=	♠'s are trumps, no slam interest
5♣	=	♣'s are trumps, no slam interest
5♦	—	♦'s are trumps, no slam interest

Everything is pretty straightforward here except that 4♥ shows ♠ slam interest. Responder's reply to this 4♥ bid is: -

After 1NT - 3♠ - 4♥,	4♠	=	no slam interest
	4NT	=	RKCB for ♠'s
	5♣	=	ERKCB for ♠'s, ♥ void

Example 1 (8.2)   3NT would be a dodgy contract here: -

West	East	West	East		
♠ KQ5	♠ A642	1NT	3♠	(1)	(1) ♥ shortage
♥ Q76	♥ 2	4♦	(2)	5♦	(2) ♦'s are trumps, slam interest
♦ AQ106	♦ K853	pass			
♣ KJ2	♣ Q1063				

Example 2 (8.3)   And 6♠ is sure to get an excellent score on this board: -

West	East	West	East		
♠ AJ108	♠ KQ7	1NT	3♠	(1)	(1) ♥ shortage
♥ Q976	♥ 2	4♥	(2)	4NT (3)	(2) ♠'s are trumps, slam interest
♦ KJ	♦ AQ976	etc to 6♠			(3) RKCB for ♠'s
♣ AJ4	♣ KQ98				

Example 3   With no slam interest, responder signs off: -

West	East	West	East		
♠ AJ108	♠ KQ7	1NT	3♠	(1)	(1) ♥ shortage
♥ Q976	♥ 2	4♥	(2)	4♠ (3)	(2) ♠'s are trumps, slam interest
♦ KJ	♦ Q9764	pass			(3) no slam interest
♣ AJ4	♣ KQ98				

But there is sometimes a slight problem when responder is looking for a slam with a void. How does he show this? There are various options but the simplest is that responder uses the bid above the Kickback bid as Exclusion RKCB, where the exclusion (void) suit is obviously the shortage already shown: -

Example 4 (8.4)

West	East	West			East		
♠ KQ6	♠ AJ98	1NT	3♠	(1)	(1)	♥ shortage	
♥ J62	♥ -	4♦	(2)	4♠	(3)	(2)	♦'s are trumps, slam interest
♦ AQ106	♦ KJ853	5♣	(4)	etc to 6♦		(3)	ERKCB for ♦'s, ♥ void
♣ KJ2	♣ Q876					(4)	1 key card outside ♥'s

Here 4♥ at (3) would have been RKCB and so 4♠ is ERKCB.

Example 5

West	East	West			East		
♠ KQJ6	♠ AJ98	1NT	3♠	(1)	(1)	♥ shortage	
♥ J62	♥ -	4♥	(2)	5♣	(3)	(2)	♠'s are trumps, slam interest
♦ AQ6	♦ KJ853	5NT	(4)	6♠		(3)	ERKCB for ♠'s, ♥ void
♣ KJ2	♣ Q876	pass				(4)	2 key cards outside ♥'s + ♠Q

Example 6   Using Exclusion RKCB (ERKCB) is sometimes absolutely necessary: -

West	East	West			East		
♠ KQJ6	♠ A985	1NT	3♠	(1)	(1)	♥ shortage	
♥ AJ2	♥ -	4♥	(2)	5♣	(3)	(2)	♠'s are trumps, slam interest
♦ Q62	♦ KJ853	5♥	(4)	5♠		(3)	ERKCB for ♠'s, ♥ void
♣ KJ2	♣ Q876	pass				(4)	1 key card outside ♥'s

Now I did say that responder's minor suits should be 4 or 5 card, but a good 3 card suit is acceptable if responder has extra values and so is almost certainly heading for slam: -

Example 7

West	East	West			East		
♠ AQ2	♠ KJ97	1NT	3♠	(1)	(1)	♥ shortage	
♥ Q976	♥ 2	4♦	(2)	4♥	(3)	(2)	♦'s are trumps, slam interest
♦ KJ87	♦ AQ10	etc to 6♦				(3)	RKCB for ♦'s
♣ A4	♣ KQJ52						

214

2- Short ♠'s (1NT - 3♣ - 3♦ - 3♥)

After 1NT - 3♣ - 3♦ - 3♥, showing ♠ shortage, opener's responses are: -

3♠	=	♥'s are trumps, slam interest
3NT	=	to play
4♣	=	♣'s are trumps, slam interest
4♦	=	♦'s are trumps, slam interest
4♥	=	♥'s are trumps, no slam interest
5♣	=	♣'s are trumps, no slam interest
5♦	=	♦'s are trumps, no slam interest

Here we use the 3♠ bid to show ♥ slam interest, responder's next bids are: -

After 1NT - 3♣ - 3♦ - 3♥ - 3♠,	4♥	=	no slam interest
	4♠	=	RKCB for ♥'s
	4NT	=	ERKCB for ♥'s (void ♠)

Example 8 (8.5)

West	East	West	East	
				(1) ambiguous splinter
				(2) where?
♠ Q976	♠ 2	1NT	3♣ (1)	(3) ♠ shortage
♥ AJ108	♥ KQ7	3♦ (2)	3♥ (3)	(4) ♥'s are trumps, slam interest
♦ KJ	♦ AQ976	3♠ (4)	4♠ (5)	(5) RKCB for ♥'s
♣ AJ4	♣ KQ98	etc to 6♥		

Example 9   And the bid above Kickback is still ERKCB: -

West	East	West	East	
				(1) ambiguous splinter
				(2) where?
♠ Q976	♠ -	1NT	3♣ (1)	(3) ♠ shortage
♥ AJ108	♥ KQ72	3♦ (2)	3♥ (3)	(4) ♥'s are trumps, slam interest
♦ KJ	♦ Q9762	3♠ (4)	4NT (5)	(5) ERKCB for ♥'s (void ♠)
♣ AJ4	♣ KQ98	etc to 6♥		

We are a little short of bids here as we have to cope with either major being trumps, so we have to use the bid of the shortage suit to show slam interest in an unspecified major: -

After 1NT - 3♣ - 3♦ - 3♠, showing ♣ shortage, opener's responses are: -

3NT = to play
4♣ = slam interest in either ♥'s or ♠'s
4♦ = ♦'s are trumps, slam interest
4♥ = ♥'s are trumps, no slam interest
4♠ = ♠'s are trumps, no slam interest
5♦ = ♦'s are trumps, no slam interest

After the 4♣ bid, it's up to responder to say whether he too has slam interest in a major.
So after 1NT - 3♣ - 3♦ - 3♠ - 4♣ responder's responses are: -

4♦ = slam interest
4♥ = no slam interest (pass or correct)
4♠ = Exclusion Blackwood (♣ void)

And after 1NT - 3♣ - 3♦ - 3♠ - 4♣ - 4♦ showing slam interest, opener then bids: -

4♠ = RKCB for ♥'s
4NT = RKCB for ♠'s.

Example 10 (8.1)

West	East	West		East		
♠ AQ105	♠ KJ3	1NT		3♣	(1)	(1) ambiguous splinter
♥ AJ5	♥ 10874	3♦	(2)	3♠	(3)	(2) where?
♦ K974	♦ AQJ85	4♠		pass		(3) ♣ shortage
♣ Q3	♣ 4					

Same contract as before. 3NT is silly and 5♦ may lose 3 tricks. 4♠ is an excellent contract that is unlikely to be reached by other methods.

Example 11

West	East	West		East		
						(1) ambiguous splinter
						(2) where?
♠ AQ105	♠ KJ3	1NT		3♣	(1)	(3) ♣ shortage
♥ AK5	♥ 10874	3♦	(2)	3♠	(3)	(4) slam interest in a major
♦ K97	♦ AQJ85	4♣	(4)	4♦	(5)	(5) I'm listening
♣ 973	♣ 4	4NT	(6)	etc to 6♠		(6) RKCB for ♠'s

With no slam interest, responder bids 4♥, pass or correct: -

Example 12

West	East	West		East		
♠ AQ105	♠ KJ3	1NT		3♣	(1)	(1) ambiguous splinter
♥ AK5	♥ 10874	3♦	(2)	3♠	(3)	(2) where?
♦ K97	♦ AJ852	4♣	(4)	4♥	(5)	(3) ♣ shortage
♣ 973	♣ 4	4♠		pass		(4) slam interest in a major

(1) ambiguous splinter
(2) where?
(3) ♣ shortage
(4) slam interest in a major
(5) no slam interest, pass or correct

So after opener shows slam interest in a major with 4♣, if responder also has slam interest he allows opener to fix the trump suit with RKCB next go. But what if responder has a void? Now there are schemes to show a void after partner has used Blackwood, but they are not 100% foolproof. The best solution is for responder to use Exclusion Blackwood.

Now responder does not know which major is trumps and so we cannot use ERKCB. Thus the options are EDRKCB (both majors) or simple Exclusion Blackwood (with no trump suit agreed); I guess that you could even dream up Exclusion Triple RKCB? Let's use the simple Exclusion Blackwood variation: -

Example 13

West	East	West		East		
♠ AQ105	♠ KJ73	1NT		3♣	(1)	(1) ambiguous splinter
♥ AKJ	♥ 10874	3♦	(2)	3♠	(3)	(2) where?
♦ Q97	♦ AJ852	4♣	(4)	4♠	(5)	(3) ♣ shortage
♣ 973	♣ -	5♦	(6)	etc	(7)	(4) slam interest in a major

(1) ambiguous splinter
(2) where?
(3) ♣ shortage
(4) slam interest in a major
(5) Exclusion Blackwood
(6) 2 aces outside ♣'s

Responder checks for kings (via whatever scheme you use) and then wants to be in a small slam. So he bids 6♥ at (7) which is pass or correct. Opener obviously corrects to 6♠.

If opener sets ♦'s as trumps (with 4♦, slam interest) and responder has a ♣ void then it's easier and we obviously use ERKCB, the bid above Kickback: -

Example 14

West	East	West		East		
♠ Q105	♠ KJ73	1NT		3♣	(1)	(1) ambiguous splinter
♥ AKJ	♥ 10874	3♦	(2)	3♠	(3)	(2) where?
♦ KQ97	♦ AJ852	4♦	(4)	4♠	(5)	(3) ♣ shortage
♣ 973	♣ -	etc to 6♦				(4) ♦'s are trumps, slam interest

(1) ambiguous splinter
(2) where?
(3) ♣ shortage
(4) ♦'s are trumps, slam interest
(5) ERKCB for ♦'s (♣ void)

4♥ at (5) would be RKCB for ♦'s (singleton ♣).

<u>4- Short ♦'s (1NT - 3♣ - 3♦ - 3NT)</u>

Here we have the same lack of bids to show slam interest in a major. It's much the same as with ♣ shortage but we still need 4♣ to show the (ambiguous) major suit slam interest. So, unfortunately, we have to use 4♦ to show ♣'s – that's usually no problem as we have just about enough room (just one above the 100% safe Kickback threshold).

After 1NT - 3♣ - 3♦ - 3NT, showing ♣ shortage, opener's responses are: -

pass = to play
4♣ = slam interest in either ♥'s or ♠'s
4♦ = ♣'s are trumps, slam interest
4♥ = ♥'s are trumps, no slam interest
4♠ = ♠'s are trumps, no slam interest
5♣ = ♣'s are trumps, no slam interest

After the 4♣ bid it's up to responder to say whether he too has slam interest.

So after 1NT - 3♣ - 3♦ - 3♠ - 4♣ responder's responses are: -

4♦ = slam interest
4♥ = no slam interest (pass or correct)
4♠ = Exclusion Blackwood (♦ void)

And after 1NT - 3♣ - 3♦ - 3♠ - 4♣ - 4♦, opener's responses are: -

4♠ = RKCB for ♥'s
4NT = RKCB for ♠'s.

Example 15

West	East	West	East		
				(1)	ambiguous splinter
				(2)	where?
♠ AQ	♠ KJ97	1NT	3♣ (1)	(3)	♦ shortage
♥ AJ108	♥ KQ76	3♦ (2)	3NT (3)	(4)	slam interest in a major
♦ Q976	♦ 2	4♣ (4)	4♦ (5)	(5)	I'm also interested
♣ K94	♣ AQJ8	4♠ (6)	etc to 6♥	(6)	agrees ♥'s, RKCB

Example 16

West	East	West	East		
				(1)	ambiguous splinter
				(2)	where?
♠ AQ	♠ KJ97	1NT	3♣ (1)	(3)	♦ shortage
♥ K94	♥ AQJ8	3♦ (2)	3NT (3)	(4)	♣'s are trumps
♦ Q976	♦ 2	4♦ (4)	4♥ (5)	(5)	agrees ♣'s, RKCB
♣ AJ108	♣ KQ76	etc to 6♣			

218

5- Opener Likes NT

Now there's one thing that we have not covered, opener may have ample cover in the short suit and wish to play in 3NT. No problem: -

Example 17

West	East	West	East		
♠ K5	♠ A763	1NT	3♠ (1)	(1)	♥ shortage
♥ AQJ9	♥ 2	3NT (2)	pass	(2)	I have good ♥'s
♦ AQ86	♦ K1053				
♣ J104	♣ Q632				

Example 18

West	East	West	East		
♠ J105	♠ AQ3	1NT	3♣ (1)	(1)	ambiguous splinter
♥ AJ5	♥ 10874	3♦ (2)	3♠ (3)	(2)	where?
♦ AJ	♦ KQ985	3NT (4)	pass	(3)	♣ shortage
♣ KJ1095	♣ 4				(4)	I have good ♣'s

And there is just one other (rather rare) possibility with these ambiguous (♠/♣/♦ shortage) splinters – opener may simply bid 3NT without asking about shortage: -

Example 19

West	East	West	East		
♠ AQJ	♠ K976	1NT	3♣ (1)	(1)	ambiguous splinter
♥ 83	♥ AQ76	3NT (2)	pass		
♦ KJ105	♦ Q982				
♣ KJ105	♣ 2				

West knows that East's shortage is not ♥'s. He is not interested in ♠'s and does not really want to play in a minor suit game – so he simply bids 3NT!

6   The 4-Level Responses

6.1   4♣ Is Gerber

Directly after a 1NT opening a bid of 4♣ is Gerber. It only really makes sense for responder to jump directly into Gerber if he is certain of the eventual strain (the suit or NT) and simply needs to check upon aces (and maybe kings).

Hand A	Hand B	Partner opens a strong NT. Hand A bids 4♣, Gerber, and then the appropriate number of NT depending upon missing aces.
♠ KQ8	♠ KQJ1074	Hand B also wants to know about aces and will then bid the
♥ K7	♥ 8	appropriate ♠ contract.
♦ K8	♦ AKQ85	
♣ KQJ986	♣ 4	

The direct 4♣ Gerber bid really is rather infrequent as it is usually better to glean more information from opener (perhaps using SARS).

There are variations on Gerber – Roman Gerber, Exclusion Gerber etc. but they really are not worthwhile as Gerber is so rarely (sensibly) used.

The direct Gerber, 1NT - 4♣, is rarely used and rather primitive. One can always find another bid before asking for aces/key cards. So you might like to consider another meaning; take a look at South African Texas Transfers – sections 6.2.1 and 7.4.

6.2   **Texas Transfers (4♦ & 4♥)**

Suppose partner opens 1NT and your hand dictates that you want to play in 4♥. You have various options. You can always transfer with 2♦ and then bid 4♥. You could also bid 4♥ directly, but it is normally better for the 1NT opener to be declarer and so we have Texas Transfers which immediately transfer opener to 4♥/♠. Transferring immediately to the 4 level is normally a sign off, i.e. not interested in slam.

There are two different versions of these Texas Transfers: -

Scheme A (South African Texas Transfer)   Scheme B

4♣ = to ♥   4♦ = transfer to ♥
4♦ = transfer to ♠   4♥ = transfer to ♠

Which is to be preferred? Presumably scheme B as this is more efficient and leaves 4♣ available for another use such as Gerber (Section 6.1). One drawback with scheme B is that opener may forget and pass a 4♥ bid! Let's assume that readers will not forget and so we will be using 4♦ and 4♥ as the transfer bids, not because I think it's better (it probably isn't) but because it is the most popular variety and people believe that they need Gerber in their arsenal (although they never sensibly use it).

So why do we want these Texas Transfers when we can always go via Jacoby? Consider these two sequences: -

                 Sequence 1   1NT - 2♥ - 2♠ - 4♠
                 Sequence 2   1NT - 4♥ - 4♠

What is the difference? Both show 6+ ♠'s and a game going hand. Sequence 1 is mildly slam interested whereas sequence 2 is not, it may even be pre-emptive in nature. If opener is max and likes ♠'s then he may bid on in sequence 1.

Example 1

West	East	West	East		
♠ A109	♠ KQJ762	1NT	4♥ (1)		(1) Texas Transfer for ♠'s.
♥ QJ84	♥ K103	4♠ (2)	pass		
♦ KQJ8	♦ 92				
♣ A8	♣ J4				

West is max and likes his hand for ♠'s, but he is not allowed to do anything more than bid 4♠ at (2). Actually, this West hand is from example 3 in section 3.1.2, where 6♠ was reached; but because East had a better hand and used the Jacoby Transfer.

Example 2

East

♠ 5
♥ KQJ654
♦ Q105   West   East
♣ 765   1NT   4♦ (1)
                4♥   pass

We met this hand back in section 3.1.2 when (the Dutch?) East incorrectly bid a 2♦ Jacoby Transfer at (1) and then invited with 3♥. The hand is worth game and a Texas Transfer is correct.

A Texas Transfer may be used with a very weak distributional hand: -

Example 3

Dealer: ♠ J3
West   ♥ AK93
Love all   ♦ 9432
               ♣ AQ3

West	North	East		South
1NT	pass	4♥	(1)	pass
4♠	pass	pass		pass

♠ A109   N   ♠ Q876542
♥ QJ84   W   E   ♥ 5
♦ KQJ8   S   ♦ 765
♣ K8   ♣ 97

               ♠ K
               ♥ 10762
               ♦ A10
               ♣ J106542

4♠ may make, but even one down is an excellent score against N-S's ♥ or ♣ partscore or game. If East hand simply transferred with 2♥ at (1) then North would have had an easy double of West's 2♠ response. Neither North nor South can really say anything at the 4 level.

As we have seen, a Texas Transfer is a weak bid or else a reasonable hand without slam interest. It is possible to have continuations by responder after the completion of a Texas Transfer, and some players do play that 4NT (or Kickback) is RKCB. This would then free the 4♣ bid in a Jacoby Transfer sequence for another use (some sort of slam try similar to our 4♦, or perhaps a splinter). Quite playable and up to you.

New suits at the 5 level by responder can also be bid. These are probably best played as Exclusion Blackwood, asking for key cards outside the exclusion suit which would be a void. But you could play this equally well after a Jacoby Transfer.

6.2.1   South African Texas Transfers

As I said just now, there is another version of Texas Transfers that utilises the 4♣ and 4♦ bids. There are a couple of advantages here: -

- Both the 4♥ and 4♠ bids are available (presumably as natural).
- Partner is less likely to forget.

So if you play South African Texas Transfers you have, directly after partner's 1NT opening: -

4♣	=	transfer to 4♥
4♦	=	transfer to 4♠
4♥	=	to play
4♠	=	to play.

Thus we have three distinct ways to reach our 4 of a major contract: -

1) Use a Jacoby Transfer and then jump to the 4 level
2) Use a South African Texas Transfer
3) Jump to 4 of the major to play.

Having three options certainly may be advantageous, consider these examples. West has opened 1NT: -

West	East	Example 1
♠ AQ6	♠ J109754	Here East is concerned with the possibility that if he transfers with 2♥
♥ Q95	♥ 76	(or a 4♥ Texas Transfer) then South may double for a lead and ♥'s may
♦ AK65	♦ Q	be wide open. A South African 4♦ prevents a double of ♥'s by South.
♣ J52	♣ AQ94	

West	East	Example 2
♠ KJ6	♠ A109754	This time East is again worried about the ♥'s but all's well if he is
♥ 952	♥ K6	declarer. Playing South African Texas Transfers means that responder
♦ AKQ5	♦ 7	can choose who declarer is. A direct 4♠ bid prevents a ♥ through from
♣ QJ10	♣ A942	North.

Conclusion?

Having three different options to get to the same 4♥/♠ contract may sometimes be beneficial. One disadvantage is that you lose the 4♣ Gerber bid (it's not really that useful). So is it a good idea?

Probably, but standard Texas Transfers are more popular and fairly well established. Quite a dilemma, I'll assume we use standard Texas Transfers in this book.

What is the sequence   1NT – 4NT ?

Traditionally this is a quantitative bid, denying a 4 card major and inviting slam. Opener should pass with a minimum NT opener; any other bid suggests slam and minor suits are bid naturally in order to establish if there is a fit there. I did, however, say 'traditionally'. With our SARS sequences, responder can find any minor suit fit below the level of 3NT and can then invite, so this traditional meaning of the direct 4NT bid is redundant. That is just something that happens when things (and people) get older.

So, let's inject some young blood into this bid (the direct 4NT over partner's 1NT). Now as the bid takes up so much bidding space it needs to be pretty specific. It is a 'spare' bid, and you could choose any meaning you like, but how about: -

'I have a hand that is totally flat (4333, any order). I have sufficient points to invite slam, about 17 pts, but my 4 card suit is so feeble (Jxxx or worse) that I don't want to suggest that suit as trumps in a slam contract. Obviously I have good holdings in all three of my 3 card suits.'

So, a similar meaning to the traditional bid, but a lot more explicit. But what about that direct 4♠ bid? Also a redundant bid so far in our system. So let's use it as a very similar bid to our jump to 4NT; we can then define these 4333 type hands even more accurately: -

a) 1NT - 4♠   =   4333 or 3433, 17 pts.
b) 1NT - 4NT   =   3343 or 3334, 17 pts.

It may be a good idea to restrict these bids to hands containing exactly two aces as the bids preclude the use of Blackwood/Gerber.
Neither bid is forcing. Any subsequent bid by opener is to play. I guess that you could invent some conventional bids, but opener should know enough to select the final contract.

Hand A	Hand B	Hand C	Partner opens a strong 1NT. Your turn …
♠ AQ3	♠ KQ7	♠ KJ76	Hand A bids 4♠
♥ J963	♥ AJ3	♥ A93	Hand B bids 4NT
♦ KQ7	♦ AQ6	♦ AQ6	With Hand C, the ♠ suit is far too good and so it starts
♣ AJ5	♣ J874	♣ QJ7	off with 2♣ and then a quantitative 4NT if there is no ♠ fit.

Example 1

West	East	West	East		
♠ K96	♠ AQ3	1NT	4♠	(1)	(1) 4333 or 3433
♥ K82	♥ J963	4NT (2)	pass		(2) let's stay out of this one.
♦ AJ9	♦ KQ7				
♣ KQ92	♣ AJ5				

Bundles of points, but West knows that there is a dodgy major, no fit, and no source of tricks.

Example 2

West	East	West	East		
♠ A9	♠ KQJ	1NT	4♠ (1)		(1) 4333 or 3433
♥ A8	♥ 9632	7NT (2)	pass		
♦ KJ72	♦ AQ7				
♣ KQ962	♣ AJ5				

(2) West knows that the KQ of one major are missing and also one jack. He can count the tricks, 5 ♣'s, 4 ♦'s, 3 in one major and one in the other.

Example 3

West	East	West	East		
♠ KJ96	♠ AQ10	1NT	4♠ (1)		(1) 4333 or 3433
♥ Q8	♥ 9632	pass (2)			
♦ A864	♦ KQJ				
♣ KQ6	♣ AJ5				

West knows that East has 3 good ♠'s or else 4 poor ones, and the same for his ♥ suit. Either way, 4♠ will play nicely, but if partner has 4 very poor ♥'s then it may be essential to play in ♠'s.

That last hand was very instructive. West knows almost everything about East's hand, and may have a good idea that a suit is unprotected. Now normally after a quantitative 4NT, a new suit at the five level accepts the slam invitation and suggests that suit as trumps. In our case, however, opener knows enough about responder's hand to make that unnecessary, and so new suits at the 5 level are to play!

Example 4

West	East 1	East 2	West	East
♠ A86	♠ KQJ	♠ KQ9	1NT	4NT (1)
♥ KQ6	♥ AJ5	♥ AJ5	pass	
♦ KJ1062	♦ AQ9	♦ 9543		
♣ Q8	♣ 9543	♣ AK10		(1) 3343 or 3334

This is a similar situation to example 3. This time West knows that it's the ♣'s that may be wide open. Does East have hand 1 or hand 2? The odds are with a hand of type 2 and a pass of 4NT is certainly a reasonable option at pairs scoring. But at teams it may be prudent to pull it to 5♦, you know that partner has 4 trumps or else 3 good ones.

All good things come to an end and here we are, with everything covered. There are just a few more pages to tidy up the loose ends: -

7.1   <u>We Open 1NT With A 5 Card Major, Do We Miss A 5-3 Fit?</u>

One of the drawbacks of opening 1NT with a 5 card major is that we may miss a 5-3 fit. One tool available for locating 5 card majors in the opener's hand is Puppet Stayman. Unfortunately, this requires responses above 2♠ and is incompatible with Garbage Stayman, our wish to be able to bid Stayman without any point requirements, SARS etc. So how does our system cope? Let's check on all of the possibilities and summarise how we can normally establish the fit after responder has bid Stayman or transferred.

West A	West B	Both of these hands open a strong NT, let's see how the bidding goes
		when partner uses Stayman or transfers to ♥'s.
♠ KQ652	♠ KQJ65	West A is declining game invitations and West B is accepting.
♥ K9	♥ K9	
♦ KJ6	♦ AJ6	
♣ K98	♣ K98	

<u>Case 1</u>   Responder has 3 ♠'s and 2, 3 or 4 ♥'s

West	Responder has invitational values		Responder has game going values	
A	1NT - 2♣ - 2♠ - 2NT - pass	(1)	1NT - 2♣ - 2♠ - 3♣ etc	(4)
B	1NT - 2♣ - 2♠ - 2NT - 3♠ - 4♠	(2)(3)	1NT - 2♣ - 2♠ - 3♣ etc	(4)

<u>Case 2</u>   Responder has 3 ♠'s and 5 ♥'s

West	Responder has invitational values		Responder has game going values	
A	1NT - 2♦ - 2♥ - 2NT - pass	(1)	1NT - 2♦ - 2♥ - 3NT	(5)
B	1NT - 2♦ - 2♥ - 2NT - 3♠ - 4♠	(2)	1NT - 2♦ - 2♥ - 3NT	(5)

(1) here we miss the 5-3 ♠ fit.
(2) when accepting game, west can show his 5 card ♠ suit if he wishes and the 5-3 fit is located.
(3) alternatively opener may have chosen a Stayman super-accept in which case the 5-3 ♠ fit would also have been located: - 1NT - 2♣ - 3♠ - 4♠.
(4) with game going hands, responder will use SARS if he is interested in a possible 5-3 ♠ fit.
(5) here we miss the 5-3 ♠ fit. There is a solution (see section 7.4) but unfortunately we have allocated the bid required (3♠) for our ambiguous splinter.

The cases when opener has opened 1NT with 5 card ♥ suit and responder has 3 ♥'s are similar:

West C   West D   Again both of these hands open a strong NT, let's see how the bidding
                                goes when partner uses Stayman or transfers to ♠'s.
♠ K9   ♠ K9   West C is declining game invitations and West D is accepting.
♥ KQ652   ♥ KQJ65
♦ KJ6   ♦ AJ6
♣ K98   ♣ K98

<u>Case 3</u>   Responder has 3 ♥'s and 2 or 3 ♠'s

West	Responder has invitational values		Responder has game going values	
C	1NT - 2♣ - 2♥ - 2NT - pass	(1)	1NT - 2♣ - 2♥ - 3♣ etc	(4)
D	1NT - 2♣ - 2♥ - 2NT - 3♥ - 4♥	(2)(3)	1NT - 2♣ - 2♥ - 3♣ etc	(4)

<u>Case 4</u>   Responder has 3 ♥'s and 4 ♠'s

West	Responder has invitational values		Responder has game going values	
C	1NT - 2♣ - 2♥ - 2♠ - 2NT - pass	(1)	1NT - 2♣ - 2♥ - 3♣ etc	(4)
D	1NT - 2♣ - 2♥ - 2♠ - 3♥ - 4♥	(2)(3)	1NT - 2♣ - 2♥ - 3♣ etc	(4)

<u>Case 5</u>   Responder has 3 ♥'s and 5 ♠'s

West	Responder has invitational values		Responder has game going values	
C	1NT - 2♥ - 2♠ - 2NT - pass	(1)	1NT - 2♥ - 2♠ - 3NT	(5)
D	1NT - 2♥ - 2♠ - 2NT - 3♥ - 4♥	(2)	1NT - 2♥ - 2♠ - 3NT	(5)

(1) here we miss the 5-3 ♥ fit.
(2) when accepting game, west can show his 5 card ♥ suit if he wishes and the 5-3 fit is located.
(3) alternatively opener may have chosen a Stayman super-accept in which case the 5-3 ♥ fit would also
    have been located: - 1NT - 2♣ - 3♥ - 4♥.
(4) with game going hands, responder will use SARS if he is interested in a possible 5-3 ♥ fit.
(5) here we miss the 5-3 ♥ fit. There is a solution (see section 7.4) but it involves re-arranging the
    responses to our 3♥ ambiguous splinter bid.

So, it is usually possible to locate the 5-3 fit if you wish. Missing the 5-3 fit is usually not a disaster,
missing 4-4 fits is the thing to be avoided.

7.2 We Locate A 5-4 Fit, But Do We Miss A 4-4 Fit For Slam?

Take a look at this example, it comes from the section super-accepts but that is irrelevant.

Example 1

West	East	West	East		
♠ AQ4	♠ 75	1NT	2♦	(1)	super-accept, no weak doubleton
♥ K984	♥ AQJ32	2NT (1)	3♥ (2)	(2)	♦ 2nd suit, looking for slam
♦ K984	♦ AQJ3	4♦ (3)	5♣ (4)	(3)	DRKCB
♣ A9	♣ 75	6♦	pass	(4)	2 key cards + ♦Q

So what is the point here?

That a 5-4 fit was located but there is a superior 4-4 fit for slam purposes. Now you can shuffle the suits around - but change both hands equally, so that we still have the same 5-4 and 4-4 fits but in different suits. What is my point? That slam should be bid in the **good** 4-4 fit.

We are concerned with the situations where opener is 4-4 in two suits and responder has 5 card support for one suit and 4 card support for the other. Both suits are robust enough for slam purposes (as the example above) and responder investigates slam.

So let's shuffle the hand a bit and we get: -

Example 2

West	East	West	East		
♠ AQ4	♠ 75	1NT	2♠ (1)	(1)	transfer to ♣'s
♥ K984	♥ AQJ3	2NT (2)	3♥ (3)	(2)	super-accept
♦ A9	♦ 75	4♦ (4)	etc to 6♥	(3)	2nd suit
♣ K984	♣ AQJ32			(4)	cue bid agreeing ♥'s

Example 3

West	East	West	East		
♠ AQ4	♠ 75	1NT	2♣ (1)	(1)	maybe no 4 card major
♥ A9	♥ 75	2♦	3♣ (2)	(2)	shape ask
♦ K984	♦ AQJ3	3NT (3)	4♦ (4)	(3)	both minors
♣ K984	♣ AQJ32	4♥ (5)	etc to 6♦	(4)	RKCB for ♦'s
				(5)	3 key cards

Example 4

West	East	West	East		
♠ K984	♠ AQJ3	1NT	2♣	(1)	shape ask
♥ K984	♥ AQJ32	2♥	3♣ (1)	(2)	4 ♠'s as well as 4 ♥'s
♦ AQ4	♦ 75	3♠ (2)	etc to 6♠		
♣ A9	♣ 75				

See what I mean? Now there are 12 permutations of this 'shuffling' process (the two non-fit suits are irrelevant) and we have to check that we will always locate the 4-4 fit for slam purposes: -

I state opener's shape first and then responder's. The x's are the 3 and 2 card suits and are irrelevant.

1	44xx - 45xx	1NT - 2♣ - 2♥ - 3♣ - 3♠ ...	The 4-4 ♠ fit is located by SARS. *(a)
2	44xx - 54xx	1NT - 2♣ - 2♥ ...	The 4-4 ♥ fit is located immediately. *(a)
3	4x4x - 4x5x	1NT - 2NT - 3♣/♦ - 3♠ ...	The 4-4 ♠ fit is located after transferring to ♦'s.
4	4x4x - 5x4x	1NT - 2♥ - 2♠ - 3♦ ...	The 4-4 ♦ fit is located after transferring to ♠'s (but see *(b) note).
5	4xx4 - 4xx5	1NT - 2♠ - 2NT/3♣ - 3♠ ...	The 4-4 ♠ fit is located after transferring to ♣'s.
6	4xx4 - 5xx4	1NT - 2♥ - 2♠ - 3♣...	The 4-4 ♣ fit is located after transferring to ♠'s (but see *(b) note).
7	x44x - x45x	1NT - 2NT - 3♣/♦ - 3♥ ...	The 4-4 ♥ fit is located after transferring to ♦'s.
8	x44x - x54x	1NT - 2♦ - 2♥ - 3♦ ...	The 4-4 ♦ fit is located after transferring to ♥'s (but see *(b) note).
9	x4x4 - x4x5	1NT - 2♠ - 2NT/3♣ - 3♥ ...	The 4-4 ♥ fit is located after transferring to ♣'s.
10	x4x4 - x5x4	1NT - 2♦ - 2♥ - 3♣ ...	The 4-4 ♣ fit is located after transferring to ♥'s (but see *(b) note).
11	xx44 - xx45	1NT - 2♣ - 2♦/♥/♥ - 3♣ ...	The 4-4 ♦ fit is located by SARS
12	xx44 - xx54	1NT - 2♣ - 2♦/♥/♥ - 3♣ ...	The 4-4 ♣ fit is located by SARS

*(a) If opener is max and you play Stayman super-accepts then he bids 3♦ to show both majors in response to Stayman and the 4-4 fit is uncovered immediately.

*(b) If opener is max and you play super-accepts then opener would presumably super-accept but responder still shows his 2nd suit (see section 3.2)

7.3.1   Responding To 1NT With Major-Major 2 Suited Hands

Strength	♠ - ♥		Section
Weak	5 - 4	Stayman, and 2♠ over responder's 2♦	2 &
	4 - 5	Stayman, and 2♥ over responder's 2♦	2.2
	5 - 5	Stayman, and either 2♥ or 2♠ over 2♦	2.2
	6 - 4	Transfer to ♠'s and pass	3.1
	4 - 6	Transfer to ♥'s and pass	
Invitational	5 - 4	Stayman, and Quest 3♥ over responder's 2♦	2.6.2.1
	4 - 5	Stayman, and Quest 3♦ over responder's 2♦	
	5 - 5	1NT - 2♦ - 2♥ - 2♠ - 2NT - 3♦/♥	3.1.4
	6 - 4	Stayman, and Quest 3♥ over responder's 2♦	2.6.2.2
	4 - 6	Stayman, and Quest 3♦ over responder's 2♦	
Game going	5 - 4	Stayman, Quest 3♥ and bid game	2.6.2.3
	4 - 5	Stayman, Quest 3♦ and bid game	
	5 - 5	1NT - 2♦ - 2♥ - 2♠ - 2NT - other than 3♦/♥	3.1.4
	6 - 4	Stayman, and Extended Texas 4♥ over 2♦	2.6.2.4
	4 - 6	Stayman, and Extended Texas 4♦ over 2♦	
Slam interest (and definitely slamming)	5 - 4	Stayman, Quest 3♥ and bid past game	2.6.2.5 & (2.6.2.7)
	4 - 5	Stayman, Quest 3♦ and bid past game	
	5 - 5	1NT - 2♦ - 2♥ - 2♠ - 2NT - other than 3♦/♥	3.1.4
	6 - 4	Stayman, Quest 3♥, re-transfer and bid on	2.6.2.6 & (2.6.2.8)
	4 - 6	Stayman, Quest 3♦, re-transfer and bid on	

7.3.2   Responding To 1NT With Major-Minor And Minor-Major 2 Suited Hands

Strength	♠ or ♥	♣ or ♦		Section
Weak	5	4	Transfer to the major and pass	3.1
	4	5	Pass	1.5
	5	5	Transfer to the major and pass	3.1
	6	4	Transfer to the major and pass	
	4	6	Transfer to the minor and pass	4.1
Invitational	5	4	Transfer to the major and 2NT	3.1.1
	4	5	Stayman and 2NT if no fit	2
	5	5	Transfer to the major and 2NT	3.1.1
	6	4	Transfer to the major and then 3 of the major	3.1.1
	4	6	Transfer to the minor and pass if no super-accept. If opener super-accepts then bid 3 of the major.	4.2
Game going	5	4	Transfer to the major and bid the minor	3.1.3
	4	5	Transfer to the minor and bid the major	4.2
	5	5	Transfer to the major and bid the minor	3.1.3
	6	4	Transfer to the major and bid the minor	
	4	6	Transfer to the minor and bid the major	4.2
Slam interest (and definitely slamming)	5	4	as game going	
	4	5		
	5	5		
	6	4		
	4	6		

7.3.3   <u>Responding To 1NT With Minor-Minor 2 Suited Hands</u>

Strength	♦ - ♣		Section
Weak	5 - 4	1NT - pass	1.5
	4 - 5	1NT - pass	
	5 - 5	1NT - pass	
	6 - 4	Transfer to ♦'s and pass/bid 3♦	4.1
	4 - 6	Transfer to ♣'s and pass/bid 3♣	4.1
Invitational	5 - 4	1NT - 2NT (via 2♣)	1.6
	4 - 5	1NT - 2NT (via 2♣)	
	5 - 5	1NT - 2NT (via 2♣)	
	6 - 4	Transfer to ♦'s and bid 3NT if super-accept	4.1
	4 - 6	Transfer to ♣'s and bid 3NT if super-accept	4.1
Game going	5 - 4	1NT - 3NT	5.1
	4 - 5	1NT - 3NT	
	5 - 5	1NT - 2♠ - 2NT/3♣ - 3♦	4.3.1
	6 - 4	1NT - 3NT	5.1
	4 - 6	1NT - 2♠ - 2NT/3♣ - 3♦	4.3.1
Slam interest (and definitely slamming)	5 - 4	1NT - 2♣ - 2♦/♥/♠ - 3♣ (SARS)	2.5
	4 - 5	1NT - 2♣ - 2♦/♥/♠ - 3♣ (SARS)	
	5 - 5	1NT - 2♠ - 2NT/3♣ - 3♦	4.3.1
	6 - 4	1NT - 2NT - 3♣/♦ - 4♣	4.3.2
	4 - 6	1NT - 2♠ - 2NT/3♣ - 3♦	4.3.1

7.4   **Alternative Options**

With most areas in this book I have been pretty adamant about the best scheme to play. There are, however, just a few areas where an alternative approach may be just as good: -

7.4.1   **The Direct Jump To 3♣/♦/♥/♠**

We have chosen BST, our Broken Suit Transfers, in conjunction with Direct Ambiguous Splinters. The other real option for these jumps is: -

6)   3♣/♦ are 6 card suits, game (3NT) invitational.
7)   3♥/♠ show a broken suit (6 or 7 cards) with slam interest.

These were described in section 5.2. These 3♣/♦ bids are clearly very useful but if you wish to use this alternative approach then you would have to try to handle the splinter type hands via transfers or Stayman/SARS – not very satisfactory. And you would also return to the problem of having the wrong hand as declarer for the broken suit jumps.

7.4.2   **Transfer To A Minor Followed By 5 Of The Minor?**

      1NT - 2♠ - 2NT/3♣ - 5♣   and   1NT - 2NT - 3♣/♦ - 5♦.

I did not come up with a realistic meaning for these jumps, a weakish hand with a very long minor should probably bid 5♣/♦ directly. So I guess that you could dream up another use; possibly some very specific sort of strong hand?

7.4.3   **Super-accepts Of A Jacoby Major Suit Transfer**

As I said earlier, there are numerous possibilities here. Showing a 2nd suit may be just as good a scheme as showing a weak suit or weak doubleton. And you have to decide if you are going to allow super-accepts with just 3 card support.

7.4.4   **Texas Transfer Or South African Texas Transfer?**

Here we are concerned with the Direct Jump to 4♣/♦/♥/♠. As I indicated in section 6.2.1, having two methods to directly get to 4♥/♠ is probably a superior method (who really needs the direct Gerber bid?). In that case we define the direct 4 level bids as: -

4♣   S.A.Texas Transfer to ♥'s
4♦   S.A.Texas Transfer to ♠'s
4♥   to play
4♠   to play
4NT   quantitative, 4333 or 3433 or 3343 or 3334

Apart from Gerber, we also lose the 4♠ quantitative bids and have to include it in 4NT. No big deal and South African Texas Transfers do have the edge in my opinion.

Note that if you do elect to play South African Texas Transfers then the Extended Texas bids (1NT - 2♣ - 2♦ - 4♦/♥) remain unchanged as the 4♣ bid here is definitely required as Gerber.

7.4.5   <u>Continuations After A Texas Transfer?</u>

So   1NT - 4♦ - 4♥ - ?   and   1NT - 2♣ - 4♠ - ?

I have said that these are hands not interested in slam. Some players, however, do play that 4NT (or 4♠ in the ♥ sequence when playing Kickback) as a 2nd bid by responder is RKCB (this applies whether you play standard Texas Transfers or South African Texas Transfers). This then leaves the 4♣ bid in the sequences   1NT - 2♦ - 2♥ - 4♣   and   1NT - 2♥ - 2♠ - 4♣   free for another use (maybe a ♣ splinter).

7.4.6   <u>Direct Splinters After A Transfer?</u>

Some players will splinter directly after transferring with a 6 card suit and game going values.

So   1NT - 2♦ - 2♥ - 3♠/4♣/4♦   and   1NT - 2♥ - 2♠ - 4♣/4♦/4♥

are all splinters. This is a quite playable scheme but I like our use of the 4♣/♦ bids and ambiguous splinters are to be preferred.

7.4.7   <u>Missing A 5-3 Fit In The Other Major?</u>

Hand A	Hand B	Now here we do have a problem that I have not yet addressed.

Hand A	Hand B	
♠ A5	♠ J104	Consider these two hands. Obviously strong 1NT openers, right?
♥ AQ976	♥ AQ976	And if one is, then the other most certainly is, right again?
♦ J104	♦ A5	But not according to some experts, let's investigate the problem:
♣ KJ8	♣ KJ8	

Example 1

West (A)	East	West	East
♠ A5	♠ KQ976	1NT	2♥
♥ AQ976	♥ K85	2♠	3NT
♦ J104	♦ 92	pass	
♣ KJ8	♣ Q106		

It's the wrong contract, but nobody's to blame. So what can be done? Most people have never even considered the problem, but I did read a 'solution' in a modern bidding book. Their answer was that you only open 1NT with a hand containing a 5 card major if you have 3 cards in the other major.

Thus you open Hand B with 1NT but Hand A with ….?

Clearly this does not solve the problem, but only moves it elsewhere. 1NT is, to me, the obvious opening with Hand A. Even if you prefer not to open 1NT with a 5 card major I'm sure that most people would agree that Hands A & B should be opened with the same bid?

So what's the real solution? .... we could perhaps use the bid of 3 of the other major here to show a reasonable three card suit with a weakness in a minor: -

Thus (a)   1NT - 2♥ - 2♠ - 3♥   =   5 ♠'s and 3 ♥'s
and (b)   1NT - 2♦ - 2♥ - 3♠   =   5 ♥'s and 3 ♠'s

So our revised bidding would then be: -

Example 1 cont.

West	East	West	East		
♠ A5	♠ KQ976	1NT	2♥		
♥ AQ976	♥ K85	2♠	3♥	(1)	(1) 5 ♠'s, 3 ♥'s + a weak minor.
♦ J104	♦ 92	4♥	pass		
♣ KJ8	♣ Q106				

Example 2   Of course opener does not have to choose the 5-3 fit if there is one: -

West	East	West	East		
♠ A5	♠ KQ976	1NT	2♥		(1) 5 ♠'s, 3 ♥'s + a weak minor.
♥ Q7632	♥ K85	2♠	3♥	(1)	(2) let them lead a minor, see if I care.
♦ AQ10	♦ 92	3NT	(2)		
♣ KJ9	♣ Q106	pass			

This works fine, but then we would unfortunately lose our ambiguous splinters and so I guess that we will occasionally land in an inferior contract.

<u>Missing a 5-3 ♥ fit after a transfer to ♠'s?</u>

So we cannot satisfactorily solve the problem, but we can solve half of it!
Consider: 1NT - 2♥ - 2♠ - 3♥ , we currently use this as an ambiguous splinter and can show either singletons or voids. But in the similar ♥ sequence there is only room enough to show a shortage (either singleton or void). This is usually quite adequate and so we can modify the ♠ sequence as follows: -

After   1NT - 2♥ - 2♠ - 3♥,

3♠ asks   3NT = 3 card ♥ suit
            4♣ = ♣ shortage
            4♦ = ♦ shortage
            4♥ = ♥ shortage

This is clearly fine, but there is no satisfactory solution to missing the 5-3 ♠ fit after a transfer to ♥'s. Perhaps don't open 1NT with 5 ♥'s and 3 ♠'s?
Only joking?

7.5   <u>What's New?</u>   Well, that's it folks. It may be a good idea to summarize the areas which are new or not yet common practice: -

1NT - 2♣ - 2♦ - 3♣	SARS. Not new but common only in Holland (I think).
1NT - 2♣ - 2♥/♠ - 3♣	SARS.
1NT - 2♣ - 2♥/♠ - 3♦	ASID.
1NT - 2♣ - 2♦ - 3♦/♥	Quest Transfers.
1NT - 2♣ - 2♦ - 3♠	4-4 in the majors, game force.
1NT - 2♣ - 2♥ - 2NT - 3♥	Max with 5 ♥'s.
1NT - 2♣ - 2♠ - 2NT - 3♠	Max with 5 ♠'s.
1NT - 2♣ - 2NT/3♣	Stayman Super-accept. Max, 5 ♦/♣'s + a 4 card major.
1NT - 2♣ - 3♦	Stayman Super-accept. Max, both majors.
1NT - 2♣ - 3♥/♠	Stayman Super-accept. Max, 5 ♥/♠'s.
1NT - 2♣ - 2♥ - 3♠	Ambiguous splinter. Not new, but not standard.
1NT - 2♣ - 2♠ - 3♥	Ambiguous splinter. Not new, but not standard.
1NT - 2♦ - 2♥ - 2♠	5-5 in the majors, either invitational or game force…
1NT - 2♦ - 2♥ - 2♠ - 2NT	… strength enquiry etc.
1NT - 2♦ - 2♥ - 2NT - 3♣/♦	Game tries. Not new, but not standard.
1NT - 2♥ - 2♠ - 2NT - 3♣/♦	Game tries. Not new, but not standard.
1NT - 2♦ - 2♥ - 2NT - 3♠	Max with 5 ♠'s.
1NT - 2♥ - 2♠ - 2NT - 3♥	Max with 5 ♥'s.
1NT - 2♦ - 2♥ - 3♣ - 3♦	Shortage ask.
1NT - 2♦ - 2♥ - 3♦ - 3♠	Shortage ask.
1NT - 2♥ - 2♠ - 3♣ - 3♦	Shortage ask.
1NT - 2♥ - 2♠ - 3♦ - 3♥	Shortage ask.
1NT - 2♦ - 2♥ - 3♠	Ambiguous splinter.
1NT - 2♥ - 2♠ - 3♥	Ambiguous splinter. * Note
1NT - 2♦ - 2♥ - 4♦	Slam try. Not new, but not standard.
1NT - 2♥ - 2♠ - 4♦	Slam try. Not new, but not standard.
1NT - 2♠ - 2NT/3♣ - 3♦ - 3♥	Shortage ask.
1NT - 2♠ - 2NT/3♣ - 3♦ - 3♠	Waiting.
1NT - 3♣	Direct Ambiguous Splinters (♠/♣/♦)
1NT - 3♦/♥	Broken Suit Transfer, slam seeking.
1NT - 3♠	♥ splinter
1NT - 4♠/NT	Precise Quantitives.

Plus a few others others: -
- More precise quantitative bids (listed in section 8.1).
- Fit Showing Quantitives after SARS.
- DRKCB with two-suited hands, EDRKCB.
- the use of 4 of the minor for the minor, or Kickback for the major.
- Two different RKCB bids with minor-major 2 suiters (one for each suit), etc. etc …

*   Note . Be wary of this one, many will take it as 5-4 in the majors (we use Quest Transfers).

In many cases we have been able to be more specific than usual about our quantitative bids. Perhaps we should name these Precise Quantitatives? : -

1NT - 4♠   is quantitative, 17 pts, 4333 or 3433.
1NT - 4NT   is quantitative, 17 pts, 3343 or 3334.

1NT - 2♣ - 2♦ - 4♠   is quantitative, contains one or two 4 card majors
                  4NT is quantitative ++, contains one or two 4 card majors
1NT - 2♣ - 2♥ - 4♠   is quantitative, contains 4 ♠'s
                  4NT is quantitative ++, contains 4 ♠'s
1NT - 2♣ - 2♠ -4♥   is quantitative, contains 4 ♥'s
                  4NT is quantitative ++, contains 4 ♥'s
1NT - 2♦ - 2♥ - 4♠   is quantitative, 5 ♥'s, 3 ♠'s. 3532 or 3523
                  4NT is quantitative, 5 ♥'s. usually 2533
1NT - 2♥ - 2♠ - 4♥   is quantitative, 5 ♠'s, 3 ♥'s. 5332 or 5323
                  4NT is quantitative, 5 ♠'s. usually 5233

1NT - 2♠ - 2NT - 4NT   is quantitative, 5+ ♣'s
1NT - 2♠ - 3♣ - 3NT   is mildly quantitative, 5+ ♣'s
1NT - 2♠ - 3♣ - 4NT   is strongly quantitative, 5+ ♣'s
1NT - 2NT - 3♣ - 4NT   is quantitative, 5+ ♦'s
1NT - 2NT - 3♦ - 3NT   is mildly quantitative, 5+ ♦'s
1NT - 2NT - 3♦ - 4NT   is strongly quantitative, 5+ ♦'s

And, of course, there are the Fit Showing Quantitatives after SARS. They are fully detailed in sections 2.5.1 and 2.5.2 and are best not listed out of context.

* Note   If you choose to play South African Texas Transfers then: -

1NT - 4♠   is to play
1NT - 4NT   is quantitative, 4333 or 3433 or 3343 or 3334

8.2   Summary Of Direct Responses To An Opening Of 1NT

2♣   Stayman,
       or a balanced 8-9 pts (i.e. a natural 2NT),   * Note 1
       or may simply be a prelude to SARS (so minor suit Stayman).   * Note 1
2♦   transfer to ♥'s
2♥   transfer to ♠'s
2♠   transfer to ♣'s
2NT   transfer to ♦'s
3♣   ambiguous (♠/♣/♦) splinter
3♦   Broken Suit Transfer to ♥'s
3♥   Broken Suit Transfer to ♠'s
3♠   ♥ splinter
3NT   to play, normally no 4 card major
4♣   Gerber
4♦   Texas Transfer to ♥'s
4♥   Texas Transfer to ♠'s
4♠   quantitative, 4333 or 3433   * Note 2
4NT   quantitative, 3343 or 3334   * Note 2

If you choose to play South African Texas Transfers then the last five bids are: -

4♣   S.A. Texas Transfer to ♥'s
4♦   S.A. Texas Transfer to ♠'s
4♥   to play
4♠   to play
4NT   quantitative, 4333 or 3433 or 3343 or 3334   * Note 2

Note 1   Because of these two possibilities, our 2♣ bid does not guarantee a 4 card major.
Note 2   The 4 card suit will be very poor (J9xx or worse) as otherwise responder would have bid
          Stayman or SARS.

238

8.3   <u>Summary Of Stayman Sequences</u>

1NT - 2♣ - 2♦ -   pass = weak, 4441 or similar
                             2♥   = weak, 45 etc to play
                             2♠   = weak, 54 etc to play
                             2NT = invitational, does not guarantee a 4 card major
                             3♣   = minor suit shape ask (SARS)
                             3♦   = Quest Transfer
                             3♥   = Quest Transfer
                             3♠   = game force; 4-4 in the majors, weak minors
                             3NT = to play, contains one or two 4 card majors
                             4♣   = Gerber
                             4♦   = transfer to ♥'s (Extended Texas)
                             4♥   = transfer to ♠'s (Extended Texas)
                             4♠   = quantitative, contains one or two 4 card majors
                             4NT = quantitative ++, contains one or two 4 card majors

1NT - 2♣ - 2♥ -   pass = weak, 44, 54 or 45 etc. to play
                             2♠   = invitational to 3NT or 4♠, contains 4 ♠'s
                             2NT = invitational, does not contain a 4 card major
                             3♣   = minor suit shape ask (SARS)
                             3♦   = shape ask, maybe a slam try (ASID)
                             3♥   = invitational, 4 ♥'s
                             3♠   = ambiguous splinter
                             3NT = contains 4 ♠'s, opener may correct to 4♠
                             4♣   = RKCB for ♥'s
                             4♦   = slam interest
                             4♥   = to play
                             4♠   = quantitative, contains 4 ♠'s
                             4NT = quantitative ++, contains 4 ♠'s

1NT - 2♣ - 2♠ -   pass = weak, 44, 54 or 45 etc. to play
                             2NT = invitational, may or may not contain 4 ♥'s
                             3♣   = minor suit shape ask (SARS)
                             3♦   = shape ask, maybe a slam try (ASID)
                             3♥   = ambiguous splinter
                             3♠   = invitational, 4♠'s
                             3NT = to play, 4♥'s
                             4♣   = RKCB for ♠'s
                             4♦   = slam interest
                             4♥   = quantitative, contains 4 ♥'s
                             4♠   = to play
                             4NT = quantitative ++, contains 4 ♥'s

Summary Of Major Suit Transfer Sequences

1NT - 2♦ - 2♥ -   pass = weak; 5+ ♥'s

                            2♠   = forcing; 5 ♠'s, 5 ♥'s   note 1

                            2NT = invitational; 5 ♥'s

                            3♣   = game force; 5 ♥'s, 4+ ♣'s

                            3♦   = game force; 5 ♥'s, 4+ ♦'s

                            3♥   = invitational; 6+ ♥'s

                            3♠   = ambiguous splinter   note 2

                            3NT = to play or correct to 4♥

                            4♣   = RKCB for ♥'s

                            4♦   = serious slam try

                            4♥   = mild slam try; 6+ ♥'s   note 4

                            4♠   = Quantitative; 5 ♥'s, 3 ♠'s. 3532 or 3523

                            4NT = Quantitative; 5 ♥'s. usually 2533

1NT - 2♥ - 2♠ -   pass = weak; 5+ ♠'s

                            2NT = invitational; 5 ♠'s

                            3♣   = game force; 5 ♠'s, 4+ ♣'s

                            3♦   = game force; 5 ♠'s, 4+ ♦'s

                            3♥   = ambiguous splinter   note 3

                            3NT = to play or correct to 4♠

                            4♣   = RKCB for ♠'s

                            4♦   = serious slam try

                            4♥   = Quantitative; 5 ♠'s, 3 ♥'s. 5332 or 5323

                            4♠   = mild slam try, 6+ ♠'s   note 5

                            4NT = Quantitative; 5 ♠'s. usually 5233

1) Both invitational and game forcing 5-5's go via the sequence   1NT - 2♦ - 2♥ - 2♠ (invitational and game forcing 54 and 45 hands use Quest Transfers)

2) The sequence is not used to show 5 ♥'s and 4 ♠'s as that is done via Stayman.

3) The sequence is not used to show 5 ♠'s and 4 ♥'s as that is done via Stayman

4) A mild slam try with 6+ ♥'s (use Texas Transfer if only interested in game)

5) A mild slam try with 6+ ♠'s (use Texas Transfer if only interested in game)

8.5   <u>**Summary Of Minor Suit Transfer Sequences**</u>

<u>Normal accept of transfer to ♣'s</u>

After 1NT - 2♠ - 3♣ - we have: -

pass = weak, 6+ ♣'s
3♦   = game force; 5+ ♣'s, 4+ ♦'s
3♥   = game force; 5+ ♣'s, 4 ♥'s
3♠   = game force; 5+ ♣'s, 4 ♠'s
3NT = natural, slam interest
4♣   = a big ♣ hand, RKCB
4♦   = splinter
4♥   = splinter
4♠   = splinter
4NT = strongly quantitative, 5+ ♣'s
5♣   = to play

<u>Super-accept of transfer to ♣'s</u>

after 1NT - 2♠ - 2NT - it's the same except: -

3♣   = weak, 6+ ♣'s

3NT = to play

4NT = quantitative, 5+ ♣'s

<u>Normal accept of transfer to ♦'s</u>

After 1NT - 2NT - 3♦ - we have: -

pass = weak, 6+ ♦'s
3♥   = game force; 5+ ♦'s, 4 ♥'s
3♠   = game force; 5+ ♦'s, 4 ♠'s
3NT = natural, slam interest
4♣   = game force; 6+ ♦'s, 4+ ♣'s
4♦   = a big ♦ hand, RKCB
4♥   = splinter
4♠   = splinter
4NT = strongly quantitative, 5+ ♦'s
5♣   = splinter
5♦   = to play

<u>Super-accept of transfer to ♦'s</u>

after 1NT - 2NT - 3♣ - it's the same except: -

3♦   = weak, 6+ ♦'s

3NT = to play

4NT = quantitative, 5+ ♦'s

<u>**Bidding Index**</u> g.f. = game forcing

The page numbers in **bold** indicate theory and the mainstream use in this book. Other entries are examples etc. The Notes column generally applies to the last bid in the sequence. I have not included all the sequences that appear in the book: -

Smolen sequences (or natural jumps to 3♥/♠ after 1NT - 2♣ - 2♦) are not included as they have been superseded by Quest Transfers.

The direct bids of 3♥/♠ to show broken suits have not been included as they have been superseded by Broken Suit Transfers.

I have also not included super-accepts of major suit transfers as there are numerous possible schemes.

And numerous other treatments which we do not use have also not been included.

O1 - R1 - O2 - R2 - O3 - R3 - O4 - R4	Page	Notes
1N - 2♣ - 2♦ - 3♦	77	Quest Transfer
1N - 2♣ - 2♦ - 3♦ - 3♥	77,78,79	weak accept
1N - 2♣ - 2♦ - 3♦ - 3♥ - 4♦	**84**	're-transfer'
1N - 2♣ - 2♦ - 3♦ - 3♥ - 4♦ - 4♥ - 4♠	**84**	DRKCB
1N - 2♣ - 2♦ - 3♦ - 3♥ - 4♦ - 4♠	**84**	DRKCB
1N - 2♣ - 2♦ - 3♦ - 3♥ - 4♥	**84**	to play
1N - 2♣ - 2♦ - 3♦ - 3♥ - 3N - 4♥	84	
1N - 2♣ - 2♦ - 3♦ - 3♠	77	3 ♥'s + ♠A
1N - 2♣ - 2♦ - 3♦ - 3♠ - 4♦	79	re-transfer
1N - 2♣ - 2♦ - 3♦ - 3♠ - 4♦ - 4♥	79,80	
1N - 2♣ - 2♦ - 3♦ - 3N	**77**	normally 3 ♠'s & 2 ♥'s
1N - 2♣ - 2♦ - 3♦ - 3N - 4♦	**85**	re-transfer, slam interest
1N - 2♣ - 2♦ - 3♦ - 3N - 4♦ - 4♥	**85**	no slam interest
1N - 2♣ - 2♦ - 3♦ - 3N - 4♦ - 4♠	**87**	DRKCB for ♥'s
1N - 2♣ - 2♦ - 3♦ - 3N - 4N	**83**	quantitative
1N - 2♣ - 2♦ - 3♦ - 3N - 4N - 6N	83	
1N - 2♣ - 2♦ - 3♦ - 4♣	77	3 ♥'s + ♣A
1N - 2♣ - 2♦ - 3♦ - 4♣ - 4♦ - 4♥ - pass	78	
1N - 2♣ - 2♦ - 3♦ - 4♣ - 4♦ - 4♥ - 5♦	**90**	EDRKCB
1N - 2♣ - 2♦ - 3♦ - 4♣ - 4♠	**83,87**	DRKCB for ♥'s
1N - 2♣ - 2♦ - 3♦ - 4♦	77	3 ♥'s + ♦A
1N - 2♣ - 2♦ - 3♦ - 4♦ - 4N - 5♥ - pass	84	
1N - 2♣ - 2♦ - 3♦ - 4♥	77	3 ♥'s (no ace to cue)
1N - 2♣ - 2♦ - 3♥	77	Quest Transfer
1N - 2♣ - 2♦ - 3♥ - 3♠	77,80	weak accept
1N - 2♣ - 2♦ - 3♥ - 3♠ - 3N	82	
1N - 2♣ - 2♦ - 3♥ - 3♠ - 4♥	**88**	're-transfer'
1N - 2♣ - 2♦ - 3♥ - 3♠ - 4♥ - 4♠ - 4N	88,89	DRKCB for ♠'s
1N - 2♣ - 2♦ - 3♥ - 3♠ - 4♥ - 4N	**88**	DRKCB for ♠'s
1N - 2♣ - 2♦ - 3♥ - 3♠ - 4♠	**88**	to play
1N - 2♣ - 2♦ - 3♥ - 3N	77	normally 2 ♠'s & 3 ♥'s
1N - 2♣ - 2♦ - 3♥ - 3N - 4♥	85	re-transfer, slam interest
1N - 2♣ - 2♦ - 3♥ - 3N - 4♥ - 4♠	85	no slam interest
1N - 2♣ - 2♦ - 3♥ - 3N - 4♥ - 4N	87	DRKCB for ♠'s
1N - 2♣ - 2♦ - 3♥ - 3N - 4♠	85	to play
1N - 2♣ - 2♦ - 3♥ - 3N - 4N	83	quantitative
1N - 2♣ - 2♦ - 3♥ - 4♣	77	3 ♠'s + ♣A
1N - 2♣ - 2♦ - 3♥ - 4♦	77	3 ♠'s + ♦A
1N - 2♣ - 2♦ - 3♥ - 4♦ - 4♥ - 4♠	82	
1N - 2♣ - 2♦ - 3♥ - 4♥	77	3 ♠'s + ♥A
1N - 2♣ - 2♦ - 3♥ - 4♥ - 4♠	81	
1N - 2♣ - 2♦ - 3♥ - 4♠	77	3 ♠'s (no ace to cue)
1N - 2♣ - 2♦ - 3♥ - 4♠ - pass	85	

246

O1 - R1 - O2 - R2 - O3 - R3	Page	Notes
1N - 2♣ - 2♠	**22,28**	denies 4 ♥'s
1N - 2♣ - 2♠ - pass	**22**	
1N - 2♣ - 2♠ - 2N	**23,28,30**	invitational, maybe 4 ♥'s
1N - 2♣ - 2♠ - 2N - pass	28,**226**	
1N - 2♣ - 2♠ - 2N - 3♣	**34**	undefined
1N - 2♣ - 2♠ - 2N - 3♦	**34**	undefined
1N - 2♣ - 2♠ - 2N - 3♠	**32,34,102**	g.f. a decent 5 card suit
1N - 2♣ - 2♠ - 2N - 3♠ - 4♠	**102,226**	a 5-3 fit
1N - 2♣ - 2♠ - 3♣	**47**	SARS
1N - 2♣ - 2♠ - 3♣ - 3♦	**47,52**	a 4 card ♦ suit
1N - 2♣ - 2♠ - 3♣ - 3♦ - 3N	**49**	to play, no fit
1N - 2♣ - 2♠ - 3♣ - 3♦ - 4♦	**49**	RKCB for ♦'s
1N - 2♣ - 2♠ - 3♣ - 3♦ - 4♥	**49**	quantitative, a ♦ fit
1N - 2♣ - 2♠ - 3♣ - 3♦ - 4♠	**49**	to play (probably a 4-3 fit)
1N - 2♣ - 2♠ - 3♣ - 3♦ - 4N	**49**	quantitative, no fit
1N - 2♣ - 2♠ - 3♣ - 3♥	**47**	a 4 card ♣ suit
1N - 2♣ - 2♠ - 3♣ - 3♥ - 3N	47,**49**	to play, no fit
1N - 2♣ - 2♠ - 3♣ - 3♥ - 4♣	**49**	RKCB for ♣'s
1N - 2♣ - 2♠ - 3♣ - 3♥ - 4♥	**49**	quantitative, a ♣ fit
1N - 2♣ - 2♠ - 3♣ - 3♥ - 4♠	**49**	to play (probably a 4-3 fit)
1N - 2♣ - 2♠ - 3♣ - 3♥ - 4N	**49**	quantitative, no fit
1N - 2♣ - 2♠ - 3♣ - 3♠	**47**	a 5 card ♠ suit
1N - 2♣ - 2♠ - 3♣ - 3♠ - 3N	**49**	to play, no fit
1N - 2♣ - 2♠ - 3♣ - 3♠ - 4♦	**49**	quantitative, a 5-3 ♠ fit
1N - 2♣ - 2♠ - 3♣ - 3♠ - 4♥	**49**	quantitative, no fit
1N - 2♣ - 2♠ - 3♣ - 3♠ - 4♠	**49**	to play
1N - 2♣ - 2♠ - 3♣ - 3♠ - 4N	**49**	RKCB for ♠'s
1N - 2♣ - 2♠ - 3♣ - 3N	**47**	4333
1N - 2♣ - 2♠ - 3♣ - 3N - pass	**49**	no fit
1N - 2♣ - 2♠ - 3♣ - 3N - 4♣	**49**	RKCB for ♣'s (3-5 fit)
1N - 2♣ - 2♠ - 3♣ - 3N - 4♦	**49**	RKCB for ♦'s (3-5 fit)
1N - 2♣ - 2♠ - 3♣ - 3N - 4♥	**49**	quantitative, a 3-5 ♣ fit
1N - 2♣ - 2♠ - 3♣ - 3N - 4♠	**49**	quantitative, a 3-5 ♦ fit
1N - 2♣ - 2♠ - 3♣ - 3N - 4N	**49**	quantitative, no fit
1N - 2♣ - 2♠ - 3♦	**40**	ASID
1N - 2♣ - 2♠ - 3♦ - 3♥	**40**	doubleton ♥
1N - 2♣ - 2♠ - 3♦ - 3♠	**40**	4333, min
1N - 2♣ - 2♠ - 3♦ - 3N	**40**	4333, non min
1N - 2♣ - 2♠ - 3♦ - 4♣	**40**	doubleton ♣
1N - 2♣ - 2♠ - 3♦ - 4♦	**40**	doubleton ♦
1N - 2♣ - 2♠ - 3♦ - 4♠	**40**	5 card ♠ suit

Transfer to ♥'s

O1 - R1 - O2 - R2 - O3 - R3 - O4 - R4	Page	Notes
1N - 2♦	**115**	transfer to ♥
1N - 2♦ - 2♥	**116**	normal accept
1N - 2♦ - 2♥ - pass	**118**	a weak hand, 0-7
1N - 2♦ - 2♥ - 2♠	**136,138**	5-5 in the majors
1N - 2♦ - 2♥ - 2♠ - 2N	**138**	relay
1N - 2♦ - 2♥ - 2♠ - 2N - 3♣	**138**	g.f. often a weak doubleton
1N - 2♦ - 2♥ - 2♠ - 2N - 3♣ - 3♦	**138**	relay
1N - 2♦ - 2♥ - 2♠ - 2N - 3♣ - 3♦ - 3♥	**138,141,144,145**	small doubleton ♣
1N - 2♦ - 2♥ - 2♠ - 2N - 3♣ - 3♦ - 3♠	**138,140,145**	small doubleton ♦
1N - 2♦ - 2♥ - 2♠ - 2N - 3♣ - 3♦ - 3N	**138,145,146**	DRKCB
1N - 2♦ - 2♥ - 2♠ - 2N - 3♣ - 3♦ - 4♣	**138,145**	weak ♣'s, ♦ void
1N - 2♦ - 2♥ - 2♠ - 2N - 3♣ - 3♦ - 4♦	**138,145**	weak ♦'s, ♣ void
1N - 2♦ - 2♥ - 2♠ - 2N - 3♣ - 3♦ - 4♥	**138,145**	5611 or 6511
1N - 2♦ - 2♥ - 2♠ - 2N - 3♦	**138**	♣ shortage, invitational
1N - 2♦ - 2♥ - 2♠ - 2N - 3♦ - 4♠ - pass	139	
1N - 2♦ - 2♥ - 2♠ - 2N - 3♥	**138**	♦ shortage, invitational
1N - 2♦ - 2♥ - 2♠ - 2N - 3♥ - 3♠ - pass	139	
1N - 2♦ - 2♥ - 2♠ - 2N - 3♠	**138**	singleton ♣
1N - 2♦ - 2♥ - 2♠ - 2N - 3♠ ...	139,143	
1N - 2♦ - 2♥ - 2♠ - 2N - 3N	**138**	singleton ♦
1N - 2♦ - 2♥ - 2♠ - 2N - 3N - 4♠ - pass	139	
1N - 2♦ - 2♥ - 2♠ - 2N - 4♣	**138**	void ♣
1N - 2♦ - 2♥ - 2♠ - 2N - 4♣ - 4♦ ...	142	DRKCB
1N - 2♦ - 2♥ - 2♠ - 2N - 4♣ - 4♥	142	sign off
1N - 2♦ - 2♥ - 2♠ - 2N - 4♣ - 4♥ - 4♠	142	DRKCB
1N - 2♦ - 2♥ - 2♠ - 2N - 4♦	**138**	void ♦
1N - 2♦ - 2♥ - 2♠ - 2N - 4♥	**138**	no slam interest
1N - 2♦ - 2♥ - 2♠ - 2N - 5♣	**138**	EDRKCB
1N - 2♦ - 2♥ - 2♠ - 2N - 5♦	**138,146**	EDRKCB

251

254

Transfer to ♣'s

Transfer to ♦'s

Alphabetic Index   Page

Printed in the United States
by Baker & Taylor Publisher Services